Flourish by Design

Flourish by Design brings together a range of established and emerging voices in design research for a collection that provides original provocations on topics of global significance. It is an insightful guide to original theory and practice concerning how we can design for a better tomorrow.

Featuring contributors from a diverse array of backgrounds and professions, this edited book explores the difference that design and design research can make for people, organisations, and the planet to prosper now and in the future. It offers a range of ideas and techniques through practical examples and ongoing projects showing how applied design research can respond to global challenges. Covering topics as diverse as artificial intelligence, bio-inspired materials, more-than-human design, sustainability, and urban acupuncture, it shares interdisciplinary and transdisciplinary design research not just to demonstrate what could be plausible in the near future but also to explain why it might be preferable. By sharing these despatches, this collection represents the very best of what design research can do, explaining how and why.

This book is intended for a wide audience of professionals, scholars, and students in design, architecture, and public policy, as well as anyone who has an interest in how we design the world and, in turn, it designs us.

Nick Dunn is Professor of Urban Design and Executive Director of Imagination, the design and architecture research lab at Lancaster University, UK. He is the founding Director of the Dark Design Lab, exploring the impacts of nocturnal activity on humans and non-humans. Nick has worked with the Alliance for Healthy Cities, Design Council European Commission, International Dark-Sky Association, and World Health Organization. He has authored numerous books, curated exhibitions, and given talks at public festivals and conferences around the world.

Leon Cruickshank is Professor of Design and Creative Exchange and a founding member of Imagination at Lancaster University, UK. His research focuses on the development of open and co-design processes in the private, public, and voluntary sectors. Past projects include leading the £13.2 million Beyond Imagination project funded by Research England and Lancaster University and the £1.2 million AHRC Leapfrog project. He is currently working on giving communities a stronger voice in an equitable move to sustainability.

Gemma Coupe is the Beyond Imagination Impact Manager at Lancaster University, UK, a bold and engaging project exploring how design research can contribute to a healthier, more prosperous, and sustainable world. Gemma has worked as the Design Manager on multiple design research projects. She develops strategic partnerships, projects, and events that demonstrate the value and impact of design-led research. Previously, Gemma was a founding member of Creative Lancashire, providing an innovative response to economic and social issues affecting creative businesses.

Flourish by Design

**EDITED BY NICK DUNN,
LEON CRUICKSHANK, AND GEMMA COUPE**

Routledge
Taylor & Francis Group
LONDON AND NEW YORK

First published 2024
by Routledge
4 Park Square, Milton Park, Abingdon, Oxon OX14 4RN

and by Routledge
605 Third Avenue, New York, NY 10158

Routledge is an imprint of the Taylor & Francis Group, an informa business

British Library Cataloguing-in-Publication Data
A catalogue record for this book is available from the British Library

Library of Congress Cataloging-in-Publication Data
Names: Dunn, Nick, editor. | Cruickshank, Leon, editor. | Coupe, Gemma, editor.
Title: Flourish by design / edited by Nick Dunn, Leon Cruickshank and Gemma Coupe.
Description: Abingdon, Oxon : Routledge, 2024. | Includes bibliographical references and index.
Identifiers: LCCN 2023018816 (print) | LCCN 2023018817 (ebook) | ISBN 9781032507682 (hardback) | ISBN 9781032507651 (paperback) | ISBN 9781003399568 (ebook)
Subjects: LCSH: Design—Social aspects. | Design—Research.
Classification: LCC NK1520 .F595 2024 (print) | LCC NK1520 (ebook) | DDC 744—dc23/eng/20230727
LC record available at https://lccn.loc.gov/2023018816
LC ebook record available at https://lccn.loc.gov/2023018817

ISBN: 978-1-032-50768-2 (hbk)
ISBN: 978-1-032-50765-1 (pbk)
ISBN: 978-1-003-39956-8 (ebk)

DOI: 10.4324/9781003399568

Typeset in Univers LT Std
by Apex CoVantage, LLC

Printed in the UK by Severn, Gloucester on responsibly sourced paper

Contents

Figures

Contributors

Mariana Amatullo's research and publishing bridge the design and management disciplines. Trained as an art historian and design theorist, Professor Amatullo teaches at Parsons School of Design and serves as Vice Provost and Academic Dean for Continuing and Professional Education at The New School, New York. Amatullo is Honorary President of Cumulus.

Jez Bebbington is a PhD student exploring the relationship between place-based co-design and public value at Lancaster University, UK. He is Lancaster University's partnership manager for NHS and public services; until May 2023 he was Lancaster City Council's lead officer for strategy, information, and partnerships.

Lee Brewster is a designer working with communities and public-sector organisations. He is also a PhD researcher based at ImaginationLancaster, the design research lab at Lancaster University, UK. He is exploring ways to help make design accessible and equitable to those who wish to participate.

Bruce Brown was educated at the Royal College of Art in London where he is currently Visiting Professor. Until 2016, Bruce was Pro-Vice-Chancellor (Research) and Professor of Design at the University of Brighton. For 20 years previously he was Dean of the university's Faculty of Arts & Architecture.

Camilla Buchanan is Co-Head of the UK Policy Lab, a highly innovative government team looking at new ways to make policy better for the people it affects. She has a PhD in strategic design, and her work is focused on bringing creative and caring techniques to policymaking. She has worked in lots of different contexts in the UK and around the world—in areas including social investment, access to education, and recidivism.

Elisavet Christou is Lecturer in Management and Organisation Studies at the Lancaster University Management School. Her work focuses on inter and transdisciplinary theories, methodologies, methods and tools across management, evaluation, design, information and communication technologies, digital arts, and biophysics.

Rachel Cooper, OBE, is Distinguished Professor of Design Management and Policy at Lancaster University, UK. Her research has focused on the future of cities and human and planetary well-being. She was a lead expert for the UK Government Foresight programme on the Future of Cities and was on the UK Academy of Medical Sciences Working group addressing the Health of the Public 2040.

Ana Rute Costa is an architect, lecturer, consultant, and researcher at Lancaster University, UK. Her research focuses on accelerating material reuse in construction and enabling circular economy strategies. As a specialist in learning and teaching spaces, her research focuses on analysing the impact of the built environment in teaching and learning through ethnographic and visual research methods.

Gemma Coupe is the Beyond Imagination Impact Manager at Lancaster University, UK, a bold and engaging project exploring how design research can contribute to a healthier, more prosperous, and sustainable world. Gemma has worked as the Design Manager on multiple design research projects. She develops strategic partnerships, projects, and events that demonstrate the value and impact of design-led research.

Leon Cruickshank is Professor of Design and Creative Exchange and a founding member of Imagination at Lancaster University, UK. His research focuses on the development of open and co-design processes in the private, public, and voluntary sectors. Past projects include leading the £13.2 million Beyond Imagination project funded by Research England and Lancaster University and the £1.2 million AHRC Leapfrog project.

Sevra Davis is Director of Architecture Design Fashion at the British Council, UK. Before joining the British Council, she was Head of Learning at the Design Museum and Director of Design at the RSA. Sevra studied architecture and urban design and worked in professional practice before moving to roles focused on design enabling and commissioning.

Nick Dunn is Executive Director of ImaginationLancaster, the design-led research lab at Lancaster University, UK, where he is also Professor of Urban Design. He is the founding Director of the Dark Design Lab, exploring the effects of nocturnal activity on humans and other species, to reduce the environmental impact of places at night.

John R. Ehrenfeld published *The Right Way to Flourish: Reconnecting with the Real World* (2020), exploring the nexus between the brain and human behaviour. After many years working in the environmental field, he returned to his alma mater, MIT, US. Now long retired, he continues to write and teach.

Katherine Ellsworth-Krebs is Chancellor's Fellow in Sustainable Design at the University of Strathclyde, Scotland, UK. Currently, she is focused on working with organisations to develop new ways to intervene in environmental sustainability issues (e.g., reduce waste, carbon, and energy) to create a 'culture of sustainability'.

Christopher Frayling is Professor Emeritus of Cultural History at the Royal College of Art and Distinguished Visiting Professor of Arts at the University of Lancaster, UK. He was formerly rector of the RCA and chair of the Arts Council of England and the UK Design Council. He was knighted in 2000 for 'services to art and design education'.

Rosendy Galabo is a research associate for the Beyond Imagination project at ImaginationLancaster, Lancaster University, UK. His research focuses on developing equitable and inclusive ways of living and working together by creating mechanisms that enable communities to collectively transform their current situations into more sustainable ones through co-design.

Rupert Griffiths is a multidisciplinary researcher at Lancaster University, UK, with a background in social and human geography, architecture and urbanism, and micro-electronic engineering. He has also worked extensively as an artist, designer, and curator in the UK and China. His work considers the cultural imaginaries of urban nature, particularly in megacities such as London and Beijing.

Naomi Jacobs is a lecturer in design policy and futures thinking at Lancaster University, UK. Her research, which often uses speculative methods, investigates how design research can be used in policymaking, particularly in the context of ensuring new technologies and digital platforms and services are ethical, transparent, and trustworthy and respect privacy.

Boyeun Lee is a post-doctoral research fellow in DigitLab at the University of Exeter Business School, UK. Her research focuses on data-driven design and responsible innovation in the context of new product/service development of emerging technologies. She holds a PhD in design from Lancaster University.

Kun-Pyo Lee is the Dean of School of Design, The Hong Kong Polytechnic University. Before joining The Hong Kong Polytechnic University, he was a professor at the Department of Industrial Design, KAIST, South Korea, and the Director of the Human-Centered Interaction Design Lab for more than 30 years. He is Co-Founder and President Emeritus of IASDR.

Joseph Lindley leads *Design Research Works*, progressing design research to address emerging socio-technological challenges. He is an alumnus of the PETRAS Centre of Excellence, the ACM Future of Computing Academy, held the AHRC's Challenges of the Future Fellowship, and has published widely on the adoption and acceptability of emerging technologies.

Marzia Mortati is Associate Professor at Politecnico di Milano—Design Department, Italy. She is vice-director of the International Master in AI for Public Services and one of the executive directors of the European Academy of Design. Her research focuses on service design applied to public-sector innovation, with special focus on the role of data and artificial intelligence in public services.

Louise Mullagh is a senior researcher (design for policy) in ImaginationLancaster, UK. Her cross-disciplinary design research explores design and its roles in the development and implementation of policy at global, national, and regional levels. Her current research explores designing policy futures for emerging technologies.

Ravi Naidoo is the founder of Interactive Africa and Design Indaba, an annual three-day design conference hosted in Cape Town, South Africa, as well as a suite of events such as Design Commons and Antenna. Naidoo is also a co-founder of the Cape Innovation and Tech Initiative (CiTi) and Rain, Africa's first 5G network.

David Perez is a lecturer in radical co-design at Lancaster University, UK. His research focuses on the emergence and adoption of new creative and collaborative practices from collaborative design projects. His research utilises a variety of methods and theories such as design-led research approaches, co-design, participatory design, and practice theories.

Paul Rodgers is a professor of design at the University of Strathclyde, UK, and was an AHRC Design Leadership Fellow (2017–2021). He explores how disruptive design interventions can enact positive change. He has more than 25 years of experience in product design research, authoring more than 180 papers and nine books on design.

Jenny Sabin is the Arthur L. and Isabel B. Wiesenberger Professor in Architecture and the inaugural chair for the multi-college Department of Design Tech at Cornell University, US. She is principal of Jenny Sabin Studio, an experimental architectural design studio based in Ithaca, and director of the Sabin Design Lab at Cornell AAP.

Laura Santamaria is Research Lead for the School of Communication at the Royal College of Art, UK. A scholar, educator, and activist, Laura specialises in sociocultural and political aspects of design, with a focus on sustainability and grassroots innovation for social change. She is founder of *Sublime* magazine and the Fair Energy Campaign.

Andrea Siodmok, OBE, is Dean at RMIT School of Design in Australia. Before this, she was chief impact officer at the Royal Society of Arts and Manufactures and commerce and design director at the Connected Places Catapult. In 2014, she founded the UK Government Cabinet Office's award-winning Policy Innovation Unit including Policy Lab, the Open Innovation Team.

Chris Speed is Chair of Design Informatics at the University of Edinburgh, UK, and Director for the Edinburgh Futures Institute. Chris has an established track record in directing large complex grants with academic, industry, and third-sector partners that apply design and data methods to social, environmental, and economic challenges.

Michael Stead is a lecturer in sustainable design futures at Imagination, Lancaster University's School of Design, UK. He creates prototypes, strategies, and tools to explore the opportunities and challenges that emerging technologies, including the IoT and AI, pose for society as we seek to transition towards sustainable futures like the circular economy and Net Zero 2050.

Deyan Sudjic, OBE, is a professor of architecture and design studies at Lancaster University, UK, and Director Emeritus of the Design Museum. He is a curator and editor. His most recent book, *Stalin's Architect*, was shortlisted for the Pushkin House Prize 2022.

Emmanuel Tsekleves is a professor of global health design innovation and the co-director of the Future Cities Research Institute at Lancaster University, UK. Emmanuel is the convenor for the Design Research Society Special Interest Group on Global Health. His research addresses the UN's Sustainable Development Goals in health and well-being.

Louise Valentine is a writer and coach. She writes about innovation and design leadership capabilities for business, society, and cultural transformation. Louise is president of the European Academy of Design and editor-in-chief of *The Design Journal*. Previously, Louise was director of fashion, design, and merchandising at Kent State University, USA, and professor of design and head of entrepreneurship at the University of Dundee, UK.

Ingrid van der Wacht works from her company Factor-I (2001), based in Eindhoven in the Netherlands, as a freelance international connector for organisations driven by (Dutch) design and on European collaboration projects. With her experience and broad network, she further develops projects with the world of design to improve life by good design of the world.

Acknowledgements

We would like to express our considerable thanks to all the authors who contributed chapters to this edited collection. We are delighted with the breadth and depth of inquiries and creative engagements with the notion of flourishing by design that they represent. They have proved to be an inspirational and attentive group and have been a pleasure to work with. Thank you, everyone.

We would also like to thank Matt Shobbrook and the team at Routledge, whose enthusiasm and support helped us to bring the book into being. Special thanks must go to Lisa Turton and Jane Quinn at Imagination, whose grace under pressure in delivering the Flourish Design Summits, with multiple speakers across different time zones, was second to none. We are grateful for the insight and skill of Bob Murison and Helen Walker during the production process of the book. We would particularly like to thank Research England and the E3 Beyond Imagination project, which funded this publication.

In addition, Louise Valentine would like to thank Drew and Rab Walker who, in 2021, set up a charity called Falling UP Together (SCIO) SC051447, and sincerely thank Drew, Rab, and Liz Walker for their kindness and conversations that helped shape her essay. Naomi Jacobs would like to thank members of the Meme Studies Research Network, whose thoughtful conversations informed the development of her essay. Finally, Mariana Amatullo would like to thank John R. Ehrenfeld for his kind permission to include the inspirational epigraph at the start of her essay.

Introduction

Flourish by design: agendas and practice for positive change

Nick Dunn, Leon Cruickshank, and Gemma Coupe

Design impacts everyday life, shaping the way we engage with the world and those around us. This is not simply limited to the 'us' as human beings but also the many other species we share the planet with. Considered in this way, our—human and non-human—collective future may seem uncertain amidst the many challenges we now face. Climate change, social inequalities, and economic and political instabilities all represent complex, often interrelated problems that require significant and urgent responses. The level of collaboration, cooperation, and coordination needed to tackle these problems is increasingly vital. Yet from the current position, we may struggle to even begin to think about how to address such matters. Our relatively short time on the planet has seen advancements that would be inconceivable to some of our ancestors. However, despite the many positive transformations and benefits we have produced, our impact upon the planet has resulted in a context in which we can all thrive becoming more and more difficult. Clearly, some of the pathways that have led us to this point are no longer desirable or sustainable. We need to rethink some of the foundational concepts of what we do, how, why, when, and for whom. Our reliance on technological ingenuity alone cannot provide a way out of this, and the inequitable approaches that continue to produce uneven distribution of resources must be questioned. This book aims to respond to these challenges.

This book is intended for a wide audience. Is it for designers? Yes. Is it for design researchers? Yes. Yet such categorisation usually suggests a professional vocation or disciplinary focus in academia. We take a much broader view, noting the influence of design across everyday life, through multiple worldviews, embedded and often embodied in the world around us. Design is thus reflexive—we design our world, and, in turn, it designs us. It powerfully influences our choices and environments, connections and conflicts, identities and values. Put this way, we all design. How and why we design and to what extent is all variable. The point here is that we really should all care what design does, how it acts, why, where and when it does so, and for whom. Design produces work that can inform structural change and cultivate entirely different realities. A big question, then, is whether such alternatives are desirable and for whom. This is the reason this book is in front of you. We believe in making things open and accessible, ideally to everyone, so we hope you enjoy the range of contributions collected here.

DOI: 10.4324/9781003399568-1

What does it mean to set an agenda?

Design and other creative practices are replete with manifestos, platforms, and proclamations. These take various forms, whether to promote new thinking, bring together perspectives in support of an approach, or offer deliberate provocations to challenge existing paradigms. In most cases, they are conceived and shared with good intentions to question current business-as-usual pathways and encourage us to rethink how our world might be. An ambition such as this is not without its consequences. Design can be disruptive, even anti-disciplinary, so it is not a surprise that its ideas and movements have not always resulted in good outcomes. In many ways, it could be argued that the world is working in the way we designed it. And it is not working well. Design, for all its positive benefits, comes with responsibility. It can profoundly alter our relationships with each other and the world around us. Yet this agency, this transformational power, can also produce unintended consequences. The design of new products, places, services, and systems has cast a long, bloody shadow on the world. Resource extraction, multiple forms of pollution, endangering human lives and those of other species towards existential risk are also part of the legacy of design. We cannot carry on this way.

The notion of flourishing

This book explores what it means to flourish. As you will discover, this idea is open to interpretation, and we use it across the collection as a springboard for different perspectives and practices to be shared. However, core to all the essays is the role of design in shaping a better world for everyone and everything. That is not to say that we all believe design and design research are innately good and able to effect positive change. Indeed, some of the contributions in this volume delve to the very heart of what design is for and seek to challenge normative attitudes to its role by asking how it can respond to global challenges or even evolve beyond its current limitations. As with all such questions, the premise of whether it *could* is typically followed by examining whether it *should*. To flourish by design, then, is the basis for several interrelated discussions that weave throughout this book. It aims to explain what the implications might be if we are to flourish by design, how it can empower us to question prevailing approaches and inspire new ones, and why it enables us to radically rethink what design can do, when, and for whom. Many of the essays explore an aspect of design to act, providing small interventions as deep system demonstrators for what might be possible.

Exploring uncharted territory and revelling in uncertain ground

Design research is a field of considerable breadth and depth. It seeks to better understand the ways in which design can contribute to situations of complexity, instability, uncertainty, and conflict. Through this open and generous remit, design research aims to provide fresh insights, new methods, and valuable knowledge for the common good. This collection explores the difference that design research can make for people, organisations, and planet now and in the future. The origins of the book were three 'flourish'-themed design summits featuring distinguished design practitioners and researchers of international standing alongside the voices of emerging scholars. While this enabled an array of speakers to come together, the book is not simply a compendium of their talks but a collection of standalone essays. This variety of contributors is reflected in the sheer diversity of perspectives and experience, topics, and practices within the book. Compiled as a series of provocative essays, *Flourish by Design* brings sharp focus to urgent and important issues. It shares interdisciplinary and transdisciplinary design research as a means of not just demonstrating what could be plausible in the near future but also explaining why it might be preferable. This book is offered as a companion for uncertain times. Many of the contributions are short, giving incisive ideas and setting out new trajectories for the world that is 'not-yet', providing stimuli for our collective future. By sharing these despatches, this collection represents the very best of what design research can do, explaining how and why.

Discovering how to flourish by design

The book is divided into three sections: Flourishing together, Flourishing organisations, and Flourishing in the world. Each of the sections responds to a core theme in relation to how we are in the world as well as how we might want to be. In doing so, the collection seeks to provide an insightful guide to original theory and practice concerning how we can design for a better tomorrow. It offers a range of perspectives and techniques through practical examples and ongoing projects for how applied design research can respond to global challenges.

The first section, Flourishing together, brings together various ways in which we can overcome division in a world of inequality and instability. This is done across a range of scales and contexts that seek to question some of the normative ways in which we communicate, connect, and create. Part of the challenge for us as we face difficult and complex global problems concerns our identity. When we think about design, who or what is doing the designing? Also, who are we designing with or for? Design is fundamental to how our lifeworlds are brought into being, and John R. Ehrenfeld presents flourishing as an ontological concept, emphasising the need for designers to reconnect people to the world around them and eschew the ongoing separation that has occurred through technological accumulation if not overload. Mariana Amatullo explores why a design attitude is vital to tackling the crises of our times, as a holistic orientation for renewed commitment and creative confidence. Unpicking the very idea of what design is, how and why it is done, and for whom, Ingrid van der Wacht, meanwhile, explains how design festivals such as Dutch Design Week can act as a testing ground for possible concepts and scenarios that contribute to the flourishing of the world.

In the second section, Flourishing organisations, a series of perspectives are given for reconfiguring approaches for blossoming ecologies. By considering why we need a design culture appropriate to the 22nd century, Andrea Siodmok urges us to decommission the assumptions that still linger from the 20th century and work toward human-connected design as the nexus of purposeful, positive change. Questioning design paradigms is core to Kun-Pyo Lee's discussion on intentionally unfinished design to enable creativity to be a public endeavour. How we do design remains distributed and uneven. The entanglements of identities now presented by more-than-human considerations suggest, as Chris Speed explores, fertile opportunity for us to create an assemblage of interactions that are just, fair, and sustainable. Laura Santamaria, meanwhile, examines the notion of decay as the premise for cultivating hope and a collective sense of purpose through which the design of flourishing cultures can be empowered.

The third section, Flourishing in the world, explores novel trajectories for how we might rethink relationships spanning society, technology, and the wider global context. In his essay, Deyan Sudjic delves into the history of design practice to inquire whether the duality of design now has the capacity to avert a world in danger of being cooked and drowned. Providing a call for slowing down, Sevra Davis posits that a focus on action rather than achievements is imperative for design to keep overstepping its boundaries in support of the collective good. Taking deep inspiration from nature, Jenny Sabin shares three projects that demonstrate radical new models of transdisciplinary collaboration, optimistic visions of what design research can produce when working in tandem with scientists and engineers. Ravi Naidoo compels us to take design out of the studio and onto the streets and into public spaces to heal a city by directly addressing issues of democracy, dignity, and gender-based violence.

Although arranged in these three sections, this book can be read in multiple ways. Rather like the major constellations in the night sky, the three core themes provide a particular arrangement of connected ideas and practices. However, there are other interrelationships within and across the sections to be discovered. You can choose your own adventure, and along the way, understand how design research offers a unique socio-technical bridge across the arts, humanities, and sciences. Our introduction has only highlighted a cross-section of the bold and brilliant voices that are brought together in this book of 32 essays. Across the collection, there is a wide array of perspectives that illustrate the creative ways that design can overcome existing barriers that prevent a safe, secure, and sustainable future for all being possible. Design has power. It has significant capacity to demonstrate and huge capability to persuade. Design (responsibly) after reading!

Part 1
Flourishing together

Chapter 1

Flourish together

Christopher Frayling

Flourish together: a theme with the commendably ambitious aim of transcending, as far as possible, the usual social, political, national, even geographical boundaries; of examining design and design research in the roundest of the round—horizontally rather than vertically. The choice of the word 'flourish' is deliberate: "to grow or develop, in a healthy and vigorous way, in a congenial environment". The usual synonyms of 'flourish'—prosper, boom, progress, shine—do not have quite the same connotations, and several of the contributions to the book usefully emphasise the differences. 'When was the last time you heard the word "flourishing"?' It's a good question. The choice of the word 'together' is also deliberate: it implies a challenge to silo thinking; a fresh sense of reconnection. John R. Ehrenfeld, a leading authority on the theme and author of *The Right Way to Flourish*: *Reconnecting to the Real World* (Ehrenfeld, 2019), has written:

> Design for flourishing must pay attention to the larger systems in which people live out their lives, all the way to the boundaries of nations, and, for some factors like the environment, to the full expanse of Planet Earth.
>
> (2020, p. 114)

It is a broad theme, and the focus should be on the role that design and design research can actually or potentially play within it. Context-setting perspectives on the theme include:

environmental—respecting nature as more than something to consume and exploit; designing for the planet rather than for the parochial—beyond the 'human-centred', even

technological—the question of whether designers are ready for the deeper implications of artificial intelligence, which may turn them into 'algorithmic wranglers' rather than creatives

communal—new thinking about 'common ownership' and 'social co-operation' as ways of counteracting exploitative tendencies: but what about IP?

communicable—the unintended consequences of messaging; how to design communications in the digital world which can make connections in a wide variety of emotional and ethical settings

DOI: 10.4324/9781003399568-3

neural—a rebalancing of personal and social considerations, within the 'two spheres' model of the brain; a 'de-colonising of design'

synthesising—design as the silent hyphen in STEM, the missing link between science, technology, and engineering, a key means of turning them into culture, and a discipline which works particularly well with contradictions and competing interests

Of course, one danger of ideas on such a broad scale is that they can all too easily turn into slogans, manifestos, bumper stickers, cheerleading for *positivity*: recent examples in the political sphere include 'where there is discord, may we bring harmony', 'the big society', 'levelling up', and 'taking back control'. They can also all too easily confuse advocacy with research. But what emerges from the book is a series of proposals about how to make them both attractive and useable within a series of compelling oppositions, attempting to turn the big ideas into pointers towards tomorrow or maybe the day after tomorrow—*through research*.

The main *leitmotif* is a strong sense that it is time to reach out to other academic disciplines; to break down boundaries and divisions; to explore fresh research landscapes; to get beyond 'user-centred design' to a much more inclusive concept of 'values-based design' or 'empathic design'; to question 'the same old ideas, to design our ways out of them'. A frustration with 'what's in it for me?' and an emphasis instead on design research as a connector between disciplines, a conduit for flows of knowledge.

personal	social
self	other
disconnect	connect
fragmentation	wholeness
linear	circular
human	nature
novelty	longevity
exclusive	inclusive
owned	shared
design	co-design
recycle	reuse

One of the contributions specifically engages with the question of what this might mean for the discipline of design research: a period of self-examination; negotiating expanded relationships (Who? Which? Why? When?), developing strategies on the basis of them, being honest about past mistakes—a sort of truth and reconciliation commission for design researchers. All of which could lead to an expansion of the boundaries, the building of a community of research and practice, as a contribution to recovery post-COVID-19: a positive progression of ideas and ideals to help heal a hurting world. When the discipline of design research first emerged in its recognisably modern form—in the 1950s, with roots going back a lot earlier—it tended to emphasise how *distinctive* it was from the usual ways of thinking about designing: in its first phase, it was centrally concerned with theorising the design process; design as a verb rather than a noun. The architect and designer Hugh Casson used to tell the story of overhearing a conversation between two well-known designers at a meeting about the design curriculum: 'Let's be philosophical about this', said one of them. 'Don't give it a second thought'. It was in this atmosphere, or something very like it, that design research began to define itself as a credible academic discipline—inevitably, with a certain defensiveness and consequent overemphasis on words and concepts which could only be comprehended by fellow researchers inside the compound (to use Tom Wolfe's word from the polemical *Bauhaus to Our House* (1981). Second thoughts included, in that first phase, a research methodology based loosely on the sciences, 'systematic design methods', and assumptions derived from Henri Dreyfuss's ergonomic reference charts, *The Measure of Man* (1960)—assumptions which have recently been challenged as 'Nietzsche marketing'.

By 1983, Donald Schön, in his stimulating book *The Reflective Practitioner* (Schön, 1983), could argue forcefully that the technical, linear model of doing things—with its scientific language, its flowchart procedures, its clear-cut problems to solve, and its optimisation—seemed inadequate to describe most processes and performances which happened in the real world, including the design process. Schön wrote of the need for 'an epistemology of practice', a discussion of the *kinds of knowledge* involved in practical activity—which could take into account intuitive ways of coping with an unstable, messy, conflicted world; which did not derive its methods from operations, systems, and management research dating from the Second World War or from an analogy with science. Or, he could have added, dating from Victorian 'grammars of ornament' and reductive attempts to conjugate design as a formal language to be learned. Schön argued for an epistemology which would be centrally concerned with *how practitioners think*. His book mainly focused on the practices of nursing and architecture—but the idea of 'the reflective practitioner', the phrase itself, was fruitful and resonant, especially in the context of design as taught and practised in the studios of art schools.

So much has changed since those early debates: from whether designers think (second thoughts; craft knowledge) to how designers think (methods) to when designers think (contexts) to what designers think (and what they don't think). In the wake of Schön's critique (and many others), 'user-centred design' morphed into co-design and a new awareness of design not just as something you do *to* things and services but something you do *in* technological, social, environmental, and cultural contexts . . . from producers to producers in relation to consumers to producers in relation to consumers within wider worlds. It was Prof. Don Norman of San Diego who introduced the term 'user-centred design' to the lexicon of design research, and when he realised that researchers and designers were interpreting 'user-centred' in far too reductive a way, he moved on in his writings to 'human-centred design' and then to 'emotional design':

The first edition of my book *The Design of Everyday Things* focused on making products understandable and useable. But the total experience of a product covers much more than its useability: aesthetics, pleasure and fun play critically important roles. . . . Emotion is so important that I wrote an entire book *Emotional Design* about the role it plays in design.

(Norman, 2013)

The book was subtitled *Why We Love or Hate Everyday Things* (Norman, 2003). Emotional ergonomics. And beyond that, to the 'why' of emotion. Along the way, there have been—as there tend to be in all families—strong divisions within the discipline, some of which have verged on the theological. Take the great debate about prepositions, the subject of countless conferences. Research through practice or research in practice; research in design, for design, through design, as design. This was matched a little later by an equivalent debate about suffixes: practice-led, practice-based, practice-related; research into practice, through practice, practice as research. Practice or praxis. Reflection or reflexivity. Some of which resembled Polonius's advice to Hamlet, where he talks about 'tragical-historical-comical', which these days is usually played for laughs (Cantor, 2004).

But now, as the contributions to *Flourish Together* reveal loud and clear, the discipline of design research seems to have moved well beyond the 'beleaguered' stage to attain a maturity and a confidence to settle its differences and reach out—stressing that like design, design research can be a very effective agent of change and that it, palpably, has much to offer. Where partnerships are concerned, the chapters point by implication towards a series of connections with groups we find attractive: with social science, environmental sciences, policy analysis, public health, artificial intelligence, and neurology, amongst others. A wide range. Research councils have always found challenging research of an inter-, multi-, or trans-disciplinary character or cross-relational projects. Their brochures say that they welcome such kinds of research—but in practice. . . . Particularly if the partner disciplines cross ingrained administrative and institutional boundaries. And then there's the territorial nature of much academic politics. But the story of design and engineering over the past ten years has shown it can be done, if the projects are attractive enough and well thought out enough and if there's perceived to be something in it for both or all parties. And as the poet T.S. Eliot once wrote, it is better to aim at the stars and miss than never to have aimed at all. Actually, he wrote: "Only those who will risk going too far can possibly find out how far one can go" (Crosby, 1931). He also wrote in *Little Gidding* what I consider to be an inspiring definition of design research, when he concluded that the purpose of serious exploration is to arrive back where we started and *to know that place for the first time* (2019, p. 54).

Reference list

Cantor, P.A. (2004) *Shakespeare, Hamlet*. Cambridge; New York: Cambridge University Press.

Crosby, H. (1931) *Transit of Venus*. Preface. Paris: Black Sun Press.

Dreyfuss, H. (1960) *The measure of man: human factors in design*. 1st edn, Folio. New York: Whitney Library of Design.

Ehrenfeld, J. (2019) *The right way to flourish: reconnecting to the real world*. Abingdon: Routledge.

Ehrenfeld, J. (2020) 'Flourishing: designing a brave new world', *She Ji: The Journal of Design Economics and Innovation*, 5(2), pp. 105–116. https://doi.org/10.1016/j.sheji.2019.03.001

Eliot, T.S. (2019) *Four quartets*. London: Faber & Faber Ltd.

Norman, D.A. (2003) *Emotional design: why we love (or hate) everyday things*. New York: Basic Books.

Norman, D.A. (2013) *Preface to the design of everyday things*. Revised and Expanded edn. New York: Basic Books.

Schön, D.A. (1983) *The reflective practitioner: how professionals think in action*. New York: Basic Books.

Wolfe, T. (1981) *From Bauhaus to our house*. New York: Farrar Straus Giroux.

Chapter 2

Flourishing, design, and the brain

John R. Ehrenfeld

The vision of all things flourishing together is compelling in a world coming loose at the seams. Many would agree that flourishing is largely absent from the modern world. This is primarily due to the way we have designed it—with a failure to understand what we mean by flourishing and a failure to regard it as the highest cultural norm.

Flourishing together

Flourishing is not some psychological state but an ontological concept: a way of being that expresses the potential of human existence—living as fully as biology and sociability permit.

Life is an emergent property of the cosmos, a miracle defined as "any event, the occurrence of which is so radically impossible as to be completely unbelievable" (Rue, 2011, p. 86). Flourishing describes the condition in which entities are achieving their potential. And while all living entities have biological potential, humans have a second dimension: an existential potential, arising from unique cognitive and physiological capabilities that drive us towards meaningful lives (Rue, 2011).

Togetherness is one of two essential aspects of flourishing. The other is every individual's historical uniqueness. Humans are autonomous but also social. To flourish, we must attain personal wholeness and social coherence (Rue, 2011). Personal wholeness describes the fullness of the expression of one's self, the authentic way of being, in Martin Heidegger's terms. Social coherence indicates how well an individual's actions conform to society's institutions—the many ways we coordinate our collective lives. It involves actions shaped by the legacy of experience, which express the undifferentiated way of being, again in Heidegger's words.

Flourishing, *eudaimonia* in Greek, was the centrepiece of Aristotle's ethics, the ultimate end of human conduct. Aristotle saw it not as momentary happiness but as a feature of a complete life. In this sense, flourishing is largely absent in the West today. My earlier work pointed to the mechanistic framing of both nature and humans as causes of our institutions' failure to provide the conditions for flourishing (Ehrenfeld, 2008). But alone, concepts do nothing. They must appear in our lifeworlds to have impact. And they do—in how we design those lifeworlds.

DOI: 10.4324/9781003399568-4

Design is how we realise the ideas floating around our brains. In effective design, what shows up resembles our intentions. Obvious unintended consequences can be remedied, but existential impacts only show much later. We cannot open up our bodies to reveal that impact, but we can infer it from the character of our actions, and its worldly outcomes are not pretty. My country is torn apart. Civility, a measure of togetherness, has evaporated. The Earth suffers.

Although we are now more aware of the dangers, we still use the same old ideas to design our way out of them. I believe this offers little hope. Design offers a way out, but only if we harness its ontological power to change our very way of being, where our actions take us towards, not away from, a flourishing world.

Flourishing and design are intimately connected because design is inherently ontological. Design designs the kind of human beings we are. In Anne-Marie Willis's words, "we design our world, while our world acts back on us and designs us" (2006, p. 70). We are caught in a perpetual hermeneutic circle. Whatever we design changes how we act but also who we are. Clearly, we need a new model. Fortunately, we have one—a model of how the brain works, with which we can design design processes that align with both aspects of flourishing.

McGilchrist's divided brain

Iain McGilchrist argues that each brain hemisphere has a distinct way of attending to the world. Whichever is dominant determines the individual's personality and the enveloping society's character:

> I believe the essential difference between the right hemisphere and the left hemisphere is that the right hemisphere pays attention to the Other, whatever it is that exists apart from ourselves, with which it sees itself in profound relation. It is deeply attracted to, and given life by, the relationship, the betweenness, that exists with this Other. By contrast, the left hemisphere pays attention to the virtual world that it has created, which is self-consistent, but self-contained, ultimately disconnected from the Other, making it powerful, but ultimately only able to operate on, and to know, itself. . . . However . . . both hemispheres take part in virtually all "function" to some extent, and in reality both are always engaged.
>
> (2012, p. 93)

His explanation begins with the ways the two sides perceive the world, independent of the observer (see Table 2.1). Whichever form of attention is active determines the nature of the things we perceive and, subsequently, how we interact with them.

Each hemisphere, therefore, produces a different way of acting out our lives (Table 2.2). A balance of both is necessary to embed a normatively proper consciousness of the world.

In my terms, the left is the Cartesian brain that captures discrete pieces of information, objectifying the world. It is aligned with the 'whatness' of the real world and 're-presents' experience as isolated chunks.

Left Hemisphere	Right Hemisphere
Overall Perceptual Field	
Re-presentation of the past/known	Presentation of the now/new
Emptied of meaning	Meaningful
Impersonal/public knowledge	Personal/private knowledge (understanding)
Decontextualised	Richly contextual
Static	Changing/evolving
Individual Parts	
Lifeless/objectified	Living/intersubjective
Generic objects	Instantiated particular objects
Disembodied in space and time/isolated	Interconnected
Explicit properties	Implicit meaning

Table 2.1 Characteristics of the inner worlds.

Left Hemisphere	Right Hemisphere
Rational/purposeful	Concerned about
Homo economicus	*Homo curitans*
Undifferentiated/inauthentic	Authentic
Outside of/disconnected from the world	Between/connected to the world
Individualistic	Social
Focused on self	Focused on others
Self-interested/willful	Empathetic
Controlling/manipulative	Collaborative
Instrumental	Creative
Needs certainty	Tolerates uncertainty
Wants to know future (probability)	Open to possibility
Optimistic/realistic	Hopeful
Analytic/reductionist	Pragmatic
Emotionally neutral/negative	Emotionally positive

Table 2.2 Characteristics of the actor, or self.

The right side cognises organic wholes, relationships, and temporal change, 'presenting' the immediate world to a person and providing meaning—a key facet of humans' cognitive powers and one that differentiates us from other species. It is, according to McGilchrist, the primal master half.

These tables reveal a close connection between the left brain's features and salient aspects of Western modernity. This uncanny match lends power to McGilchrist's bi-hemispherical model to explain the origin and persistence of the fundaments of modernity. Significantly, this means the aspects of flourishing align with the brain hemispheres: personal wholeness with the right and social coherence with the left.

The right connects us to the now and is the seat of empathy and care. It underpins personal wholeness, which requires authenticity. The left hemisphere provides the means for social coherence which, in turn, requires knowledge of social institutions' rules and beliefs. It retrieves decontextualised knowledge from experience and re-presents it back to the right side, where it is combined with its understanding of the present to produce whatever action ensues.

A quick look at the modern world indicates left-side dominance.

- Primary societal goal: economic well-being
- Objective universe composed of decontextualised abstractions—a big, complicated machine
- Science as the method to reveal the nature of the Cartesian mechanistic world, including human nature
- Technological hubris
- Human nature: *Homo economicus* or economic rationality
- Focus on the individual

Alternatively, a flourishing world would reflect right-side dominance.

- Primary societal goal: flourishing
- Subjective universe composed of contextually interconnected parts—a garden
- Pragmatism as the method to understand the nature of the complex world, including human nature
- Technological realism
- Human nature: *Homo curitans* or caring
- Focus on relationships

When the two sides are balanced, individuals can flourish in both their autonomy and social/institutional relationships. But when one dominates and suppresses the other, the individual and culture become one-sided (an apt adjective). Today, we are stuck in a left-brain culture, living out of the detritus of the past—ignorant of, uncaring about, and unable to face the present. The suppressed right cannot add its contextual awareness of the present. Truth as a meaningful expression of the 'real' world vanishes, as does caring. The consequences should be obvious.

McGilchrist has his theory on how we arrived here, but for designers, the reason lies in the power of [ontological] design. From the beginning, virtually all design has strengthened the left brain. Our worlds have become abstract—disconnected from what's out there.

Designers must restore balance, carefully distinguishing between design for institutional settings and social coherence and design that influences how we relate to the world in extra-institutional settings, contributing to personal wholeness.

Heidegger's ontological phenomenology

At the risk of becoming too philosophical, Heidegger's phenomenology can elucidate the relationship between design and the two aspects of flourishing (Heidegger, 1962). He examined the special way that human beings 'be': how we appear in the world relative to all other kinds of objects. He dubbed humans' Dasein, translating roughly as being-in-the-world. Dasein exhibits a unique mode of being that seems closely tied to personal wholeness. The two broad categories, Dasein and other entities, are so distinct that Heidegger uses 'existence' only for Dasein, as opposed to the usual forms of 'be'.

> The being that exists is man. Man alone exists. Rocks are, but they do not exist. Trees are, but they do not exist. Horses are, but they do not exist. Angels are, but they do not exist. God is, but does not exist.
>
> (Heidegger, 1956, p. 214)

Further, the divided-brain model would have Dasein correspond to the dominance of the right side and the other modes to the dominance of the left, almost as if humans have embodied two distinct actors. Given the need to design differently for these two aspects, the dual-personality metaphor may be helpful.

By far, the task of [industrial] design is to produce practical tools. These range from Heidegger's simple example of a hammer to computers, blackboards, and even space vehicles. Their primary setting is institutional, where they are part of the institution's structure, along with the beliefs and norms (Giddens, 1984). Institutions could be described as structures created to guide intersubjective behaviours, and reflect our inherent social aspect, forming the normative framework for our lives. Family, work, school, sports, religious organisations, and more are all parts of our social being; flourishing depends on cohering to these institutions' rules. Coherence, not rigid compliance, allows us to be creative and make choices as to our actions so long as they conform to the rules and norms.

Heidegger (1962) calls such tools 'equipment'. In their normal mode of being—availableness—they are used transparently for routine tasks. His description of the way we understand such equipment is uncanny in its parallel to the way the left brain operates.

> Where something is put to use, our concern subordinates itself to the "in-order-to" which is constitutive for the equipment we are employing at the time; the less we just stare at the hammer-thing, and the more we seize hold of it and use it, the more primordial does our relationship to it become, and the more unveiledly is it encountered as that which it is as equipment.
>
> (Heidegger, 1962, p. 98)

He calls this way of understanding, 'manipulation', the same word McGilchrist uses to describe the left hemisphere's primary features. Heidegger's example of the hammer, which we will be conscious of as an object when we first encounter it, will become abstracted and categorised as it is used and, subsequently stored in the left brain, waiting for the next time something needs hammering.

This mode of being, 'available' is the primary mode involved in social coherence and the more common object of design. The mode of action that is mediated by such equipment is labeled 'absorbed intentionality', and, again, fits the way the left hemisphere works. Far from being neglected, this form of design has become so dominant that it largely suppressed designing for the other half, personal wholeness.

Interestingly, Heidegger's argument that there are three kinds of disturbances (breakdowns) which render (available) equipment 'unavailable' also fits into the divided-brain model. All change the mode by which we both encounter the world and act within it, and each corresponds closely to a different combination of left/right hemispheric dominance. (This should be read as illustrative, not necessarily as an exact description of the brain in action.) The first form of disturbance is 'malfunction' or 'conspicuousness' and occurs when the equipment malfunctions and action is interrupted. Heidegger suggests a hammer too heavy for the job. If the left brain has stored knowledge about an alternate means of coping—say, picking up a smaller hammer—it can restore action without breaking stride. The left brain remains fully in charge.

If there is no such available alternate, the second mode of unavailableness, a temporary stoppage—'obstinacy'—occurs, and the action shifts from absorbed intentionality to practical deliberation. Heidegger suggests a hammer that loses its head. Computer use also offers examples, such as pop-up ads appearing as you read a web page. The right brain becomes active, takes in the scene, and, in conjunction with the left, initiates an alternate way of coping, that is, completing whatever action had begun. The left side gives the right a role but remains dominant.

The third kind of disturbance, permanent breakdown or 'obtrusiveness', occurs when no alternate route can be discovered. The actor remains involved with the action but is helpless to move forward. The institutional setting in which the action was taking place becomes present. The right brain is now more fully engaged, but the actor cannot continue without help.

Heidegger offers another mode of the being besides availableness and unavailableness, 'occurrentness'. In this mode, practical action within an institutional setting has come to an unplanned halt, and the decontextualised world becomes present to the actor. Computer users are familiar with this, as computers often stop mid-task for unknown reasons. Action stops while the user puts the task aside and tries to figure out how to resume work. Contextual features, apprehended by the right brain, are added back to the categorical representations driving the task, but the left brain remains dominant.

As for flourishing, perhaps designers have become too proficient, so thoroughly competently designing equipment that they subvert social coherence to social slavery. Once again, Heidegger comes to mind. In later works, he pointed out the danger that the dominance of technology was framing the way humans attended to the world in such a way that Dasein, the mode of being peculiar to humans, was being concealed (Heidegger, 1977). We, along with every other thing, were nothing but 'standing reserve' for the maw of modernity. Images of life in an Amazon warehouse, prominent in the US news recently, could not be more graphic in portraying humans as standing reserve, virtually lacking agency.

Recent scholarship by Sherry Turkle and Shoshana Zuboff points to the immense power social media and associated devices have for manipulating our behaviours, damaging our personal wholeness and flourishing. Turkle (2015) argues that smart phones diminish interpersonal conversations, the primary way we relate to other people, greatly reducing our capability for acting out of empathy. Zuboff (2019) claims that the massive collection of personal data, coupled with the deliberate, persuasive power of the media, is changing who we are. Personal wholeness has little chance to emerge, since these technologies so completely engage the left brain to their purposes with little or no care for those using them that the right brain is virtually asleep. One might even say that users have become part of the equipment.

All this discussion about equipment and its modes centres on the primacy of the left brain and its relevance to the social coherence, but what about personal wholeness? Heidegger had something to say here too. As noted, our being shows up as Dasein, a form of existence in which our actions are fundamentally different from those involving equipment. Dasein's most salient characteristic is exhibiting care, attending to the world. But this world, unlike that contained within the left brain, is the external world in which the actor dwells and is connected to. The right brain is in control but needs to design specific responses based on the particular aspects it apprehends. It may be able to do this on its own but, alternatively, may have to call on the left for suggestions. In either case, it remains the dominant hemisphere. The authentic actions of Dasein constitute personal wholeness and obviously require actors capable of using their right brains in opposition to the controlling tendencies of the left.

Caring acts occur in extra-institutional contexts, including breakdowns within institutions when the context shifts from the routine to the immediate present, a key for any flourishing-oriented design. The intended outcome is designed to fit the needs of the recipient, not some instrumental institutional purpose. An action's effectiveness depends on the understanding the right brain gleans from the context, coupled with knowledge drawn from the left. In interpersonal actions, empathy is key, like knowing when a hug is in order. Watering the garden, tutoring students, showing a stranger respect, and picking up litter are all caring acts. No institutional voice is directing the actor. Metaphorically, a voice may call, but it is the actor's own.

The intention behind caring acts, unlike instrumental acts, depends on context. Although an actor may exhibit similar responses to similar situations, every caring act stands alone. In a sense, the actor must design the act to fit the circumstances. I believe 'design' is a more precise word in this case than the frequently used 'choose' and is closer to Heidegger's use of authentic to describe such acts. Not all extra-institutional acts are authentic; the actor may pluck some generic response from the left brain. Heidegger calls this mode inauthentic. Here, the right brain continues to be dominant, but the left provides a plan of action. This does not mean inauthentic acts are not appropriate; the word refers only to the way the acts were cognitively constructed. However, only authentic acts contribute to personal wholeness and, consequently, to flourishing.

Conclusion

McGilchrist's earlier quote continues with a warning about left-brain dominance.

These gifts of the left hemisphere have helped us achieve nothing less than civilisation itself, with all that that means. But these contributions need to be made in the service of something else, that only the right hemisphere can bring. Alone they are destructive. And right now they may be bringing us close to forfeiting the civilisation they helped to create.

(McGilchrist, 2012, p. 93)

Without a deliberate effort to reverse the left's takeover and rebuild the right, our march toward the abyss will continue. Designers' role is to undo this mess. One part is preventive: to avoid converting social coherence to social capture, but that also involves decisions made prior to design. At the least, we can become aware of artefactual design's impact on flourishing and decide if we will be complicit in continuing to commoditise human beings.

Designers can also bring forth Dasein and its associated authenticity. Cognitively, that means getting the right brain to dominate. Practically, it means breaking transparency, affording presence. People can care only when they are connected to the immediate world. One example is the two-button toilet, which forces the user to stop, think about the impact of the waste, and make a deliberate choice. Similarly, speed bumps wake the driver out of the transparent mode of driving and force a deliberate act that elicits care for the potential danger ahead. A quick perusal of design literature shows that works relating to this aspect of design—empowering the right hemisphere—are small compared to those that relate to the left brain.

The balance between social coherence and personal wholeness—the left and right hemispheres—is idiosyncratic and incommensurate. Everyone must find their own balance. As to the first of these two, work must be done to find coherence instead of capture. This involves questions about the design of the political economy and society writ large. Such questions are now being asked about broad concerns over inequality, global warming, racial justice, and more in my country.

On the personal wholeness side, I have coined my own label, *Homo curitans*, as the equivalent of Dasein to make the connection to care more evident (Ehrenfeld, 2020). I have offered broad categories to guide actors toward person wholeness, reflecting the panoply of extra-institutional encounters over normal life: (1) myself, (2) other human beings, (3) the non-human material world, and (4) transcendence (Ehrenfeld, 2020, pp. 103–104). Authentic action in these domains generally involves the use of artefacts but artefacts that fit the context and that maintain the connectedness and meaningfulness of the moment, beyond any role as equipment.

I hope I have articulated the critical role for design in creating flourishing together. Of course, whatever role depends on the definition of flourishing. I believe that mine represents the unique potential that only humans possess among all living species. The uncanny correspondence between the aspects of flourishing and the two brain hemispheres opens a window on a new framework for designing for flourishing.

In closing, let us circle back to ontological design. Designers must always keep in mind that flourishing is an existential quality. It is easy to lose this in the technological, utilitarian haze of modern cultures. Since I am not a designer by profession, I thought it more appropriate to end with a quote from someone who is, Anne-Marie Willis:

> The ontological claim that "design designs" (Fry's formulation) is a much stronger claim than 'design affects' or 'has an influence on'. It includes the designing of design processes, whereby outcomes are prefigured by the processes deployed and where-in the activation of particular design processes inscribe within designers' particular ways of working. "Design designs" also includes the designing effects of that which designers design (objects, spaces, systems, infrastructures). The significant point here is that all these designings are of the same order. That is, no distinction is being made about the nature or relative significance of determinations; neither object, process nor agent is granted primacy. Traditionally agency has been posited with the designer—the assumption being that the designer's intentions are embedded within the designed object which then causes the object's user to do things in certain ways. But the problem here is a flawed model of causality based on a linear temporality, in which it is assumed things can be traced back to origins further back in time—there is no particular need for this assumption when attempting to explain phenomenologically the designing that is going on in a particular situation. The fact that teams of designers worked on the configuration of the screen and keyboard I am now using cannot really help me to understand that my using this equipment is at the same time this equipment designing what I am doing. Once the comfortable fiction of an originary human agent evaporates, the inscriptive power of the designed is revealed and stands naked.
>
> (2006, p. 95)

Reference list

Ehrenfeld, J. (2008) *Sustainability by design: a subversive strategy for transforming our consumer culture*. New Haven, CT: Yale University Press.

Ehrenfeld, J. (2020) *The right way to flourish: reconnecting with the real world*. New York: Routledge.

Giddens, A. (1984) *The constitution of society*. Berkeley, CA: University of California Press.

Heidegger, M. (1956) 'The way back into the ground of metaphysics', in Kaufmann, W. (ed.) *Existentialism from Dostoevsky to Sartre*. New York: Meridian Books.

Heidegger, M. (1962) *Being and time*. New York: Harper and Row.

Heidegger, M. (1977) *The question concerning technology and other essays*. New York: Harper & Row.

McGilchrist, I. (2012) *The master and his emissary: the divided brain and the making of the Western world*. New Haven: Yale University Press.

Rue, L. (2011) *Nature is enough: religious naturalism and the meaning of life*. Albany, NY: State University of New York Press.

Turkle, S. (2015) 'Stop googling. Let's talk', *New York Times* [online]. Available at: www.nytimes.com/2015/09/27/opinion/sunday/stop-googling-lets-talk.html (Accessed: 10 April 2021).

Willis, A.-M. (2006) 'Ontological designing', *Design Philosophy Papers*, 4, pp. 69–92.

Zuboff, S. (2019) *The age of surveillance capitalism: the fight for a human future at the new frontier of power*. New York: Public Affairs.

Chapter 3

Designing more-than-human urban places

Nick Dunn

The idea that design should be human centred seems increasingly precarious, if not downright preposterous given the anthropogenic impacts we have made and continue to make on the planet. Our relentless quest for the future has produced an astounding array of beneficial places, products, and services for our species. In some instances, design has literally been lifesaving. It has, however, also resulted in widespread resource extraction and led to serious damage to the environment, destruction of ecosystems and habitats, multiple forms of pollution, and putting animal lives at risk, and it continues to contribute towards climate change. There is no doubt that as a species, we are unusual. Our lives carry a characteristically different sense of purpose, and this has encouraged us to view the world with human values, overlooking the qualities of place that enable flourishing of other species in different ways (Lopez, 1986). This separation from the rest of the living world has increased over time. Yet while this may initially appear to be positive, commonly understood as an important transition for our primitive origins, it can also be recognised as highly problematic and in urgent need of redress.

Much of this transformation has been driven by culture and notions of progress. The capacity of culture to store information outside the human body has enabled us to advance in countless ways, and other species do this differently. Ants, for example, have reached their global success by diversifying into more than 14,000 species. As humans, we have very few environmentally specific adaptations. Instead, we have speciated our culture. Parallel to this development, more and more of the world's human population have sought to live in urban environments, with 68% predicted to be living in urban areas by 2050 (UN DESA Population Division, 2018). Urban environments are complex. Their amalgamation of people, economy, and technology is frequently positioned as a triumph, offering as it does the opportunities for us to flourish and change our lives in positive ways. At least this is the theory. In reality, however, it is also the dynamic interactions between these elements that result in many of the problems in urban environments. This is before we even begin to consider the other species we share the planet with.

For most of us, living in cities has served to further our detachment from the rest of the living world, often simply referred to as 'nature'. The versions of nature we find within our cities raise important, and increasingly urgent, questions about what is good or better. If we follow Bruce Braun's (2005) assertion

DOI: 10.4324/9781003399568-5

that urbanisation is a particular spatialisation of nature, what is made visible in such places is a highly sanitised version of urban nature. This is due to the development of urban landscapes which integrates, perhaps more accurately subsumes, distinctive characteristics within a single socio-ecological system and thereby profoundly alters nature in the process. Certain aspects of nature, therefore, are considered to be compatible with urbanisation and are included in the design of urban places, while others are not, being deemed problematic or completely omitted. In particular, the manicured aspect of urban green spaces results in questionable decisions where the wildlife value of them is dismissed. In the UK, for example, exotic tree species are deliberately planted as no native wildlife can benefit from them, so they are low maintenance and favour neatness. Other plants that are useless for pollinators, meanwhile, are used in urban parks, limiting their use to insects. Why should this matter?

Renewed focus on the places where we live and work has encouraged us to rethink our relationship with them. Amidst the plethora of new agendas advising us to connect to green and blue spaces for our health and well-being, especially in urban environments, are a flurry of visions for how this metropolitan life should be. We are presented with azure skies and verdant districts in cities. These representations are alluring but also elusive, since the natural world does not stop beyond the buildings and streets. Rather, it lives on, above, around, underneath, and away from our homes and places of work. Of course, it also lives on the surfaces of the city, in the cracks, out of view or undetectable by human eyes. More-than-human life is a multi-scalar phenomenon, from the microscopic to the global networks of migration by numerous different species. I use the term 'more-than-human' in this essay to avoid the pejorative dimensions of the term 'non-human' when referring to other living beings so as to not diminish their status in relation to our species. A more-than-human approach to urban places can provide new insights since it considers other-than-human agency, in that people are not the only ones shaping urban landscapes. For example, the Städte wagen Wildnis (Cities Venturing into Wilderness) project in Germany, where a hands-off approach to green spaces means that new habitats for plant and animal species will be created in Dessau, Frankfurt, and Hanover. Acknowledging the significance of biodiversity opens new worlds of possibilities for reimagining cities in more sustainable and resilient ways to help mitigate the climate crisis. Multispecies urbanism is useful because it "shifts our vision to include other modes of urban creation and fields of political contestation and can alert us to the ways that urban nature itself helps is to locate and site the city" (Sharma, 2021, p. 2).

Developing an approach for the design of more-than-human urban places means also being cognisant of those existing sites of urban nature that may appear empty, neglected, or unproductive. Although there is growing demand for acknowledging that such untamed natures exist, can add value, and have a right to the city, their qualities can provoke derogatory and even hostile responses from humans (Mattoug, 2021). Existing practices by built environment professions and policymakers typically overlook these kinds of places until it is profitable for them to undergo regeneration. Urban regeneration is a process which, in its current forms, will inevitably have a range of ecological impacts, for good or ill, depending on the species of flora and fauna. I therefore argue that it is useful to turn our attention and open up sensitivities to those elements that are usually underrepresented or excluded from design. Viewed from this perspective, it is becoming increasingly urgent and important for us to consider how we might account for our "unexpected neighbours" (Stoetzer, 2018) and, in doing so, establish a framework through which the more-than-human city can be supported. This would involve a dynamic and ongoing process that adopts agile design principles and practices, including a more temporally sensitive approach to architecture, urban design, and urban planning.

The theory regarding more-than-human approaches for rethinking nature in cities (Maller, 2021) is still nascent. By making such urban natures legible through practice-based methodologies (Pollastri et al., 2021), accounts of multispecies encounters enrich our understanding of how urban environments and atmospheres are coproduced. I contend that such knowledge can not only enhance but essentially transform built environment design practices and policy, rendering them attentive to the various ways in which coexistences of humans and more-than-humans shape our cities. This is imperative amidst an era of climate emergency where we need to protect and support biodiversity both within and beyond our cities. This is where design can make a difference, empowering approaches such as the implementation of corridors of coexistence and the rewilding of cities to become the baseline for how we develop urban environments. To conclude, we need to fundamentally rethink the ways we develop and deliver urban places to inform how design can have greater sensitivity toward and responsive principles and practices for the coproduction of urban environments. This would enable *all* of us to move towards ethical and convivial more-than-human cities and flourish together.

Reference list

Braun, B. (2005) 'Environmental issues: writing a more-than-human urban geography', *Progress in Human Geography*, 29(5), pp. 635–650. https://doi.org/10.1191/0309132505ph574pr

Lopez, B. (1986) *Arctic dreams: imagination and desire in a northern landscape.* New York: Charles Scribner's Sons.

Maller, C. (2021) 'Re-orienting nature-based solutions with more-than-human thinking', *Cities*, 113, 103155. https://doi.org/10.1016/j.cities.2021.103155

Mattoug, C. (2021) 'Dwelling in an urban wasteland: struggles for resources', in Di Pietro, F. and Robert, A. (eds.) *Urban wastelands: a form of urban nature?* Cham: Springer, pp. 115–134.

Pollastri, S. *et al.* (2021) 'More-than-human future cities: from the design of nature to designing for and through nature', in de Waal, M. and Suurenbroek, F. (eds.) *MAB20: proceedings of the 5th media architecture biennale conference.* New York: ACM, pp. 23–30. https://doi.org/10.1145/3469410.3469413

Sharma, A. (2021) 'The city under stress. Waking to a multispecies urban', in *Position paper, Urban environments initiative*, 11 January. Available at: https://urbanenv.org/the-city-under-stress/

Stoetzer, B. (2018) 'Ruderal ecologies: rethinking nature, migration, and the urban landscape in Berlin', *Cultural Anthropology*, 33(2), pp. 295–323. https://doi.org/10.14506/ca33.2.09

UN DESA Population Division (2018) *World urbanization prospects: the 2018 revision, key facts*. New York: United Nations.

Chapter 4

Why a design attitude matters in a world in flux

Mariana Amatullo

The vision of all things flourishing together is very compelling in a world that seems to be coming loose at the seams.

(John R. Ehrenfeld, 2019)

Scientists have coined the second decade of the 21st century *the decade of determination*: one in which the stakes could not be higher to come to terms with planet Earth's finite nature and fragility. In the face of the current climate emergency, an era of climate mitigation and gradual solutions is giving way to calls for significant transformations in the ways our global society functions and interacts with our natural ecosystems (Ripple *et al.*, 2020). Meanwhile, economic and energy supply pressures dominate many political agendas, powering net-zero and low-carbon technology investments. A profound reckoning with systematic racism has ignited new efforts to confront ingrained legacies of discrimination. Geopolitical strife with the Russian war on Ukraine, a tense and broadly competitive relationship between the US and China, and global populism threats against democracy fuel a sense of interdependence and resolve to confront insecurity and uphold human rights values worldwide.

These recent events have created a confluence of challenges and multiple crises that most of us have not experienced before. The complexity we face elevates our shared consciousness about the gravity of these trials and the importance of finding new sources of resiliency. In this context, the United Nations and other global actors are renewing commitments for resolution as COVID-19 transitions from pandemic to endemic and ahead of the mid-point for the Sustainable Development Goals implementation agenda (SDG Summit, 2023). As we contend with this VUCA world by addressing volatility, uncertainty, complexity, and ambiguity, many forces–social, economic, environmental, political, and technological–are coming together in new ways that make our relationship to change a constant. In the fluid circumstances under which we must operate, change becomes a regular part of our daily lives rather than the exception. Our outlook must be prospective (Rittel, 1988). As we increasingly observe the limitations of the linear and reductionist models of thought that often govern our traditional management practices, the cognitive flexibility we find in design

DOI: 10.4324/9781003399568-6

as a field of knowledge and research promises new opportunities for optimism, learning, and hope.

Celebrating the positive core

David Cooperrider, the founder of Appreciative Inquiry (Ai), a theory of change for organisations grounded in positive psychology, reminds us that one of humanity's greatest gifts is that new perspectives are forged in times of shock and disruption (Cooperrider and Selian, 2021). Cooperrider has been a long-time champion of organisations as centres of human connectivity and collaboration. A body of research shows that institutions can harness their positive cores to magnify strengths and bring forward a full spectrum of human flourishing (Elkington and Upward, 2016). Ai is founded on the premise that we excel only by amplifying strengths, never by simply fixing weaknesses (Cooperrider and McQuaid, 2012). Ai involves the art and practice of asking positive questions and generating 'life-giving stories' that can energize all stakeholders by creating shared and lasting agendas for positive change. Ai interventions focus on the power of imagination and innovation instead of dwelling on the negative and deficit-based approaches that we tend to fall back on, with the prevailing focus on solutionism that abounds in our organisations (Cooperrider, Stavros and Whitney, 2008).

As we contend with our planet's critical challenges, we can draw parallels between the positive principles underpinning Ai and the relationships that John R. Ehrenfeld draws between the concept of flourishing and design. His conceptualisation of the latter situates design "at the heart of a move toward a flourishing world"; it characterises design as "perhaps the most critical of all intentional activities that govern human life" (Ehrenfeld, 2019, p. 115).

Richard Buchanan's classic definition of design also highlights the actionable nature of design as a force for human betterment. He provides a valuable framing that brings to light the humanity and purposefulness core to the design act. He underscores the transversal quality of design that cuts across domains: "the human power of conceiving, planning, and bringing to reality all of the products that serve human beings in the accomplishment of their individual and collective purposes" (Buchanan, 2005, p. 504). This framing invites an inherent sense of optimism. It points to the agency of design—leveraging the potentiality of design for organisational transformation. Design emerges as the connective tissue for collaboration and the basis of a shared understanding across differences. This is a field in which practitioners and researchers alike are uniquely positioned—by virtue of their capacity to craft user experiences and shape artefacts of all kinds— to make tangible visions of plural futures and bring those futures to life, creating new ways to explore and experiment.

Embracing a design attitude to flourishing together

Ehrenfeld suggests that 'flourishing' is an emergent property of a complex system supported by design (Ehrenfeld and Hoffman, 2013). If we assume that the best in our human systems comes about most naturally when people collectively experience the wholeness of their system, and, as Ai suggests, when strength ignites strength across complete configurations of relevant and engaged stakeholders, internal and external, and top to bottom (Cooperrider and McQuaid, 2012), design becomes paramount to flourishing. In other words, our prerogative is to design for flourishing and to build a framework of inclusive and holistic possibility (Laszlo *et al.*, 2012).

What might be the stance to respond to such an urgent call to action?

Based on more than two decades of design research and practice in social innovation, I would like to emphasise the importance of embracing a design attitude as a possible path forward (Amatullo *et al.*, 2021). Design attitude is a multidimensional construct that can be sourced to Richard Boland and Fred Collopy's (2004) view of 'managing as designing', which draws on Herb Simon's (1969) claim that design as intelligence is separate from decision-making (i.e., choice)—albeit both necessary elements of effective organisational change. Specifically, design attitude is a composite of distinct abilities (skills, capabilities, aptitudes) that designers apply during designing; the dimensions of these abilities are (1) ambiguity tolerance, (2) engagement with aesthetics, (3) connecting multiple perspectives, (4) creativity, and (5) empathy. Several empirical and mixed-method studies have shown that design attitude is the cognitive orientation designers take when they engage with complex situations (Boland and Collopy, 2004; Michlewski, 2008; Amatullo, 2015; Amatullo, Lyytinen and Tang, 2019). Thus, a design attitude is a mindset that opens spaces of new possibilities for creating alternatives, accelerating outcomes in fluid innovation processes. By drawing on design attitude, designers augment design thinking as behaviours that exhibit intellectual and formal depth, catalyse unexplored possibilities, and foster creativity and the potential for social innovation.

Concluding provocation

If we embrace design attitude as a holistic orientation that underlies design praxis, we can also start advocating for the concept of flourishing with renewed commitment.

Flourishing individuals and organisations go beyond the limits of incentives and rational attempts to disrupt the status quo. They are able to tap into something much more profound and powerful. Like the act of designing, they unleash our capacity to imagine together and harness our shared humanity. This promise is worth holding onto as we meet the challenge of the coming years with creative confidence—and by design.

Reference list

Amatullo, M. (2015) *Design attitude and social innovation: empirical studies of the return on design.* Cleveland, OH: Case Western Reserve University.

Amatullo, M., Boyer, B., May, J. and Shea, A. eds., 2021. *Design for social innovation: Case studies from around the world*. Abingdon: Routledge.

Amatullo, M., Lyytinen, K. and Tang, J. (2019) 'Measuring a design attitude in accelerating social innovation: scale development and validation', *Academy of Management Proceedings*, 2019(1), p. 13907. Briarcliff Manor, NY: Academy of Management.

Boland, R. and Collopy, F. (eds.) (2004) *Managing as designing*. Stanford, CA: Stanford Business Books.

Buchanan, R. (2005) 'Design ethics', in Mitcham, Carl (ed.) *The encyclopedia of design, technology, and ethics*. Farmington Hills, MI: Thomson Gale.

Cooperrider, D.L. and McQuaid, M. (2012) 'The positive arc of systemic strengths: how appreciative inquiry and sustainable designing can bring out the best in human systems', *Journal of Corporate Citizenship*, (46), pp. 71–102.

Cooperrider, D.L. and Selian, A. (eds.) (2021) *The business of building a better world: the leadership revolution that is changing everything*. Oakland, CA: Berrett-Koehler Publishers.

Cooperrider, D.L., Stavros, J.M. and Whitney, D. (2008) *The appreciative inquiry handbook: for leaders of change*. Oakland, CA: Berrett-Koehler Publishers.

Ehrenfeld, J.R. (2019) 'Flourishing: designing a brave new world', *She Ji: The Journal of Design, Economics, and Innovation*, 5(2), pp. 105–116. https://doi.org/10.1016/j.sheji.2019.03.001

Ehrenfeld, J.R. and Hoffman, A.J. (2013) *Flourishing: a frank conversation about sustainability*. Redwood City, CA: Stanford University Press.

Elkington, R. and Upward, A. (2016) 'Leadership as enabling function for flourishing by design', *Journal of Global Responsibility*, 7(1), pp. 126–144.

Laszlo, C., Brown, J., Sherman, D., Barros, I., Boland, B., Ehrenfeld, J., Gorham, M., Robson, L., Saillant, R. and Werder, P. (2012) 'Flourishing: a vision for business and the world', *Journal of Corporate Citizenship*, (46), pp. 31–51.

Michlewski, K. (2008) 'Uncovering design attitude: inside the culture of designers', *Organization Studies*, 29(3), pp. 373–392.

Ripple, W.J. *et al.* (2020) 'World scientists warning of a climate emergency', *BioScience*, 70(1), pp. 8–12. Available at: https://academic.oup.com/bioscience/article/70/1/8/5610806

Rittel, H.W. (1988) *The reasoning of designers*. Boston, MA, USA: IGP.

SDG Summit (2023) Available at: www.un.org/en/conferences/SDGSummit2023/

Simon, H.A. (1969) *The sciences of the artificial*. Reprint, Cambridge, MA: MIT Press, 2019.

Chapter 5

Flourish(ing) by design?

Paul Rodgers

The word 'flourish', like the word 'design', is both a noun and a verb. As a verb, flourish means to grow or develop in a healthy or vigorous way (especially as the result of a particularly congenial environment); develop rapidly and successfully; be working at the height of one's career during a specified period. Flourish as a noun means a bold or extravagant gesture or action, made especially to attract attention; an elaborate rhetorical or literary expression; an impressive and successful act or period.

The etymology of the word flourish[1] c. 1300 (as a verb) is '*to blossom, grow*' from the Old French *floriss-*, stem of *florir* '*to blossom, flower, bloom; prosper, flourish*' and similarly from Latin *florere* '*to bloom, blossom, flower*'; figuratively '*to flourish, be prosperous*'.

Interestingly, in the 1550s, flourish (as a noun) takes on the meaning '*an ostentatious waving of a weapon*' and from c. 1600 '*excessive literary or rhetorical embellishment*' in reference to decorative curves in penmanship as '*a fanfare of trumpets*' c. 1650.

Design as a noun refers to a plan or drawing produced to show the look and function or workings of something before it is made; the art or action of conceiving of and producing a plan or drawing of something before it is made; the arrangement of the features of an artefact, as produced from following a plan or drawing; a decorative pattern; purpose or planning that exists behind an action, fact, or object. As a verb, design means to decide upon the look and functioning of (a building, garment, or other object), by making a detailed drawing of it; do or plan (something) with a specific purpose in mind.

The etymology of design[2] (as a noun) from the 1580s means '*a scheme or plan in the mind*' from the French *desseign, desseing* meaning '*purpose, project, design*' from the verb in French, especially '*an intention to act in some particular way*' often to do something harmful or illegal. Earlier, in the 1630s, the artistic sense of the word 'design' was taken into French as *dessin* from the Italian *disegno*, from *disegnare* '*to mark out*' from the Latin *designare* '*mark out, devise, choose, designate, appoint*', which is also the source of the English verb. The general (non-scheming) meaning '*a plan or outline*' is from the 1590s, '*the practical application of artistic principles*' is from the 1630s, and '*artistic details that go to make up an edifice, artistic creation, or decorative work*' is from the 1640s.

DOI: 10.4324/9781003399568-7

Design (as a verb) originates from the late-14th-century meaning '*to make, shape*' from the Latin *designare* '*mark out, point out; devise; choose, designate, appoint*'. The Italian verb *disegnare* (16th century) developed the senses '*to contrive, plot, intend*' and '*to draw, paint, embroider etc.*' French took both these senses from Italian, in different forms, and passed them on to English, which uses *design* in all senses.

So to flourish involves growth, development, and success, the very same outcomes that many design projects set out to achieve. As such, one might argue that a key aim of design and designing (be that a new product, service, system, space, or strategy) is to flourish—in an economic, social, cultural, and/or environmental sense. Flourishing in this world, however, is not achieved by dealing with these things in isolation. A nation's economic development, for example, cannot and should not come at the expense of its people's health and well-being. Nor should it harm the planet's natural environment and resources. Gordon Brown, ex-prime minister of the United Kingdom, stated in a speech on climate change in 2005:

> If our economies are to flourish, if global poverty is to be banished, and if the wellbeing of the world's people enhanced—not just in this generation but in succeeding generations—we must make sure we take care of the natural environment and resources on which our economic activity depends.
> (Full text: Gordon Brown's Speech on Climate Change, 2005)

In essence, Brown is suggesting that we, as designers and design researchers, strive to achieve a harmonious and sustainable balance between our natural environment and resources and our economic development. In a design context, this challenge is not new. Designers and researchers such as Victor Papanek, Donella Meadows, Dieter Rams, and others have acknowledged the significant impact of their work and the responsibility of balancing economic development with the health and well-being of people and the planet. In recent years, Papanek's primary argument around design's responsibility has become central to many designers' ethical stance in the design, production, and consumption of products, systems, and services. The notion of 'responsibility' has been embraced by many contemporary design researchers and practitioners working towards positive social and environmental outcomes, which is acknowledged explicitly in three of Dieter Rams' 10 Principles for Good Design (Lovell, 2011):[3]

- Good design is long-lasting—it avoids being fashionable and therefore never appears antiquated. Unlike fashionable design, it lasts many years—even in today's throwaway society.
- Good design is environmentally friendly—nothing must be arbitrary or left to chance. Care and accuracy in the design process must show respect towards the user(s). Design makes an important contribution to the preservation of the environment. It conserves resources and minimises physical and visual pollution throughout the life cycle of the product.

- Good design is as little design as possible—less, but better, because it concentrates on the essential aspects, and the products are not burdened with non-essentials. Back to purity, back to simplicity.

More recently, however, Arturo Escobar's critical questioning of Papanek's 'Real World' highlights a lack of representation of all experiences of reality and all worlds. Escobar proposes a decolonial and pluriversal approach instead, one that designs for many worlds rather than the usual one world of the Global North (Escobar, 2018).

From another perspective, Franco 'Bifo' Berardi, founder of the renowned 'Radio Alice' in Bologna and an important figure of the Italian Autonomia Movement, points out that the endless thirst for economic growth and profit and the denial of our planetary limits makes us extremely tired (Berardi, 2011). Berardi believes that for our future world to flourish, it will not be driven by energy but by slowness, reminding us that we were first advised of the finite physical resources of the planet when the Club of Rome commissioned the book *The Limits to Growth* over 50 years ago (Meadows *et al.*, 1972).

Today, we witness a world that is seriously unprepared to deal with the mounting crises we face because we have based our ways of life on the identification of energy and goods; have an overriding obsession with accumulation, property, and greed; and strive for continual growth, expansion, and social well-being. For example, currently in the United Kingdom, 300,000 households could be forced into homelessness because of the rising cost of living and the ongoing economic and social impacts of the COVID pandemic (Crisis UK, 2023). Also, pollution and pollution-related deaths are increasing; we see rising levels of poor mental health, workplace discrimination, depression, and high suicide rates (particularly amongst young men); significant increases in violent crime and hate crime have been reported in the aftermath of the Brexit vote; and sustainability and transformation plans (STP) designed to make improvements to health and social care across the UK will actually mean a loss of services.[4]

But if we were to contemplate a creative consciousness of slowness, as Berardi proposes, the current crises and other issues may mark the beginning of a massive abandonment of competition, consumerist drive, and dependence on work and help address our contemporary malaise.

In their book *Slow Wonder: Letters on Imagination and Education* (2022), Peter O'Connor and Claudia Rozas Gómez develop Berardi's concept of slowness further by proposing creative alternatives to current orthodoxies that privilege technocratic approaches to education, which, they claim, have strangled discussion about what it might mean to make education good and right or even beautiful. O'Connor and Rozas Gómez posit the imagination as a powerful site of resistance within education and other walks of life through marrying the poetic and the academic, the rational and the affective, to model a slow approach to wondering about the joy, beauty, and possibilities of life. In so doing, they contemplate new ways for us to think (design) and live.

Returning once more to Papanek, this year (2023) sees the 100-year anniversary of the birth of the Austrian-born American designer and educator who became a leading advocate of socially and ecologically responsible design. Papanek's book *Design for the Real World*, originally published in 1971, has been translated into more than 24 languages and has sustained its impact among design scholars and researchers all over the world. Papanek's radical ideas on design and his global approach to educational and other issues at the time was a fresh shift away from the existing design movements of the 1960s and '70s—a time of significant individual self-expression and personal emancipation. Papanek perceived design as an object or system, specifically as a political tool and how it might directly affect people, society, and the environment. He considered much of what was being designed and manufactured to be inconvenient, often frivolous and thoughtless (Papanek, 2019).

As we face a series of interrelated global crises of climate emergency and serious public health issues, financial inequalities and challenges to democratic processes across the world, the need for designers and design researchers to develop impactful interventions takes on ever greater importance. This does not mean we overlook important qualities such as care, responsibility, and rigour but that we are wary of economic-driven quick wins and of doing things in a rush solely for a fast profit. Currently, we inhabit a world (at least from a UK perspective) that cannot be described as flourishing—in an economic or environmental sense, nor in a health and well-being or a political or any other sense. Indeed, Adam Smith, the revered Scottish economist and philosopher, wrote in *The Wealth of Nations* (1776): "No society can surely be flourishing and happy, of which the far greater part of the members are poor and miserable" (Smith, 2014).

So the call is for design researchers to take the lead on impactful interventions where our purpose and focus is on caring for life rather than on extraction, consumption, and production. If we are to flourish in the future, we need to privilege 'Earth Care' where an ethics of care for humans applies to all-of-life design. Stephanie Carleklev describes this as a careful theory of design(ing) that "has fewer answers and embraces the life we care for in a rather inconsistent, inaccurate and unpredictable manner" (2021, pp. 244–245).

What is needed, then, is a repurposing of design to focus on innovative ways and methods that open up new possibilities for our lived experiences and imaginations. New ways forward that advance the understanding of design from the perspective of social responsibility. Ways that support design as an innovative and creative practice that can transform communities and societies and enhance human well-being. Perhaps a caring theory of design that seeks to make a difference in the world, bringing greater care to what we look to design and make. As Jen Archer-Martin writes, "a caring theory of design is an embodied, living practice of caring for, about, with and through design" (2021, pp. 220–221). New designed ways forward that help us flourish collectively and not at the expense of any group or individual nor at the expense of any more-than-human entity. This is ***the*** challenge facing us all.

Notes

1 Online Etymology Dictionary. *Flourish entry*. See www.etymonline.com/
2 Online Etymology Dictionary. *Design entry*. See www.etymonline.com/search?q=design

3   Dieter Rams. *Ten principles for good design*. See https://readymag.com/shuffle/dieter-rams/?gclid=EAIaIQobChMI39DE5o_5_AIVCZntCh1fOw0-EAAYASAAEgLmn_D_BwE

4   Grayling. See https://grayling.com/news-and-views/a_look_at_the_biggest_social_issues_facing_the_uk/

Reference list

Archer-Martin, J. (2021) 'A caring theory of design[ing]', in Rodgers, P.A and Bremner, C. (eds.) *118 theories of design[ing]*. Delaware, United States: Vernon Press, pp. 220–221.

Berardi, F. (2011) 'Time, acceleration, and violence', *e-flux Journal*, (27), September. Available at: www.e-flux.com/journal/time-acceleration-and-violence/

Carleklev, S. (2021) 'A careful theory of design[ing]', in Rodgers, P.A and Bremner, C. (eds.) *118 theories of design[ing]*. Delaware, OH: Vernon Press, pp. 244–245.

Crisis UK (2023) 'Crisis homelessness charity | together we will end homelessness'. Available at: www.crisis.org.uk/ (Accessed: 21 March 2023).

Escobar, A. (2018) *Designs for the pluriverse: radical interdependence, autonomy, and the making of worlds*. Durham: Duke University Press.

Full text: Gordon Brown's Speech on Climate Change (2005) *The Guardian* [online], 15 March. Available at: www.theguardian.com/politics/2005/mar/15/economy.uk (Accessed: 3 March 2023).

Lovell, S. (2011) *Dieter Rams: as little design as possible*. London: Phaidon Press.

Meadows, D.H. *et al.* (1972) *The limits to growth: a report for the club of Rome's project on the predicament of mankind*. New York: Universe Books.

O'Connor, P. and Gómez, C.R. (2022) *Slow wonder: letters on imagination and education*. Cambridge: Cambridge University Press.

Papanek, V. (2019) *Design for the real world*. 3rd edn. London: Thames and Hudson Ltd.

Smith, A. (2014) *The wealth of nations*. London: CreateSpace Independent Publishing Platform.

Chapter 6

Memes—designed to flourish or doomed to divide?

Naomi Jacobs

Our world is infused with digital content. We can now create, access, share, and transform this content at incredible speeds. From the now-defunct Vines to GIFs, tweets and TikToks, there are many new forms of highly shared and shareable media, which Jenkins, Ford and Green (2013) call 'spreadable'.

When the so-called Web 2.0 arrived, it was believed to be a way of democratising the spread of information. The ability to create and upload became open to almost anyone—all you need is a device with an internet connection.

In this new digital space, technology is bringing us together; by making these connections, we have the ability to thrive. It is helping us to flourish by broadening our understanding and allowing us to connect with others who might previously have been beyond our reach. And so as designers and design researchers, we should consider the value that this spreadable media can bring to our work, particularly with regards to communication design. But do all memes have positive impacts, and is this still the case once these memes escape the control of the creator? Can you design internet memes? Should you? How might designers use internet memes in their work? What makes something a meme in the first place?

Design in the age of memes

Memes are not new, and in fact, the idea of transmissible ideas is even older. When Richard Dawkins coined the term in 1976, it was these spreadable ideas he was thinking of. But in the digital world, once something starts to spread, it infects much more widely and at a much more rapid pace.

It is still unclear what makes a certain idea spread when others do not, what makes something 'catchy'. Even defining something as being a meme is difficult. Is it a digital image, perhaps including words, that can be copied and shared on social media? Is it the format of that image rather than the single instance that people can adapt in multiple ways? Or is it the idea and concept that go into making something that people want to interact with and share with others, going back to Dawkins's self-replicating cultural unit?

Creating something that is appealing or useful—something people might feel compelled to share—is a key aspect of design. Dawkins suggests that "Examples of memes are tunes, ideas, catch-phrases, clothes fashions, ways of making pots or of building arches" (1989, p. 192). Several of these are also clearly

DOI: 10.4324/9781003399568-8

examples of design. Daniel Dennett (2017) goes further, describing memes as "design worth stealing or copying" (p. 206). Perhaps design research is therefore perfectly placed to consider what features a meme might need to spread.

Designers might incorporate aspects of digital memes into their designs—particularly if the goal is appealing to and reaching people on a wider scale and transmitting information. How we design media content to educate and convey data, for example, might take inspiration from popular memes.

Affective digital design

Limor Shifman (2015) differentiates between two different ways to research memes: first focussing on the way they spread then on the way they are used to support shared communities of meaning. Both should be of interest to design researchers.

How people create and receive messages, particularly digital ones that spread so widely and rapidly, depends on values and emotional attachment. These are not only intensely personal but shaped by our experiences and context. In an increasingly fragmented digital reality, not only do we not all have the same experience, but it may not be possible to know what others are seeing, as algorithms serve us all up a uniquely created digital space. Demirkol Tonnesen (2021) has written about how 'ambient context' can create a unique time and space in which digital expression has meaning; a tweet about something happening at that moment will no longer be interpretable days or weeks later, or if one is not situated in that particular ambient context.

Multiple layers of meaning embedded in media content is not new; any visual or language-based communication relies heavily on context and, in part, on the meaning brought by the recipient. There may be surface levels of understanding, with meaning and depth added when particular cultural points of reference are understood. But because memes combine images, text, and format in simplified, limited immediacy, their representational features can easily be transferred to give a meaning which may be different from that intended by the person who made it. This can be problematic if those meanings are in conflict.

Dangerous memes

The use of symbolic and representational content online has many purposes. Among these is the ability to build a shared vocabulary and language that cements communities, forming an important part of expression both on- and offline. This is particularly crucial in the case of subcultures, countercultures, and underground movements. When they spill over into visibility on the wider stage, these symbolic trappings can appear nonsensical or even ridiculous. But in some cases, they can be subsumed into the wider culture, at which point they may lose interest for and be distanced by the original subculture that created them (Pelletier-Gagnon and Pérez Trujillo Diniz, 2021).

In this way, identical imagery and symbols that are incorporated into memes can be used by different groups in very different ways. An example of this is *Pepe the Frog*, a cartoon created by artist Matt Furie, coupled with the catchphrase

"Feels good, man". The image appears online and offline in many different guises and has become particularly associated with offensive material posted by far-right online groups and factions of former US President Donald Trump's supporters (Pelletier-Gagnon and Pérez Trujillo Diniz, 2021). Within these groups, the character was used as a rallying cry. For those opposed to these groups, seeing Pepe therefore evokes strong negative reactions. But this is not the only use of Pepe—the character also appears as a symbol of pro-democracy protesters in Hong Kong, many or most of whom likely have no knowledge of alternative uses.

As designers, we must be careful when we work with memes to consider how they may be received, used, and appropriated for those whose values differ from our own and how division and exclusion can be the basis for connection. Working in our new porous digital/physical hybrid space, our key concern must be to acknowledge these challenges and to not make assumptions about understanding. What meanings, values, and understanding do those receiving and using our designed objects and services bring or create, and how does affect interact with design? What if the meanings are not those we intended and, in fact, are counter to our own ideals? How might we even know if this was happening?

What's next for memes and design?

We cannot design for everyone. Rather than try to design for an implausible, imaginary universal audience, memes could be designed to target specific groups, harnessing the power of shared understanding. Combining cultural referents, symbology, and often humour, memes can be a more effective tool in the designer's toolbox for reaching unique subcultures. But we must be cognisant of the dangers in this approach and how fragmented communities and unseen understandings can have negative—even damaging—impacts in the world. We can't predict or even necessarily comprehend the full reach of what we design: what happens when our tame memes escape and evolve beyond the places and groups we designed them for?

Put simply, can we really flourish together if we cannot understand each other?

We might want to consider how design research can be an important tool for understanding memes, both their features and their spread, and how they impact the world. In this way, perhaps we can support empathy and shared understanding across these divides. Digital memes are as much a part of our world and the way we communicate as catchy ideas and concepts have always been. As designers, we must ensure that we are fully engaged with making sense of digital memes and are able to use digital memes to make sense of the world, in a way that helps us flourish.

Reference list

Dawkins, R. (1989) *The selfish gene*. 2nd edn. Oxford: Oxford University Press.

Demirkol Tonnesen, N.O. (2021) 'Perceived interconnectedness and the dependence on ambient context on twitter during elections', *AoIR Selected Papers of Internet Research*, 2021.

Dennett, D.C. (2017) *From bacteria to Bach and back: the evolution of minds*. New York, NY: W.W. Norton.

Jenkins, H., Ford, S. and Green, J. (2013) *Spreadable media*. New York: New York University Press.

Pelletier-Gagnon, J. and Pérez Trujillo Diniz, A. (2021) 'Colonizing Pepe: internet memes as cyberplaces', *Space and Culture*, 24(1), pp. 4–18.

Shifman, L. (2015) Memes as ritual, virals as transmission? in praise of blurry boundaries. *Memeology Festival 05*. Available at: https://culturedigitally. org/2015/11/memeology-festival-05-memes-as-ritual-virals-as-transmission-in-praise-of-blurry-boundaries/ (Accessed: 7 April 2022).

Chapter 7

Can designers and AI flourish together?

Boyeun Lee

Artificial intelligence (AI) is a computer's ability to simulate how humans think and act. Ever since its emergence in the 1950s, it has been the subject of intense interest, offering the possibility of disrupting industries across a range of sectors. For instance, generative AI uses algorithms to produce novel data, texts, videos, and images based on patterns and relationships identified in existing data. In design industries, generative AI is used as a design process to write design briefs or create a number of possible design solutions. For instance, Airbus partnered with Autodesk, the design and engineering software company, to design components of planes of the future using generative design in 2015 (Autodesk, 2015). In 2018, Autodesk introduced an interactive visual analysis tool called Dream Lens to help designers explore a large array of 3D design solutions at the Computer–Human Interaction conference. With this system, they were able to create a number of 3D-printed monitor stand design variations (Figure 7.1). Recently, AI has been in transition from these 'brute force' approaches of creating billions of designs to effective approaches of providing optimal design solutions. Superficially, there is the potential for an artificial designer to only bring positive impacts that enable the creation of designs with better efficiency and speed than when the task was given to a human designer. However, design AI is now being faced with a number of new challenges as to what it means to be a designer and for the role of design in future. This provocation highlights some of the critical issues designers will have to consider if they are to flourish alongside AI, which then suggests the potential for critical contributions of design research towards value creation.

In terms of protecting the ownership of AI-inspired design, the key issues of flourishing alongside this technological revolution are copyright and the ownership of work produced by algorithms. In the past year, the most well-known artificial intelligence models to produce content have been released by OpenAI: ChatGPT (a chatbot that mimics human conversation) and DALL·E (a tool for AI-generated art that generates digital images from text descriptions). Generative AI uses existing content to train a machine-learning model to produce new works. The training data for ChatGPT is largely pulled from the internet—from Wikipedia to Reddit, the BBC, blog posts, books, and more. Similarly, DALL·E uses the vast corpus of images found online. Hence, the output generated by AI from copyright-protected data might infringe copyright and could face serious legal challenges. Indeed, a

DOI: 10.4324/9781003399568-9
39

Figure 7.1
Conceptual illustration of a collection of design variations for a single task: lifting a computer monitor 80 mm off a desk.
Image courtesy: **Matejka, J.** *et al.* **(2018) 'Dream lens: exploration and visualization of large-scale generative design datasets',** *Proceedings of the 2018 CHI conference on human factors in computing systems (CHI '18).* **Association for Computing Machinery, New York, NY, USA, Paper 369, pp. 1–12. https://doi.org/10.1145/3173574.3173943. Fig.1, with permission.**

group of artists have filed a lawsuit against the companies behind AI art generators, Stable Diffusion (Chen, 2023).

Regarding commercial implications, these generative AIs also raise another significant question: 'Who has the ownership of output generated by AI?' This ambiguity can cause great confusion and potentially undesirable consequences. If the works generated by AI are not protected by copyright, the obvious question is, 'Does this mean work created by AI can be freely used and reused by anyone around the world?' which is not very hopeful for the company that invested in the design. To address this, OpenAI has attempted to transmit its ownership of the generated content as part of the product's terms of use if the outputs are original. However, 'original' is somewhat unclear, as it is unlikely that you would know whether the AIs have ever generated the same outputs before. Moreover, it is likely to be ineffective in Spain, Korea, Australia, and the US, where only work produced by human beings can be granted copyright protection. On the other hand, if the designer contributes to AI-generated work with some level of intervention, 'What level of copyright can the designer have?' Clearly, we are at a transitional stage of rapid AI development and implementation in which notions of originality are understood differently.

Apart from the problematic questions surrounding copyright and commercial implications, artificial intelligence may pose an imminent threat to designers' livelihoods, because design is one of the most creative human activities. For instance, in generative design, AI creates thousands of options based on the requirements of structures and substructures. It then identifies and suggests the top few options that best fit the design requirements. AI-generated design solutions can be cost-effective and efficient and result in more manufacturable products. In this process, a designer's contribution is to assess the results and select the most effective, best-performing and aesthetically pleasing design. However, would designers value this role over the existing one that more readily involves their imagination and creative practice? As creative thinkers, problem-finders, -solvers, and innovators, designers are regarded as highly valuable assets to any business. They make their ideas tangible by sketching, drawing, prototyping, building, and experimenting, which sometimes involves uncomfortable, challenging, and complex processes. While developing designs through these creative activities, designers also find the meaning of what it is to be designers and continuously build on their creative thinking. Although hundreds of novel designs can be generated by AI algorithms, which might be perceived as beneficial to the business, it would diminish what it means to be a designer by using what is, in effect, a 'brute force' approach to replace the skills of designers going through the creative process and essentially turning them into algorithm wranglers.

Despite the concerns that artificial designers may well eventually replace human designers, the author argues that a human designer's ability in problem-finding and -framing is needed more than ever. It is evident that AI would bring several advantages, such as cost-effective businesses and improving the customer experience by analysing users' behaviour patterns in real time. However, when we look at the design process thoroughly, there are distinct advantages that human designers bring. These are the design research activities in the early stages of the process, such as empathising with others, problem-finding and -framing based on a thorough understanding of the context, and making sense of subtle nuances and complexities in decision-making. Humanity has been critically valued through the design process, specifically when tackling a wicked problem. Most likely, a design process begins with comprehending the real-world situation, identifying an opportunity, revealing underlying needs, and understanding the context of a challenge. Empathy for the users is critical at this early stage of the design process, which is not yet embedded in algorithms, and true empathy may prove to beyond AI development for some time. It may even prove to be a fundamental limitation. Designers learn as much as possible about users' wants, needs, anxieties and difficulties and turn these into an actionable problem statement which identifies the gap between the current situation and the desired one of a process or a product. AI can confirm if the problem statement is accurately framed based on an understanding of the users. However, without a human designer's empathy, the problem statement will only be superficial, missing important details of the challenges.

Designers' ingenuity and value judgements are also qualities in which AI is unable to surpass human designers. The design process is an iterative journey in which we transform disorder into order, generate diverse ideas, and creatively synthesise them to generate pleasing outcomes. While we transform disorder into order, we make numerous difficult decisions, particularly when there is no clear answer due to a conflict of interest or uncertainty, which could have an unforeseen impact. For example, when designing an application or website, there are several well-known UI (user interface) design principles, including clarity, consistency, simplicity, user control, usability, accessibility, and delight. AI may help to develop an application or website, but it is challenging to develop one that satisfies all these principles, because some may conflict and require a subtle balance. For instance, a user interface with information density and overload to nurture the users' feeling of control would harm the value of simplicity. As such, a human designer's intervention based on value judgement can make sense of the complexities and uncertainty based on a thorough understanding of the design context. Moreover, designers' ingenuity is critical in improving the details of the features, style, feel, and forms as they are created in the process of synthesising different ideas and judging their value. Although AI generates many proposed design options at high speed, these lack finesse or reflection. Because of the human designers' sensitivity, the subtle nuances of design generated by AI can be adjusted.

AI is bringing more complexity into current design practices, notions, and a small fraction of what we are going to be faced with. Whether easy or difficult, the future is coming faster than we think, and AI will be a part of our creative practice. Although this advanced technology is proliferating rapidly and seems to be a threat to designers, this chapter argues that designers cannot be replaced by AI without the human capabilities of empathy, problem-finding and -framing, ingenuity, and value judgement, attributes that will always be utilised over the design process. In the early phase of the design process, finding and framing a design problem based on empathising with users and comprehending the context is critical. Later in the design process, designers making sense of uncertainty and subtle nuances are required to make the appropriate design decision and improve the user experience. AI is an intelligent tool that designers can exploit rather than combat. It is a stepping stone to something more useful, meaning we designers need to think about how we will use it. That is the challenge, but we shall bring design ingenuity to how we utilise this tool, shaping a new generation in this way of creating innovation rather than being threatened by it.

Reference list

Autodesk (2015) *Autodesk and Airbus show the future of aerospace design and manufacture in pioneering generatively designed 3D printed partition.* Available at: https://adsknews.autodesk.com/en/news/autodesk-and-airbus-show-the-future-of-aerospace-design-and-manufacture-in-pioneering-generatively-d/ (Accessed: 9 March 2023).

Chen, M. (2023) *Artists and illustrators are suing three A.I. art generators for scraping and 'collaging' their work without consent.* Available at: https://news.artnet.com/art-world/class-action-lawsuit-ai-generators-deviantart-midjourney-stable-diffusion-2246770 (Accessed: 8 March 2023).

Chapter 8

Challenging capitalism through design for commonism

Rosendy Galabo

The dominant paradigm of capitalism is fundamentally unfair. It nurtures inequalities and establishes power in the hands of a few people who have or who inherit control over the private or state resource systems (e.g., land, real estate, industry) that make up the wealth of nations and shape social, economic, and political processes. Whoever has or inherits the power to control these resources and to influence these processes is in an advantageous social condition to have better health, education, and access to employment. Social inequalities are driven by this unequal distribution of wealth, income, and power, which leads to inequities in people's social conditions and differences in many aspects of life, such as housing and health. To tackle these inequalities, there is a need to provide support for alternative ways of distributing power and wealth to progress the equity agenda and increase collective control over the aspects that shape the lives of communities, particularly those that are socially disadvantaged and deprived. Design research has the potential to support new equitable social practices and thus contribute to changes in the direction of politics, social relations, and economies through the new design practices that empower communities to have agency in economic and political processes that affect their everyday life. Although design research has historically addressed control over decision-making (political agency), a new design practice that addresses the distribution of wealth (economic agency) across communities and has attracted the attention of the design research community is called design for commonism.

Nico Dockx and Pascal Gielen define the term *commonism* in the book *Commonism: A New Aesthetics of the Real* (2018) as "a new radical, practice-based ideology . . . based on the values of sharing, common (intellectual) ownership and new social co-operations". The term *commons* was originally applied in land management practice that dates back to 1215 and was used as a legal term for common land, where certain tenants and others held the rights over a specific piece of land. These people, called commoners, had a sense of 'sharing' and joint ownership. In present times, a commons includes a shared natural or human-made resource system and sustainable governance strategies used by a community as the primary stewards rather than a government entity or private organisation. Shared resource systems or common goods exist at all scales, and the resource units used or withdrawn by commoners can be material or immaterial, such as physical or digital tools, infrastructures, spaces, knowledge,

DOI: 10.4324/9781003399568-10
43

or information. Fisheries and forested land (e.g., national parks) are two natural resources that have long been managed as commons. Linux and Wikipedia are well-known examples of digital commons. Examples of urban commons are parks and community gardens managed by local residents. In this sense, commonism is defined as a new political belief system based on self-sufficient modes of production, new social relationships, trust, and shared ownership of resource systems.

Literature on the commons offers robust analytical frameworks to understand the infrastructure of existing functional commons but is lacking in approaches to support communities in creating or improving commons infrastructures (Sacks and Galabo, 2022). These infrastructures are physical and digital materials or institutional structures that people use to manage a shared resource and monitor the behaviours of commoners in order to protect the commons from depletion, enclosure, privatisation, or commodification. Design research can support communities interested in creating or improving commons infrastructures and commoning practices to support the maintenance of shared resources, such as production, distribution, monitoring, and enforcing resource-use rules. Design researchers can develop open spaces, tools, and approaches that frame the way communities engage with commons situations and conditions for self-governance, enabling people to creatively participate in modifying and enforcing the rules for sustainably managing a commons. Commons action situations or commoning practices involve individuals' actions taken and outcomes obtained that directly affect day-to-day decisions. For example, in an action situation in which a member of a community garden breaks a piece of gardening equipment, a community can explore how this member might repair the equipment through the use of creative engagement tools to develop rules to manage the situation. Another way design can support commonism is by creating new extensions to a digital platform to improve the management of resources and people, such as gadgets for Wikipedia.

In essence, only resource systems can be considered commons and should involve community-led management of the shared resources and self-managed networks, which are decentralised and protected by commoners. Commons literature focuses on self-governance and the aspects and conditions that affect the success of community members sustainably governing commons but lacks approaches for community-based action to solely create and manage commons. Design for commonism involves supporting commoning practices that can nurture commons, value cooperation rather than aggravate inequalities, and exploit social relations in a capitalistic way. Supporting such collective actions creates social cohesion, mutual responsibility, and community resilience and encourages the development of partnerships with those affected by inequality and exclusionary processes. Design research can empower people in commoning practices through the design of creative spaces, tools, and approaches that enable communities to have political and economic agency over the wealth that shapes processes that can affect their lives. These designs can facilitate different notions of power (WHO, 2010), enabling excluded groups to participate and influence existing economic and political structures (power over); become more active in transforming these structures (power to); improve their capacities to exercise collective action (power with); and recognise their fundamental human rights (power within).

Commonfare.net is an example of a co-design project, in which the main goal was to foster and facilitate a social welfare approach based on social cooperation with local communities in Croatia, Italy, and the Netherlands (Bassetti *et al.*, 2019). The project was aimed at tackling societal challenges, such as precariousness, low income, and unemployment, in collaboration with citizens at risk of material deprivation and social exclusion who were committed to re-appropriating the common good. The research outcomes include the recognition of the common values that are important for the successful creation of cooperative communities, such as fairness, justice, dignity, autonomy, and the design and development of a digital platform that challenges the dominant socioeconomic paradigm. The design of Commonfare.net reflects these common values, providing a space to support autonomous cooperation, where a community can share resources, practices, and information to deal with issues they are concerned about.

The Grange Pavilion project in Cardiff, UK,[1] is an example of participatory architecture that started with community engagement events to gather stories in 2012, which informed the design brief of the place that guided the final design and its opening in October 2020. In this project, design researchers and students from Cardiff University worked in partnership with residents, policymakers, local businesses, and health professionals to take over and redevelop a vacant public facility into a community-led and community-owned multifunctional pavilion and garden, where people of all backgrounds could connect and feel welcome. Before initiating the architectural and design briefs, the research team focused on building the community and developing a common ethos by gathering stories through creative engagement events to increase awareness and build capacity in residents and community groups and organisations (McVicar and Turnbull, 2018). The research outcomes include increased community resilience, social cohesion, improvements in the built environment, and an increase in activities offered for well-being, employment, and youth provision.[2]

From a design research perspective, the main implication of designing for commonism is that researchers should empower communities to take over and manage their local assets and resources produced as part of design projects. This could involve developing approaches that enable voluntary or community groups to take over land, buildings, or structures owned by a public body or to run a particular service. Researchers should frame their work or interventions beyond design and architecture outputs, looking at the sustainability, legacy, and long-term impact of their projects towards socioeconomic and political alternatives that can nurture commons and value cooperation and social relations. This involves citizens taking ownership and control over the commons design after researchers leave the project. Some questions around these challenges include how can communities self-manage the commons once research funding is over? Which capabilities are required to enable people to self-manage shared resources?

To sum up, design for commonism becomes a viable alternative to allow us to flourish together and overcome inequality, injustice, and instability generated by capitalism. This approach can empower communities to have control over resources to reduce inequalities and differences in access to such resources instead of commodifying material or immaterial resources and keeping them under the control of public and private organisations.

Notes

1   Grange Pavilion Project. See http://dcfw.org/case-study-creating-a-community-led-and-community-owned-facility/
2   Grange Pavilion Impact. See http://www.designforthecommongood.net/dcg-exhibition/curated-works/grange-pavilion/

Reference list

Bassetti, C., Sciannamblo, M., Lyle, P., Teli, M., De Paoli, S. and De Angeli, A. (2019) 'Co-designing for common values: creating hybrid spaces to nurture autonomous cooperation', *CoDesign*, 15(3), pp. 256–271. https://doi.org/10.1080/15710882.2019.1637897

Dockx, N. and Gielen, P. (eds.) (2018) *Commonism: a new aesthetics of the real*. Amsterdam: Valiz.

McVicar, M. and Turnbull, N. (2018) 'The live project in the participatory design of a common ethos', *Charrette*, 5(2), pp. 117–135.

Sacks, J. and Galabo, R. (2022) 'A framework for infrastructuring commons creation', in Bruyns, G. and Wei, H. (eds.) *With design: reinventing design modes: proceedings of the 9th congress of the international association of societies of design research (IASDR 2021). IASDR: congress of the international association of societies of design research*, 9, Springer, Singapore: IASDR 2021, pp. 1016–1036. https://doi.org/10.1007/978-981-19-4472-7_67 (Accessed: 5 December 2021).

World Health Organization (2010) *A conceptual framework for action on the social determinants of health*. World Health Organization. Available at: https://apps.who.int/iris/handle/10665/44489 (Accessed: 15 March 2023).

Chapter 9

How cross-relational design research can foster pandemic recovery

Elisavet Christou

The COVID-19 pandemic has challenged us all to examine what lessons we can learn from this period and to reflect on how we can collectively build back better futures. As researchers, scientists, artists, and designers, how can we engage with wider design research and practice ecosystems—finding our place in this new landscape? In short, how can our research communities work together to build resilience and recovery?

An opportunity for 'cross-relational' collaboration?

The pandemic has forced us to set new research priorities, engage with pressing issues and address challenges. But we should also acknowledge that the last couple of years have offered a historic opportunity for building better systems and approaches for collaboration within our ever-evolving research ecosystems.

Whether to meet those new priorities or to make the most of that opportunity, it is vital that we work together: recovery demands cross-relational efforts, global solidarity, and innovation (UN Research Roadmap for the COVID-19 Recovery, 2020). But to understand how we can better support efforts for both resilience and recovery, we first need to understand the true meaning of 'cross-relational' collaboration.

Does this mean prioritising collaborations between industry, the public sector, and researchers? Is it about investing in knowledge bridging between disciplines? Should we look to build partnerships and align efforts within our research communities? Or do 'cross-relational' efforts cover all these possibilities?

These are important questions for design researchers to consider. Exploring avenues for more effective research collaboration not only is timely in terms of fostering resilience and recovery but will also ensure that design expertise has greater impact, recognition, and reach across the research landscape for the longer term.

Building networks in a changed world

Design processes are by their nature processes of synthesis. When we design, we bring together elements from different parts—disciplines, groups of people, and practice fields. As such, they are collaborative and co-creation processes,

DOI: 10.4324/9781003399568-11

where participation and input from various stakeholder groups are valued and prioritised; design research fundamentally invites cross-relational interactions.

However, examining what cross-relational means for design research in the context of resilience and recovery means re-examining the existing networks across design research in a world changed by the pandemic at both a micro and macro level.

We must recognise and harness our agency in forming new connections across and within our networks while adopting a pragmatic approach to a research landscape altered and refocused by an urgency for practical solutions in the face of the pandemic.

In the UK in particular, the complexity of both the research and innovation and the research and development landscapes is a fundamental issue when developing plans and strategies for resilience and recovery (UKRI Corporate Plan, 2020–21). Finally, examining what cross-relational means for design research in the context of resilience and recovery also means facing our limitations and correcting mistakes of the past.

Practical steps for cultivating cross-relational collaboration

In the face of changing ecosystems, landscapes, and priorities, how can design researchers and design research groups develop cross-relational efforts for resilience and recovery? We can offer five avenues to explore:

1 **Increase literacy in design research ecosystems**

Developing our understanding and awareness of our design research ecosystems is not only about charting their different elements but also understanding of how these operate and connect to each other. The potential list of elements is extensive. This includes the industries, organisations and institutions, communities and social groups that already use design research and practice in their services, operations and applications. It also extends to the relevant government bodies and research-funding bodies as well as our own virtual and physical design research infrastructures. Better understanding of how our work as designers is positioned and connected to these ecosystems and identifying under-explored connections could support us in realising new cross-relational collaborations. This could be achieved through activities like design-research ecosystems mapping, design-research landscape workshops or cross-organisational networking events.

2 **Expand community ties**

Design researchers are part of existing research communities, both design focused and otherwise. Community-based relations are often more inviting of input by others and allow for more direct communication between members. Expanding our community ties could mean inviting others (such as organisations, communities, and other research groups) into our existing community networks by making networking and collaborative activities part of our programmes. It could, however, also mean actively seeking to participate in external community networks, whether by developing new strategies for new cross-sectorial research or by prioritising a more inter/cross/multi- and trans-disciplinary research agenda.

3 Develop strategies for cross-relational collaborations

Strategy development starts with identifying opportunities for both existing and new collaborations. Design research environments like conferences, societies, and associations are prime opportunities for discourse and strategising around new research. This is especially true since the COVID-19 outbreak, where many conferences have introduced new formats for discussion and networking, increasing participation through various virtual environments. However, it is equally important to look beyond traditional or familiar forums to settings open to more interest groups. This not only helps us expand our communities (as per point 2) but also creates broader opportunities for working with partners beyond the usual research or academic circles for strategic-thinking and strategic-planning processes.

4 Develop infrastructures for collaboration

Infrastructure development has become a priority in research and innovation agendas in the UK in recent years. By developing better research infrastructures, we will promote cross-disciplinary and cross-sectoral collaborations—fostering cross-relational efforts for now and for the future. This could be achieved by investing in supporting technologies like virtual platforms, open-access databases, and research and practice that promote collaborative interactions and improve research capacity.

5 Develop applied ethics for cross-relational collaboration

For our cross-relational efforts to truly foster resilience and recovery, it is essential that they are built on an unshakable ethical foundation. How can we ensure that we are relationally inclusive, multi-directional and committed to building a better and more equitable, resilient and sustainable design research infrastructure for the future? By using existing ethical frameworks for applied ethics—or developing new ones where needed—our cross-relational strategies and operations can encourage better collaboration, build trust, and foster a professional culture of respect, responsibility, and accountability among participating parties. At the same time, sound ethical frameworks will enhance the integrity of our research activities for the public and for all stakeholders.

Harnessing design research for a post-pandemic future

In the wake of the greatest challenge of our generation, it is vital that we consider our role and, in doing so, examine our methods, approaches, and frameworks, even if that means turning to unfamiliar ground or crossing traditional boundaries.

As design researchers, we have an opportunity to make our skills vital tools in building a better post-pandemic world. Ours is a discipline rooted in innovation in both its methods and its results. As such, design research should embrace the opportunity to forge new networks—growing both our communities and our impact.

The five steps outlined here offer a start—practical suggestions for speeding recovery and fostering resilience.

Reference list

UKRI Corporate Plan (2020–21) Available at: www.ukri.org/wp-content/uploads/2020/10/UKRI-091020-CorporatePlan2020-21.pdf (Accessed: 10 March 2023).

UN Research Roadmap for the COVID-19 Recovery (2020) Available at: www.un.org/en/coronavirus/communication-resources/un-research-roadmap-covid-19-recovery (Accessed: 10 March 2023).

Chapter 10

Flourishing in joyful discovery

Scaffolding new thinking

Lee Brewster

We lean heavily on the umbrella term 'design'. It helps us paint over the gaps that such a sweeping label might expose, the bits we either do not understand or are unable to adequately explain. We expect that everyone has some understanding of what we mean when we say 'design', but that understanding might not necessarily be the same or even similar as anyone else's. Design researchers often invite their partners to playfully engage in the game of design without providing them with the rules, and this method does not inspire confidence.

We know from the literature and successful, tangible collaborative projects like Leapfrog: Transforming Public Sector Engagement by Design (Lancaster University, 2018) and Empowering Design Practices (Open University, 2021), that confidence is a key element if we intend to explore uncertain ground together. Designers spend years building a resilience to uncertainty and repositioning and valuing their understanding of failure, both essentials for doing design. It is unreasonable to expect partners to do this in a short period of time, during a workshop or similar intervention, without providing some secure scaffolding, e.g., that of explicit and accessible language.

Designers and researchers often draw on a huge range of literature and examples to explain what design is and its component methods for doing. However, this is an unwieldy and complex archive to navigate that offers more questions than answers for those participants and partners keen to be engaged as agents of change in their social contexts.

Explicit language will help us to continue the demystification of design. Designers are reliant on the tacit knowledge that they have assimilated over many years. If designers had a better grasp of what they do and were able to explain and contextualise how they do design, perhaps designers and partners alike would more easily believe in what they were doing. They might find the confidence to be disruptive with their own thinking, take risks and joyfully think the unexpected, not only when doing design but in everyday activities, like learning and problem-solving.

It is not enough to say 'this stage is about divergent thinking', 'thinking outside the box', and 'being out there'. These terms do not mean anything without being explicit in how and why to do them. There are multiple annotated diagrams the design researcher can refer to in order to try and explain how to do design, and they provide a visual notion of the overall design process that can be theoretically adopted. The Design Council promotes the adoption of the Double Diamond Framework (Design Council, 2021), for example. Even so, the conversation

DOI: 10.4324/9781003399568-12

continues as to: What is design? What does it do? How is it done? with little in the way of common language and understanding filtering through academia to the world beyond. Outside academia, it is still common place for design to be categorised by subject area or specific household objects, furniture design, textile design or interior design. This is how most people understand it; they see design as a thing, not a process. The process is hidden while the object is visible.

Doing collaborative design and participating in workshops is beginning to help make process visible. Using engagement tools and collaborative design methods, observing them and writing about how much agency they were afforded does provide and disseminate valuable knowledge and understanding, but on its own, it is not enough.

Collaborative design values the diverse individuals who are engaged in the process; this is played out and exemplified time and again in the projects that tussle with societal issues. However, these diversity-led projects seem to consistently begin at the messy front end that Sanders and Stappers (2008) describe as the creative, chaotic thinking process that happens at the beginning of design projects. Let us be in a position to provide an adequate—no, an inspirational— explicit language and understanding that facilitates the confidence, awareness, and mindset to grapple with this designerly thinking. Let us nurture confidence that encourages risk, disruption, and failure as essential elements of design before we get to the chaos of creative thinking. The confidence to be playfully irreverent and disruptive is an element of designerly thinking that is seldom recognised or communicated, perhaps due to lack of recognition or from fear of consequence.

Figure 10.1
Collaborative designers exploring how to unlock an open and playful disposition.
Source: **Photograph by Robyn Saunders.**

Figure 10.2
Young people and teachers from West End Primary School (Morecambe) and Lancaster University student ambassadors being welcomed to ImaginationLancaster's design research lab.
Source: Photograph by Robyn Saunders.

Figure 10.3
Collaborative designers exploring the fundamental elements needed for designerly ways of thinking.
Source: Photograph by Robyn Saunders.

Let us strive to remove this fear of consequence and replace it with playful, open-minded pursuit of imaginative and unexpected ways of thinking. We all understand that we have a responsibility to provide impactful outcomes and that tangible good-quality outcomes are of paramount importance. However, for those outcomes to be more frequent and of a higher quality, the confidence to be disruptive must be encouraged. The FUSE project (ImaginationLancaster, 2022), undertaken at ImaginationLancaster, exemplifies joyful discovery through thinking irreverently and mischievously. This way of thinking also extends beyond design through a cross-disciplinary research team that used language to identify design fundamentals (Brewster *et al.*, 2022).

This language emerges from challenging the tacit behaviour of the designer to make their processes visible. FUSE has begun to explore this tacit knowledge through workshops that have invited designers to identify the fundamental elements of practice that cannot be distilled any further.

This knowledge is being shared through collaborative design workshops with primary-school children and teachers, and it is disrupting thinking and learning, not just in design but across the curriculum. The children who have attended the FUSE workshops are happy to call themselves agents of change and to apply a new way of thinking wherever they decide it is needed. They are asking What if? and Why not? And they are valuing the power of failure and informality to gain confidence, to do the unexpected. Providing explicit and accessible design language is not supporting us to identify solutions to societal issues, it is prompting us to ask the right questions in order to make the best-informed decisions about our futures.

"You've turned my world upside down."—FUSE project co-designer age 9.

Let's provide the scaffolding for everyone to be an agent of change. It's not difficult! We just need to do it.

Reference list

Brewster, L. *et al.* (2022) *Using design to connect children through playful discovery ISSN: 2758–0989—The European conference on arts, design & education 2022 official conference proceedings.* https://doi.org/10.22492/issn.2758-0989.2022.24

Design Council (2021) *Framework for innovation.* Design Council. Available at: www.designcouncil.org.uk/news-opinion/what-framework-innovation-design-councils-evolved-double-diamond (Accessed: 1 December 2021).

ImaginationLancaster (2022) FUSE. Available at: https://imagination.lancaster.ac.uk/project/fuse/ (Accessed: 22 November 2022).

Lancaster University (2018) *Leapfrog: transforming public sector engagement by design.* Available at: https://imagination.lancaster.ac.uk/leapfrog-tools/ (Accessed: 14 July 2023).

Open University (2021) *Empowering design practices: historic places of worship as catalysts for connecting communities.* Available at: www.empoweringdesign.net (Accessed: 24 February 2022).

Sanders, E.B.-N. and Stappers, P.J. (2008) 'Co-creation and the new landscapes of design', *CoDesign*, 4(1), pp. 5–18, Taylor & Francis.

Chapter 11

Build together a flourishing world

Let's give a shit and plant seeds

Ingrid van der Wacht

It is obvious that our planet is far from flourishing and is, indeed, decaying in an even more rapid tempo over recent decades. The Club of Rome published *The Limits to Growth* in the early '70s about the necessity to stop the continuous striving for economic growth and to impose limits on ourselves and our production of material goods (Meadows *et al.*, 1972).

But humankind, especially in the northern hemisphere, seems to be addicted to a lifestyle that is responsible for the deplorable state the world is in. We take more from nature than it can regenerate. This is represented in Earth Overshoot Day[1] by marking the date when humanity has used all the biological resources that Earth regenerates during the entire year. Since 1971, this date moved from the end of December to July 28th in 2022 on a global perspective.

As John R. Ehrenfeld states, "Sustainability has failed. Instead, the positive image of flourishing has the power to reverse the course of environmental and social deterioration. . . . The ultimate goal of every designer should be to foster flourishing. But as an emergent property, it cannot be obtained directly by technological or institutional design" (2020, p. 114). Ehrenfeld calls for humans to live more mindfully and for any institutions or objects that are being re-designed to "enhance *presencing*: the perception of being connected to the contextually rich surrounding world. Design for flourishing must therefore pay attention to the larger social and environmental systems in which people live out their lives" (2020, p. 114).

The science is there, but how to make humanity aware of it and act on it?

Some examples of bringing the message across to larger audiences over the last 12 years include:

- "You have doubled the consumption of my resources in the last thirty years" exclaims our exhausted planet Earth, played by actor Stephen Fry in the short animation movie Costing the Earth.[2] And he shrewdly adds: "You need me more than I need you". The film created by Accounting for Sustainability explained the thoughts behind the need to embed sustainability into an organisation's DNA.
- Economist Kate Raworth,[3] with the help of creatives, transferred her knowledge and ideas about abandoning the economic growth perspective and created the model of The Doughnut of social and planetary boundaries. Numerous

DOI: 10.4324/9781003399568-13

explanatory Doughnut movies have followed and been shown in classrooms, boardrooms, and policy offices.

- Dutch product designer Babette Porcelijn comes up with a true footprint calculation in her book *Hidden Impact*.[4] Clear visuals make the impact of our present consumption perfectly clear. If everyone in the world reached the average consumption of a Dutch person, we'd devour more than the equivalent of three Earths.

However, it is very likely that these actions do not directly reach the wider public.

This must have been one of the reasons that, during her first State of the Union address in the European Parliament, EU President Ursula von der Leyen launched a call to all Europeans, and specifically the creative industries and the building sector, to create a New European Bauhaus (NEB). The aim: to kickstart a European renovation wave and make the European Union a leader in the circular economy. NEB should not be just an environmental or economic project but "a new cultural project for Europe. Every movement has its own look and feel. And we need to give our systemic change its own distinct aesthetic—to match style with sustainability".[5]

It started a chain reaction fuelled by the Commission's Joint Research Centre (JRC) team, responsible for policy innovation. The team's designers, architects, and experts elaborated on contributions from European researchers in design for policy to write about the New European Bauhaus "as a school of thought and practice for the European Green Deal", stating "Design and architecture, as they concern culture and identity as much as technology and materiality, can play a fundamentally powerful role here, helping transform an avant-garde into a 'new wave' of systemic change" (Bason *et al.*, 2021). JRC launched a website to engage partners from all over Europe through digital conferences and meetings. They have launched an NEB Compass to guide decision-/project-makers with a framework at the design phase for all types of NEB projects encompassing the three pillars: Beautiful, Together, Sustainable. They also drew participants in NEB Prizes (2021/22) and the NEB Festival (2022) representing a diversity of organisations and communities across Europe. To mention two projects from over 3,000 applicants: The 2022 nominee in the 'Reconnecting with Nature' category was the Jume Garden Class Room in Latvia,[6] a community-driven and -curated outdoor classroom that brings new ways of accumulating and sharing knowledge through permaculture. In the 'Shaping a Circular Ecosystem' category, the 2022 winner was Flaux Flower leather.[7] Around 40% of commercially grown flowers are thrown away before reaching consumers. Flaux—Flower Matter is a research project by graduates of two Finnish/German institutions aiming to divert flower waste from landfill. 'Flaux' is an innovative 'bioleather' made from discarded petals that could generate a positive environmental impact in the fashion industry by replacing leather.

As the 2021/2022 European Commission's New European Bauhaus Progress Report states: "Only two years after its launch, NEB has become a catalyst for the European Green Deal transformation, ensuring social inclusion and participation. The initiative has grown into a movement with an active and growing community from all EU Member States and beyond".[8]

Based on over 20 years' experience on advocating integration of (Dutch) design to make better companies, better lives, and better futures, I'd like to put in a plea for more transitional cross-over projects between organisations in all sectors of economy, society, education, ecology, and, of course, design. As John R. Ehrenfeld advocates, designers are indispensable in creating projects and concepts that foster flourishing, which is also a starting point for Dutch Design Foundation (DDF), the organisation I work for as an international liaison and project developer.

Over the last 10 years, DDF changed from an international design innovation platform to a true propagator of radical transition driven by design towards a sustainable future. Over the last five years, DDF developed the format called World Design Embassies (WDE), uniting stakeholders for a longer period of time to co-design new scenarios around specific topics narrowly connected to the Sustainable Development Goals like the Future of Urban Mobility, Health, Water, Circular & Biobased Building, Inclusivity, and Food. Designers take up roles as visualisers, storytellers, and material developers. They lift the scenarios from paper and engage the end users through prototypes and experiences.

One embassy that seamlessly connects with what New European Bauhaus aims to achieve and resonates with the theme of Flourishing is the WDE of Circular and Biobased Building, programmed and designed by Biobased Creations. It came to fruition over the last five years with a growing number of participants from industry and audiences queuing at live Dutch Design Weeks and other exhibition sites. Their storytelling for co-design programmes encompasses stakeholders at every level and across the full breadth of the building sector: the small producing or designing pioneers and the big building companies planning their transition; the government that needs to change regulations to permit the use of local and renewable resourced building materials; researchers for experimentation and knowledge. Their latest programme is possible landscapes[9] for exploring and developing local building materials with stakeholders, from end users to constructors.

The results of a year of good design for hundreds of designers (2,600 in 2022) are annually presented and discussed during DDF's design festival, which, as a journalist once said, is not the best *of* the world, but it strives to be one of the best *for* the world. Dutch Design Week, initiated by designers in 2001 in Eindhoven (NL), brings together a diversity of audiences through a programme of exhibitions, experiences, exploration tours, and exchanges. For the (inter)national participants, DDW is also a test ground for concepts and scenarios, for the work of outstanding graduates and professionals that might contribute to reducing negative impact and increasing good actions, leading to the flourishing of the world. One example is the Solar Pavilion of DDW 2022 Ambassador Marjan van Aubel,[10] an award-winning innovative solar designer who brings solar energy into daily life. Designing for a positive future through combining the fields of sustainability, design, and technology, van Aubel initiated the idea of a solar movement in 2022 aiming to engage every energy consumer.

Through experimental design, visitors of every age and from all backgrounds can live the change, learn, get active, and become drivers of change. They Get

Set (theme of DDW 2022) by being inspired and empowered through the entire experience and the energy of DDW that fuels and inspires.

There are many exciting design festivals around the globe that are united by the World Design Week's network established during DDW in Eindhoven in 2016.

Like Gdynia Design Days in the North of Poland on the Baltic Sea, a small festival in the 'smallest and happiest city of Poland'[11] but where the content is international, inspirational, and forward thinking. It is the cooperative product of the minds of the contributing designers and sponsors, like the city, the Technology Park and the passionate organisers at the Design Centre. I had the opportunity to speak twice: live in 2019 and online in 2021. The themes of these festival editions acknowledged the challenges and needs of Poland, Europe, and the world today: Polarisation (2019), Attention (2020), and Solidary (2021). They illustrate the complex issues and the transition needed, from signalling design solutions for a Polarised world where self-centredness needs to be changed toward empathy and Attention. Design that awakens and makes people aware of today's challenges that need the attention and care of everyone is what Solidary is all about: to begin working on reaching shared goals. It is a word coloured by the movement in the region of Gdynia, Gdansk, where people organised themselves to fight for better rights with Solidarność. Through courageous actions, they succeeded and created a wave of change throughout the world.

Can design festivals turn their audiences into brave and solidary citizens? Can participating organisations stand shoulder to shoulder to work on the recommendations of the Intergovernmental Panel on Climate Change to transform our planet in crisis into planetary well-being (IPCC, 2022)? Now, this needs transformation of political agendas as well, and in our democracies, this means support by the people. Can the political design approach of New European Bauhaus be intensified, multiplied, and transferred to other places? Can design communities and festivals start positive movements?

Social designer Fides Lapidaire,[12] a specialist in offering unexpected perspectives on complex issues to housing cooperatives and government, is investigating how the nutrients/phosphates that are lost in our sewer systems can be 'harvested' to feed our soil. Fides also goes into the field with her food truck and participates in design and music festivals, where she sells 'shit' sandwiches, in which the bread and ingredients come from the land fed by human excrement donated by visitors.

For a flourishing world, we should give a shit, our shit.

It is more urgent than ever to stop the endless lust for growth, for having and needing, and to transform it into lust for life: being and caring.

Notes

1 Earth Overshoot Day. See www.overshootday.org/
2 Costing the Earth Film. See https://youtu.be/-ElsIpLsPX8
3 Doughnut Economics. See www.kateraworth.com/doughnut/
4 Babette Porcelijn. *Hidden impact.* See https://thinkbigactnow.org/en/what-is-hidden-impact/
5 Ursula von der Leyen. *State of the union*, September 2020. See https://ec.europa.eu/commission/presscorner/detail/ov/SPEECH_20_1655

6 Garden Classroom Jume. See https://2022.prizes.new-european-bauhaus.eu/application/garden-classroom-jume

7 Flaux—Flower Matter. See https://2022.prizes.new-european-bauhaus.eu/finalists/

8 New European Bauhaus Report. See https://new-european-bauhaus.europa.eu/about/progress-report_en

9 Biobased Creations. See https://biobasedcreations.com/project/possible-landscapes/

10 Marjan van Aubel. See https://marjanvanaubel.com/

11 Gdynia Happiest City. See www.thefirstnews.com/article/is-gdynia-cool-yes-it-is-but-its-also-so-much-more-19429

12 Fides Lapidaire. See www.fideslapidaire.com/about

Reference list

Bason, C. *et al.* (2021) *A new Bauhaus for a green deal.* UCL Institute for Innovation and Public Purpose. Available at: www.ucl.ac.uk/bartlett/public-purpose/publications/2021/jan/new-bauhaus-green-deal

Ehrenfeld, John R. (2020) 'Flourishing: designing a brave new world', *She Ji: The Journal of Design Economics and Innovation*, 5(2), pp. 105–116. https://doi.org/10.1016/j.sheji.2019.03.001

IPCC (2022) 'Climate change 2022: impacts, adaptation, and vulnerability', in Pörtner, H.-O. *et al.* (eds.) *Contribution of working group II to the sixth assessment report of the intergovernmental panel on climate change.* Cambridge, UK and New York, NY: Cambridge University Press, p. 3056. https://doi.org/10.1017/9781009325844

Meadows, D.H. *et al.* (1972) *The limits to growth: a report for the club of Rome's project on the predicament of mankind.* New York, NY: Universe Books.

Part 2

Flourishing organisations

Chapter 12

Flourishing organisations

Bruce Brown

Creating the conditions in which people and communities may flourish has always been a challenge for designers to get right. Success in this respect may depend on a complex intermingling of external and internal factors—that is, the design of the physical environments in which people live and work and how these link with those intangible systems of thought and belief that unite and motivate people.

Until recently, the modus operandi for professional design practice was a derivation of behavioural science in which anything that matters should be measurable—and if it is not measurable, then it may not matter. Emerging in the 1930s, behavioural science rejected any explanation of human behaviour that could not be measured, such as those based on mental states or internal representations as described by Freud and Jung. So this approach gave emphasis to the design of tangible stuff in the physical environment at the expense of more intangible representations such as memories, imaginings, beliefs, desires, or plans. Though the behaviourists did not necessarily reject the importance of internal representations, they simply believed—in terms of empirical science—that these could not be measured in the same way that human responses to external stimuli could be. So the focus of design, especially in the support of business and commerce, tended to be on the design of physical environments and their assembled artefacts.

The behaviourists went on to develop a view that people were (or so they thought) simple behaving systems that were conditioned by the complex environments of an increasingly technological and media-saturated age. In this version of life, it followed that the complexity of human behaviour is simply a reflection of the increasingly complex environments in which we live. For example, in 1969, Herbert Simon (who has had a significant influence on contemporary design practice) wrote in his influential book, *The Sciences of the Artificial*,

> I have argued that people—or at least their intellective component—may be relatively simple, that most of the complexity of their behaviour may be drawn from their environment, for their search for good designs. If I have made my case, then we can conclude that, in large part, the proper study of mankind is the science of design.
>
> (1996, p. 138)

DOI: 10.4324/9781003399568-15

As a seemingly rational extension of this principle the (perhaps naive) assumption was that the good design of all things in which our daily lives are immersed will naturally help communities and individuals to flourish in a better, more modern(ist), world. Le Corbusier reflected this thought when writing in his journal, "I am quite simple, even transparent. It's the events swirling around me that are twisted" and "all art must have as its ultimate aim the regeneration of society"[1] These comments may, in part, have been Le Corbusier's belated defence against criticism of his presumed sympathies for the Fascist regime. Indeed, here, it is also worth reminding ourselves that design may be used for both good and evil ends—the Holocaust was, after all, a designed programme that utilised images, objects, buildings, and narratives to influence the mass behaviour of a populace.

In the aftermath of war, two issues surfaced in the minds of politicians and industrialists. First, the factories, which had been geared up to mass produce armaments in support of the war effort, were now in danger of standing idle at a time when the machinery of capitalism needed to keep churning out goods if bankruptcy was to be avoided. Second, two world wars had demonstrated that human behaviour could not always be counted on to be rational or predictable. In this latter respect, a major shift in the concept of democracy began to take shape. This was in some large part engineered by Edward Bernays, who was born of Jewish parents in Vienna in 1891 and was the nephew of Sigmund Freud. Bernays moved with his parents to America, where he came to have a significant influence on US presidents Calvin Coolidge, Theodore Roosevelt, and Woodrow Wilson along with the captains of major industrial corporations such as Procter & Gamble, American Tobacco, Columbia Broadcasting System (CBS), General Electric, Dodge Motors, and so on.

Learning from his uncle Sigmund and the experience of two world wars, Bernays concluded, like the behaviourists, that human beings were simple behaving systems but, additionally, were also driven by deep impulses that could lead either to a civilised society or to a barbaric one. So he developed a conviction that the proper functioning of an orderly and stable society should be based upon what some of the leaders of today's most populous nations would describe as managed democracy. Bernays concluded that there had to be an intelligent elite, charged with the responsibility of managing and designing society's affairs. He wrote that,

> Universal literacy was supposed to educate the common man to control his environment. Once he could read and write he would have a mind fit to rule. So ran the democratic doctrine. But instead of a mind, universal literacy has given him rubber stamps, rubber stamps inked with advertising slogans, with editorials, with published scientific data, with the trivialities of the tabloids and the platitudes of history, but quite innocent of original thought.
>
> (Bernays, 2005)

In the interests of both a stable society and the accumulation of industrial wealth, Bernays successfully persuaded senior politicians and industrialists that people's baser instincts could be controlled and further aggression avoided by satisfying their inner desires through well-designed products. These, in one way or another, could serve as tangible anchors to represent more intangible systems of self-identity through, for example, social or religious affiliation, position, status, and so on.

Here, the utilitarian value of an artefact, though still important, was overshadowed by its desirability in satisfying people's inner needs along with bestowing the sense of well-being that would accompany an affluent modern(ist) society. This gave rise to the post-war consumer boom in which a fledgling design profession witnessed its own exponential growth and rise to power in response to industry's demand for desirable products. Initially, this focused on the design of all those tangible artefacts making up our physical environment such as buildings, domestic products, visual communications, cars, trains, planes, and so on. Indeed, with the consumer society that emerged after World War II, one of its star designers, Raymond Loewy, would be able to claim to have designed all classes of material products from lipsticks to locomotives (Industrial Designer Raymond Loewy, 2007). By the latter half of the 20th century, however, discontent began to emerge at the behaviourist techniques being used to manipulate people's responses along with the material waste this created through the production of consumer goods having redundancy designed in. This unease first emerged in 1957 with Vance Packard's book *The Hidden Persuaders* (Packard, 1975) followed, a decade later, by Ken Garland's 1964 manifesto, *First Things First*, in which he wrote "we have reached a saturation point at which the high-pitched scream of consumer selling is no more than sheer noise . . . we are proposing a reversal of priorities in favour of the more useful and more lasting forms of communication . . . for worthwhile purposes" (Garland, 1964). In 1972, this growing howl of outrage was cemented with the publication of industrial designer Victor Papanek's seminal book *Design for the Real World*, in which he wrote,

> There are professions more harmful than industrial design, but only a very few of them. . . . Industrial design, by concocting the tawdry idiocies hawked by advertisers, comes a close second. . . . As long as design concerns itself with confecting "trivial toys for adults", killing machines with gleaming tailfins, and "sexed-up" shrouds for typewriters, toasters, telephones, and computers, it has lost all reason to exist.
>
> (1974, pp. 9–10)

Around the same time, Herbert Simon sought to establish a new science of design that would shift its focus from business and commerce to society and welfare. However, unlike Garland and Papanek, Simon was not a designer of tangible stuff but a scientist whose work in decision-making and artificial intelligence (for which he received the 1978 Nobel Prize in Economic Sciences) emphasised the design of intangible systems. This approach was neatly summed up in Simon's influential phrase: "everyone designs who devises courses of action aimed at changing existing situations into preferred ones" (1996, p. 53). Indeed, this phrase has become something of a mantra for contemporary designers, having had considerable influence on the shape of current design practice. The bold assertion of post-war designers to have designed everything from lipsticks to locomotives may seem modest against current design parlance. As Simon shifted the focus of design from tangible stuff to intangible systems, a new space for fresh approaches to design—such as service design and social design—opened up. Today, we hear about the design of publics, of democracy, government strategy, corporate responsibility, the design of healthcare and business, of local communities, cities, nations, and cultural identities. The practice of design now seems to have few defining edges—seemingly boundless, it is everywhere, and anyone who acts to change things is thought to be a designer.[2]

All of this said, the roots of Simon's influential approach are not always recognised by designers. For example, elsewhere in *The Sciences of the Artificial*, Simon also makes clear his position within the tradition of behavioural science in writing, "Human beings, viewed as behaving systems, are quite simple. The apparent complexity of our behaviour over time is largely a reflection of the complexity of the environment in which we find ourselves" (1996, p. 53). This approach is within the traditions of behavioural science pioneered by B.F. Skinner who, in his 1971 book *Beyond Freedom and Dignity*, took the debate one alarming step further when writing: "We need to make vast changes in human behaviour, and we cannot make them with the help of nothing more than physics or biology . . . what we need is a technology of behaviour . . . comparable in power and precision to physical and biological technology" (1971, p. 2).

Skinner's quest for a 'technology of behaviour' and Simon's mission to design intangible systems that would change 'existing situations into preferred ones' (along with the behaviourist approach per se) are underpinned by a number of flawed assumptions. The first is that we now know more than our predecessors about how to influence human behaviour. The second is that design will only and always deliver a social good (at times, design being presented as the panacea for all deficits and ills). The third is that people will behave rationally and predictably in response to external stimuli. And the final flawed assumption is that we can always be certain of our ultimate aims and their outcomes when seeking to influence human behaviour.

The shift of focus from the design of tangible things to intangible systems has had positive effects for the contribution of design in areas of public life and citizenship such as, for example, healthcare, governance, or commerce. Though this approach remains within the tradition of people as behaving systems, there has recently been some interest in exploring the invisible systems of belief, memory, and imagination through which people give meaning and shape to their surroundings. In *Placebo Project*,[3] Anthony Dunne and Fiona Raby designed a series of objects to elicit the narratives that people might create in order to explain and relate to them. As with a medical placebo, the artefacts themselves had no inherent meaning but served to stimulate narratives within the mind of each person—the consequent effects being as tangible as if they were real. Again, in his book, *Meaningful Stuff: Design that Lasts*, Jonathan Chapman writes,

> Never have we wanted, owned, and wasted so much stuff. Our consumptive path through modern life leaves a wake of social and ecological

destruction—sneakers worn only once, bicycles barely even ridden, and forgotten smartphones languishing in drawers. By what perverse alchemy do
our newest, coolest things so readily transform into meaningless junk?

(Chapman, 2021, back cover)

In response to this, Chapman explores how meaning can emerge through
designed encounters between people and the tangible stuff in their environment.
In learning how material things can be designed to have personal attachments in
the mind of each person, the ultimate aim is to end up with less stuff and more
meaning—reducing landfill waste and satisfying inner needs.

The conditions that enable people and communities to flourish are both complex and fragile. If left to their own devices, the outcomes may be unpredictable
and, if overdesigned, they could be instrumental in shaping behaviour. Overall,
any design intervention, or lack of it, will bring a responsibility to observe ethical
principles that govern the potential effects of design on human behaviour. Given
the history of designed systems, these ethical principles have, in the past, been
lacking, with little to no evidence for public accountability. Knowing how to design
tangible artefacts and intangible systems that, together, help individuals to flourish in a civilised state is a work in progress that will benefit from further research.

Notes

1 Le Corbusier. See https://forward.com/culture/422333/le-corbusierrevolutionary-architect-
  nazi-apologist/#:~:text="I%20am%20quite%20simple%2C%20even%20transparent.
  %20It's%20the,revolutionary%20ideas%20and%20crowded%20life%20would%20
  eventually%20inspire.
2 In *Exploring if a Design is Good, Beautiful and True* (a presentation given at the conference *Exp'19—Experience and Principles of Design* at Tongji University College of Design
  and Innovation, Shanghai, China, in May 2019), Tim Fife described design as "the creation of compelling arguments that move people to action". This sits in stark contrast to
  preceding definitions of designs such as "a plan to make an artefact". Also, in his introduction to *Design, When Everybody Designs*, Ezio Manzini writes, "In a changing world,
  everyone designs: each individual person and each collective subject, from enterprises
  to institutions, from communities to cities and regions, must define and enhance a *life*
  project" (Manzini, E. (2015) *Design, when everybody designs, an introduction to design
  for social innovation*. London: MIT Press, Cop).
3 Placebo Project. See www.nomads.usp.br/pesquisas/design/objetos_interativos/arquivos/
  restrito/DUNNE_the%20placebo%20project.pdf (Accessed: 27 November 2021).

Reference list
Bernays, E.L. (2005) *Propaganda: with an introduction by Mark Crispin Miller*.
    New York: Ig Publishing, p. 48.
Chapman, J. (2021) *Meaningful stuff: design that lasts*. Cambridge, MA: MIT Press.
Garland, K. (1964) *First things first* [online]. Available at: https://web.archive.org/
    web/20070701150225/www.kengarland.co.uk/KG%20published%20writing/
    first%20things%20first/index.html (Accessed: 23 November 2020).

Industrial Designer Raymond Loewy (2007) *Subject of new exhibition at the National Heritage Museum, Lexington, MA* [online]. Available at: www.prweb.com/releases/2007/09/prweb552888.htm (Accessed: 27 February 2023).

Packard, V.O. (1975) *The hidden persuaders*. Harmondsworth: Penguin.

Papanek, V. (1974) *Design for the real world*. 2nd edn. Boulder, CO: Paladin Press.

Simon, H.A. (1996) *The sciences of the artificial*. 3rd edn. Cambridge, MA: MIT Press.

Skinner, B.F. (1971) *Beyond freedom and dignity*. New York: Bantam Books.

Chapter 13

What organisations will flourish in the future and why we need a new design culture that is fit for the 22nd century

Andrea Siodmok

It has been over two hundred years from the epoch of the Industrial Revolution to where we sit today. Two hundred remarkable years of relative warp-speed progress that has delivered great benefits for much of the world and yet has also brought incalculable waste and growing inequalities—a waste of both talent and resources. As William Gibson has reportedly once said, "The future is here—it's just not evenly distributed".

As different countries' governments are collectively considering their responses to climate change, many UK local authorities have already declared a climate emergency. Other organisations across the public, private, and social sectors are reviewing and investing in alternative technologies as the race to net zero heats up. Some are going beyond, to carbon negative operations, and fewer still are looking to reimagine a wholly restorative economy in one form or another. Whatever the motivation, there is little doubt that it is time for change. But who will lead that change? And how will we ensure that the future is fit for purpose?

Design in its many guises has been at the service of our modern economy since its inception, shaping, forming, and responding to the demands of clients and commissioners. It has evolved alongside the changing needs of industry. But have we reached the limits of the modernist design paradigm and of the usefulness of human-centred notions of progress? Do we need a new roadmap for design that will break free from the 20th-century intellectual cubbyholes and models of value creation? And how might intellectual property (IP) and other legal devices need to change in order to accelerate the spread of new ideas across different contexts?

At the heart of this provocation is the simple premise that for our hyperconnected and polarising times, we need a new notion of design, which is better described as *human-connected design* (Dargan, Fox and Hartung, 2021). And along with that will flow new research questions, practice, and opportunities. If we look backwards for precedent, and with an eye on the future, we need the same kind of energy and spirit of the Enlightenment but directed through the prism of today's technologies, today's human awareness, today's climate, and directed at today's concerns.

DOI: 10.4324/9781003399568-16

This chapter sets out to briefly ask what kind of technologies will shape future organisations in the short, medium, and longer terms and how design might enable organisations to respond to the challenges that lie ahead. It will argue that designers have an important role to play in shaping the transition to a new economy and in bringing to life the idea of 'purposeful innovation' through their collective practice. It will state that purposeful innovation means moving beyond problematising and 'simple solutions' to complex challenges, to embracing complexity by creating more emergent propositions that are responsive, inclusive, systemic, and effective (RISE). In this context, it will argue that design practice also needs to adapt and evolve.

It will conclude by suggesting that design should move beyond the 20th-century idea of 'user-centred design' to embrace a broader concept of 'human-connected design' shaping our relationship with technologies, with people, and with the planet.

It will note that design achieves this by acting as an agent for change, encouraging informed collaborative processes, that are regenerative, inclusive, and just—equipping clients, policymakers, place leaders and citizens with proposals, processes, methods and (future) propositions that are shaped with our physical, digital, natural, and social infrastructure. However, it will also note the power asymmetries of the current intellectual-property environment in this context. Finally, it will highlight the importance of bringing together the key components of an emergent design practice by seeking to blend strategic, circular, regenerative and inclusive design principles, described through a reimagined 'design helix' model.

What will it mean to thrive in the 22nd century, and how will we get there?

In the short term, we are experiencing a rapid intensification of the pace of the Fourth Industrial Revolution (Schwab, 2017), building on the digital revolution of the last half century, propelled further by the COVID-19 pandemic and the arrival of next-generation technological infrastructure. In the West, this revolution is characterised by its fusion, commodification, and the extraction of value from intangible 'knowledge assets'.

The Fourth Industrial Revolution is not about any one technology but the convergence and conversion of a number of different technologies into something new, blurring the boundaries between our physical, digital, and biological worlds. The third platform[1] that results is created by interdependencies between things like mobile computing, social media, cloud computing, and big data to name a few. Additive manufacturing remains in relative infancy, but, along with micro-factories and intelligent factories, it is changing the landscape of production and reconfiguring supply-chain logistics.

We are only just beginning to see the potential of Fourth Industrial Revolution technologies. In 2021, machine-generated data is the lifeblood of the Internet of Things (IoT) and in the not-too-distant future, more data will be generated by machines than by humans. As noted by CISCO, this will mean significantly more

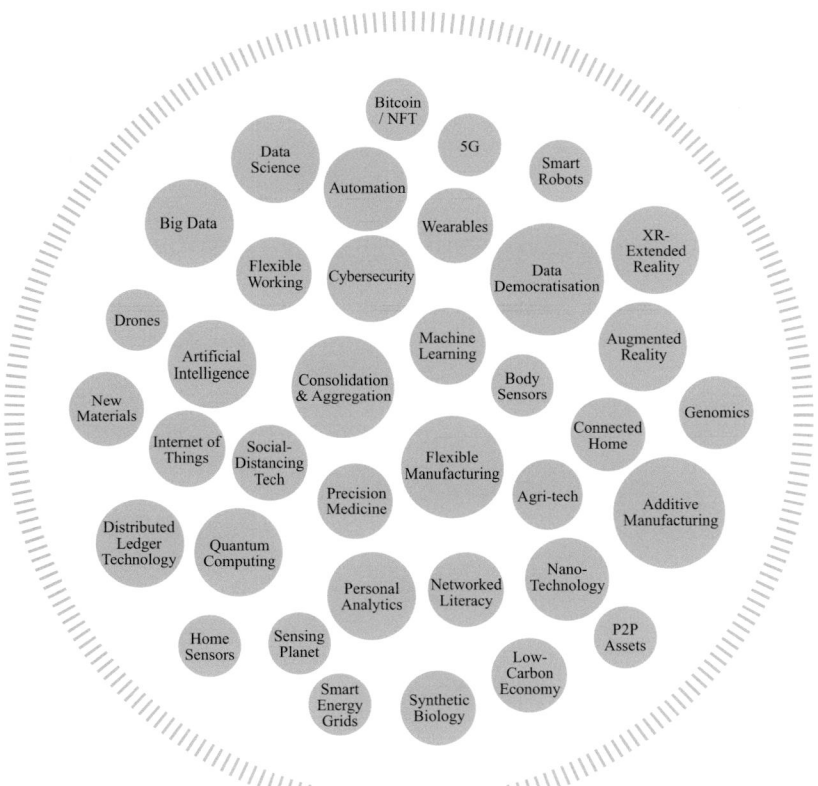

Figure 13.1
**Converging
technologies.**
Source:
**Diagram by the
author.**

connected devices than people on the planet, "The number of devices connected to IP networks will be more than three times the global population by 2023" (CISCO, 2020). And yet simultaneously, we have more people on the planet and more potential synchronicity than at any time in history, offering the potential for tapping into the deep seams of social capital held in communities.

In the medium term, next-generation technologies such as 5G telecommunications promise to reduce the impact of latency that has been holding back automation and robotics, further enabling real-time sensing, connected intelligent devices and mobile computing. Such 'ultra-wideband' connectivity offers exciting possibilities and, in turn, will mobilise and accelerate the development of an array of applications including virtual reality (VR), augmented reality (AR), mixed reality (MR), and cross reality (XR) along with increasing the value of artificial intelligence (AI), big data, and cloud computing. The new 'metaverse' as envisaged by Facebook and others is one step towards commercialising these future environments. However, when these advances are combined with more sophisticated sensor technologies and analytics, they will continue to fuel the uptake of technologies like connected autonomous vehicles (CAVs) and a whole host of as-yet unimagined Internet of Things (IoT) applications.

This great convergence (Baldwin, 2016) is not just limited to technologies; it is likely whole industries and sectors will blend as the third wave disrupts business models and enables new entrants to markets. We are seeing, for example, the merger of edtech and gaming; e-tail and fintech; logistics and clean energy (power by the hour); agri-tech and geo-tech; big pharma and big data (internet of medical things); construction and MMC (modern methods of construction); entertainment and virtual reality. As noted, this has been underpinned by huge advances in data, sensors, robotics, and connectivity, with the resulting servitisation of whole industries, creating offers like Software-as-a-Service (SaaS) and Mobility-as-a-Service (MaaS) to name just two—business models by the hour fuelled by Infrastructure-as-a-Service (IaaS). Whole new industries are on the cusp of being born, the flying Internet of Things; crypto-collaborations enabled by cryptocurrency; augmented-intelligence sensing; lidar and simulation industries (such as the much-hyped concept of digital twinning).

But we are only just beginning to see their potential because many of these technologies are in their relative infancy. Governments around the world are increasingly focusing their R&D efforts on the race for artificial intelligence dominance, even reaching the point of 'singularity' (Shanahan, 2015). While the jury is out on predictions of reaching artificial general intelligence (AGI), quantum computing is gaining momentum, for example for military AI applications. Today, ChatGPT is raising questions about intellectual property and plagiarism in education and beyond. If this is simply the beginning, can we peek a little further around the corner and shape a powerful agenda for our future generations to inherit?

In the longer term, energy-intensive technologies like distributed ledger technology (DLT), more commonly known as blockchain, promise to move us from the Internet of Information (IOI) to the Internet of Things (IOT) and beyond to the Internet of Value (IOV). The Internet of Value is a notional online space where people can transfer value directly between each other, even as strangers, with complete trust. Such 'transactional' advances would, in effect, eliminate the need for the 'middlemen', much bureaucracy, and make many of our most recognisable institutions redundant. Whether it is banks, universities or even governments, some are pointing to a future where these organisations of 'trust' no longer broker as much transactional value. As these technologies gain power and momentum, we are seeing a number of 'institutional bypasses' as the boundaries of organisations are eroded. Powered by DLT, assets like currency, intellectual property rights (like royalties), scientific discoveries, qualifications, and even physical objects (like houses) could be exchanged one-to-one through disintermediated immutable transactions. The trend towards increasing atomisation, in which society is made up of self-sufficient and self-interested individuals, also has significant consequences for organisations and institutions. Enabled through network technologies, we have seen the emergence of a grey/informal economy, empowering the long tail of prosumers and making government and governance as we know it impossible due to declining trust in democracy, tax revenues, and fundamental breakdown of the social contract (Leadbeater, 2000).

These new hybrid technologies have themselves produced new forms of design, from interaction design to digital design and from service design to experience design. But then what? As always, design will first imagine and then shape our possible futures in as-yet unimagined ways, offering to sustain organisations that demonstrate the vision, tenacity, and agility to move with the times and harness latent opportunities.

Decommissioning 20th-century assumptions

This white heat of technology is increasingly the time of the tech entrepreneur, the moment for the makers, the vanguard of the venture capitalist, and the playground for the pioneers. In short, it favours brave innovators who will put everything on the line to shape their and our collective futures.

There are many paradoxes and rifts forming as these technologies collide and our existing business models and sources of power and investment are pushed to the limit. Changes in finance and venture capital (VC) are likely to follow. With next-generation seamless platform logic, many of the economic constructs of the industrial economy are also likely to be tested. Consider, for example, the following potential economic effects:

Next-generation seamless platform logic changes the rules of enterprises, organisations, and institutions

Artificial intelligence = end of information asymmetries?

Cloud computing = end of global employment elasticity and foreign direct investment?

Cybersecurity = end of national control 'bordered' policy?

Internet of Things = end of the hegemony of human intelligence?

Blockchain = end of institutions, intellectual property, and bureaucracy?

COVID-19 and social distancing = end of agglomeration benefit?

As a result, the ways we do business will inevitably evolve. The pursuit of economic reward is only one value by which success might be measured. It is clear that we may need new goals for organisations of all kinds to thrive as we move beyond the legacy of the carbon economy.

Do we need new mechanisms to measure progress that are fit for purpose?

As the industrial society (and its organisations and institutions in all their forms) comes to terms with the negative externalities of the modern economy and limits of our planet, what is next? How might we rethink 'common good' to avoid the pitfalls of the tragedy of the commons?

Design has been the handmaiden of the industrial economy. Designers' intellectual property as captured in patents, and subsequently trademarks and designs, was a crucial legal foundation for the acceleration of the Industrial Revolution (Leaffer, 1990), providing the blueprint for innovation and value creation. There were significant power asymmetries in this value system, for example: before

1965, women represented between 2% and 3% of patent awards. Intellectual property gender inequality is just one aspect, the other being the way this 'command and control' model of protecting knowledge assets prevents progress being shared more widely to benefit all parts of the world economies more evenly. How might we approach dispersal of intellectual property to reduce the inequalities in the current system?

In the internet era, Creative Commons and other forms of shared ownership have opened-up new possibilities for collective imagination and problem-solving. Intellectual property that is shared is essential to avoid issues of reinventing things over and over. Sharing, shaping and collaborating through our intellectual property will be vital to the future of creative problem-solving.

Purposeful innovation

Designers have an important role to play in shaping the transition to a new low-carbon economy, as the UK's Design Council have set out in their recent Design for Planet agenda: "galvanising and supporting the UK's 1.69 million design community to address the climate emergency" (Design Council, 2021). This transition to a more circular economy[2] will require many forms of innovation, from service re-design to the development of whole new business models. This expanded idea of innovation goes beyond the idea of technology as a pre-requisite for innovation to include many other behavioural drivers and blockers of innovation. Thinking of maturity not only in terms of technology readiness levels (Banke, 2010), that is common in innovation funding, but also of 'societal readiness levels' will be a critical feature of purposeful innovation. The concept of societal readiness level has been growing in interest because it incorporates ethical, legal, social, and economic factors and can be applied to both technological and social innovations that are likely to be important in a transition to a low-carbon economy (Büscher and Spurling, 2019).

In a VUCA world (Bennis and Nanus, 1985), that is volatile, uncertain, complex and ambiguous, mission-led innovation (Mazzucato, 2022) offers one way to approach complex problems at pace. However, I prefer the idea of 'purposeful innovation' as a way of describing new forms of inclusive innovation that go beyond the technological determinism of Silicon Valley–era thinking and practice and don't carry the negative connotations associated with Christian and colonial ideals and power.

Purposeful innovation could of course mean many things. When I was working at the Policy Lab in the UK government, I broke it down into four components, namely responsive, inclusive, systemic, and effective (RISE).

- **Responsive** to societal needs—Responds quickly and positively to changing social patterns. Responsive innovation seeks to put citizens' needs in context with wider societal and environmental trade-offs and co-benefits. It applies explorative experimental methods to develop new thinking in an agile, open, adaptable and flexible way and also considers regenerative and resilient outcomes that can be generated as positive spillovers.

- **Inclusive** and open in its approach and outcomes—Prioritising impact that will re-distribute power, resources and opportunity to address inequality—impacts focusing on improving health, well-being, security, service quality, and building human capital.
- **Systemic** in its ambition, embracing complexity and opportunities for collaboration. Many of the future challenges will be systemic and require action at a governance level, activating actors across the system. Anticipatory innovation (Roberts, 2018) enables such proactive systemic dialogue including local, national, and international effort: applying new thinking from first principles to the front line.
- **Effective** in delivering significant measurable impact and learning for the future. This seeks to measure innovation effectiveness, providing an evidence-based approach to taking innovations to scale and ensuring sufficient feedback loops enable a culture of learning to be maintained.

Taking a more holistic and systemic approach to innovation also means moving beyond problematising and 'simple solutions' to complex challenges. Applying an explorative and experimental mindset and approach to innovation in this context embraces complexity by creating more dynamic and emergent propositions. In this broadened context of innovation, it could be argued that design practice also needs to adapt and evolve. In this context, it seems fitting to lift our horizons and ask what next for design? What is the contribution design and the design research agenda can provide to create the foundations for this change? Design shapes new possibilities, but through economies of scale, it also amplifies. It amplifies messages, and it amplifies impact. Design has always been a catalyst for change and an enabler of progress.

An urgent need for a new design paradigm and design culture

Culture refers to the cumulative deposit of knowledge, experience, beliefs, values, attitudes, meanings, hierarchies, religion, notions of time, roles, spatial relations, concepts of the universe, and material objects and possessions acquired by a group of people in the course of generations through individual and group striving.

(Samovar and Porter, 1994)

User-centred design, a term that emerged in the late 1990s, was an explicit attempt to move from a technology-driven approach to one that espouses putting people before machines. User-centred design brought with it a new vocabulary of 'users', usability and accessibility, for example. However, it could be argued that design too often retains old outmoded dogma and mantras, forged in the Bauhaus-era thinking that no longer serve a purpose in these challenging times (Young, Blair and Cooper, 2001).

Central to this provocation is the suggestion that for our hyper-connected times, we need a new notion of *human-connected design*, a broad tent in which designers can explore new possibilities and pathways yet also a new narrative for design theory. To both imagine and create a vibrant, optimistic and prosperous future will require our collective human creativity, ingenuity, and endeavour in ways more akin to the flourishing of the Enlightenment-era thinking not just within our organisations but across the whole of our society and economy. A viable way to approach this would be by utilising a design praxis to unleash bold thinking and to deliver a "restorative future" (Warden, 2021) based on renewing and reconnecting the natural, built, digital and biological ecosystems and socio-economic environments (Design Council, DFP, 2021). Just as the industrial economy created new design job titles like industrial designer and the service economy created job titles like service designer, once again we will see the connected economy create job titles like connected designers. From this new vantage point of human-connected design, we might look back on human-centred design as a relic of an outmoded world view that put humans before humanity and people before the planet.

What will human-connected design entail?

In contrast to the myopic connotations of user-centred design, *human-connected design* will put design at the nexus of positive, purposeful change—for example, thinking about taking multiple human and non-human perspectives into account:

- How humans are connected to artificial intelligence (data systems design)
- How humans are connected to the planet/organic intelligence (circular design)
- How humans are connected to other agendas, disciplines and worldviews (strategic design)

With a new paradigm for design, we will need a reformed *design culture. Human-connected design* is systems thinking and doing, embracing multiple perspectives, acknowledging the essential human perspective of 'human-centred-design' but also understanding that humans are not limited to being at the centre.

For this bold new design agenda, we will also need a new design praxis, beyond the Bauhaus with its machine-like efficiency to ecologies of change that cross existing boundaries, finding value in the space between—in the transitions—and in the novel. This will require a new generation of professionals characterised as boundary spanners and hybrid designers with skills that overlap economics, sociology, organisation design, and more. But that's not enough, as designers we will need to be relevant, we will need to be vibrant, and we will need to be confident if we are to face the ambiguities and uncertainties that 'field-building' entails. More than that, we will need to collaborate and avoid the 'horizontal hostilities' and infighting that can occur between groups which you might otherwise assume have common interests.

We need a 'big tent' culture of design that amplifies effectiveness through adaptation, creating belonging through shared purpose and progress through harnessing our common passions. Such a design praxis would be underpinned by five core beliefs of empathy, equality, ecologies, emergence, and effectiveness. Through *human-connected design*, we aim to create and develop broader narratives and strategy for achieving equitable, post-carbon development as the interconnections of social, economic, and environmental issues and challenges intensify nationally and globally. From this starting point, we will see new design disciplines such as circular designers, inclusive designers and data systems designers, amongst others. But more significantly, we will also see creative skills and practice become more common-place in other professions from law to economics.

Human-connected design unites forward-looking design, thinking-doing and approaches. It moves from 'design for' to 'design with' and from 'centred' to 'connected'. In doing so, it also offers an umbrella-term that can embrace and interlink with Design for Planet (Design Council), Planet-Centred (Jackson, 2022), Humanity-Centred (PARK), Beyond-Human-Centred (Superflux), and Regenerative Futures (RSA).

In my view, this new *design culture* would have three key cornerstones, namely circular, inclusive, and strategic design:

1 **Circular design**—Circular design to support the circular economy—reimagining design's role as a catalyst for change. Linking service design and new business, finance and governance models that increase economic, environmental, and social value for organisations. Accelerating the transition to a low-carbon economy through the effective use of design for circularity by reinventing business models and redesigning 'business as a service' to unlock the potential for closing the loop on resources. Understanding how hybrid value chains (HVC) across sectors have the potential to move from questions to quests through common purpose. Organisations as a platform to attract likeminded, talented individuals to connect and enable new ecologies for ideas to blossom. Near-term priorities might include encouraging research and training in practical methods for circular design. This could lead to a new praxis, curriculum, and pedagogy for circular designers to bring about responsible change.

2 **Inclusive design**—Inclusive design to improve all our lives. This would incorporate considerations of the impact of investment in hard and soft infrastructure (social infrastructure). Converging technologies (AI-assisted design) combined with COVID-19 will transform our homes and places of work as well as blurring those two domains. Improving the independence of older people or anyone who requires adaptive or inclusive design would be an important feature of such an approach. Appropriate responses might be reflected in the growth in the Internet of Things and smart product markets. Near-term priorities might include designing for our future selves (Coleman, 1993)—reducing the stigma of an ageing population and 'reinventing the experience of living longer'. Inclusive design encompasses both human and more-than-human domains. For example, design for the marginalised, giving much-needed voice to those excluded from decision-making power; design for inclusive 'community designers' and designing for empathy; while also establishing design for an AI world, redesigning design, and business. This cornerstone would evolve a new praxis, curriculum, and pedagogy that is interlinked with social innovation and social design.

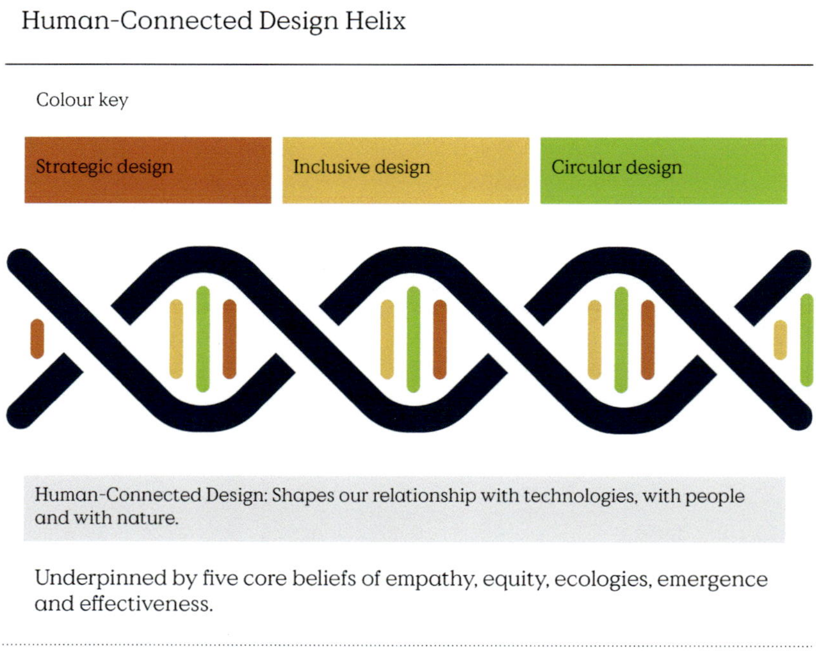

Figure 13.2
Human-connected design helix.
Source: **Diagram by the author.**

Human-Connected Design Helix

Colour key

| Strategic design | Inclusive design | Circular design |

Human-Connected Design: Shapes our relationship with technologies, with people and with nature.

Underpinned by five core beliefs of empathy, equity, ecologies, emergence and effectiveness.

3 **Strategic design**—bold ambition to work across boundaries to improve organisational productivity efficiency and effectiveness. Future-oriented design principles that increase an organisation's 'value' to customers and citizens. Including analysis of external and internal trends and data, enabling design decisions to be made on the basis of facts and design effectiveness. Near-term priorities: adding design to R&D investment (RD&D), showcasing the role of design in purpose-led business such as B Corps, providing design foresight and market intelligence to accelerate business opportunities and opening up design to broader communities of purpose from law (The Legal Design Lab, 2021) to policy (Knight and Kimbell, 2022).

With this approach, we can inspire and create Resilient & Human-Connected Places (HUB-IN framework, 2021)—striving for 'environmental balance', 'empowering communities' and creating truly 'liveable and connected places'.

The diagram in Figure 13.2 sets out how these elements come together to make a design helix.

Conclusion

In summary, there is one common denominator that unites individuals, communities, institutions and organisations worldwide, and that is our desire for greater human connectivity, our belief in human agency and our awareness of our interdependency. We need a culture of design that amplifies effectiveness through adaptation, creates belonging through shared purpose and fosters progress through harnessing our common passions. Such a design praxis would be underpinned by five core beliefs of empathy, equality, ecologies, emergence, and effectiveness.

When we look at the emerging domains of design together, the concept of *human-connected design* offers a tantalising glimpse of a future paradigm that will befit a post-industrial hyper-networked economy that goes beyond net zero.

My final provocation is that we don't need more design, we need *better* design—*human-connected design*—which combines circular design, inclusive design, and strategic design. Because design is too important to be left to designers.

Notes

1 Third Platform. See www.zdnet.com/article/third-platform-shift-triggers-enterprise-soft ware-evolution/
2 Circular Design Guide. See www.circulardesignguide.com

Reference list

Baldwin, R.E. (2016) *The great convergence: information and the new globaliza- tion*. Cambridge, MA, Belknap Press.

Banke, J. (2010) *Technology readiness levels demystified*. NASA. Available at: www.nasa.gov/topics/aeronautics/features/trl_demystified.html. (Accessed: 20 March 2023).

Bennis, W. and Nanus, B. (1985). *Leaders: strategies for taking charge*. New York: Harper & Row.

Büscher, M. and Spurling, N. (2019) *Social acceptance and societal readiness levels*. DecarboN8. Available at: https://decarbon8.org.uk/social-acceptance- and-societal-readiness-levels/ (Accessed: 20 March 2023).

CISCO (2020) *Annual Internet Report (2018–2023)*. White paper. Available at: www.cisco.com/c/en/us/solutions/collateral/executive-perspectives/annual- internet-report/white-paper-c11-741490.html (Accessed: 23 March 2023).

Coleman, R. (1993) *Designing for our future selves*. Editorial. Available at: www. academia.edu/26131398/Designing_for_our_future_selves (Accessed: 22 March 2023).

Dargan, L., Fox, M. and Hartung, G. (2021) 'HUB-IN framework: an overview of our shared context, vision and values towards "HUB-IN Places"', *HUB-IN project—hubs of innovation and entrepreneurship for the transformation of historic urban areas*. H2020-SC5–2019, GA 869429.

Design Council & The Point People (2021) *System-shifting design. An emerg- ing practice explored*. Available at: www.designcouncil.org.uk/our-work/ skills-learning/resources/download-our-systems-shifting-design-report-1/ (Accessed: 22 March 2023).

Jackson, C. (2022) *What is planet-centric design? We create futures*. Available at: www.wecreatefutures.com/blog/what-is-planet-centric-design (Accessed: 22 March 2023).

Knight, A. and Kimbell, L. (2022) *Next generation public policy design*. Civil Service. Available at: https://publicpolicydesign.blog.gov.uk/2022/05/19/next-genera tion-public-policy-design/ (Accessed: 22 March 2023).

Leadbeater, C. (2000) *Living on thin air: the new economy*. Delhi: Penguin Books India.

Leaffer, M.A. (1990) 'Inventing the industrial revolution: the English patent system 1660–1800', *American Journal of Legal History*, 34(4), pp. 422–423. https://doi.org/10.2307/845835

The Legal Design Lab (2021) *Stanford Law School* [online]. Available at: https://law.stanford.edu/organizations/pages/legal-design-lab/ (Accessed: 22 March 2023).

Mazzucato, M. (2022) *Mission economy*. London: Penguin Books.

Roberts, A. (2018) 'Innovation facets part 6: anticipatory innovation', *OECD Blog*. Available at: https://oecd-opsi.org/blog/innovation-facets-part-6-anticipatory-innovation/#:~:text=Anticipatory%20innovation%20is%20essentially%20about%20recognising%20and%20engaging,work%2C%20which%20then%20inform%20what%20should%20be%20done (Accessed: 22 March 2023).

Samovar, L.A. and Porter, R.E. (1994) *Intercultural communication. A reader*. Belmont, CA: Wadsworth.

Schwab, K. (2017) *The fourth industrial revolution*. London: Portfolio Penguin.

Shanahan, M. (2015) *The technological singularity*. Cambridge, MA: MIT Press, p. 233.

Warden, J. (2021) *Regenerative futures: from sustaining to thriving together*. Royal Society of Arts. Available at: www.thersa.org/reports/regenerative-futures-from-sustaining-to-thriving-together (Accessed: 22 March 2023).

Young, R., Blair, S. and Cooper, A. (2001) 'Redesigning design education: the next Bauhaus? Exploring emerging design paradigm', *Proceedings of ICSID educational seminar 2001*, Seognam, Korea, ICSID. Korea: Korea Institute of Design Promotion, pp. 26–33.

Chapter 14

Flourishing for all

The imperative for design research to go beyond academia

Leon Cruickshank

This provocation calls for design research to engage with societal issues in a manner that has a tangible positive impact, that design research contributes to making things *better* in addition to posing questions and contributing to knowledge and the academy of design.

While there are notable examples in which impactful engagement does occur in some centres of design research, there is also a great deal of research that does not look beyond the borders of the discipline and a self-congratulatory exploration of novel but ultimately frivolous ideas. This is not a result of a lack of partner working but often a mismatch, a lack of equitable, productive relationships between design research and external partners. While working with these partners often has a semblance of participation, letters of support, attendance at events and feel-good quotes, there is often a disconnection between the outcomes of the project and benefits to partners, business or wider society. Too often, partners are sources of data, approval, insights or resources without tangible benefits to them, where designers run creative sessions with 'users' but then take these findings away and do the synthesising, often proposing ideas that do not demonstrate a connection to the participants' contributions.

It is also not new for designers to adopt a mode of enquiry that purports to go beyond the profession and practices of design while, in fact, merely reinforcing these practices. While the 1980s radical design group Memphis praised the aesthetics of the nightclub, of cheap plastic furniture and leopard print, they only took from this design-led vernacular to reinforce elitist design as art. This is appropriation dressed up as accessibility, resulting in furniture that is impossibly expensive and often implausibly too large for a mere mortal's house. In a more contemporary context, as academics, we share knowledge and understanding of contemporary issues, often including sustainability issues, by travelling across the globe to meet together with all the environmental damage this entails. It's pleasing to see new models appearing to explore how we can keep the physical nature of knowledge exchange in academia without having to fly, for example the European Academy of Design's 'Hub' approach to their conference in 2023 in which regional hubs across the world are working together to create a single, distributed conference.

DOI: 10.4324/9781003399568-17

The position here is not to say that design research should not engage with theory, with concepts or challenging ideas, whether it's new materialism, decolonisation, generative design, AI or something else. As design researchers, though, we have a greater responsibility to go beyond this because, ultimately, most of our activities are funded by public money, the taxes of cleaners, carers, builders, and hairdressers. How does design research repay this investment from the earnings of these people? Design research often finds it difficult to either achieve or articulate its tangible contribution to the wider society.

We have an ethical responsibility to look for ways to make a positive impact on society, business, and the public sector. There is an argument that we also need the pure creativity of exploration, and while this is valid for genuine pioneers, the real leaders in a field, let's take an honest look at ourselves and our discipline. Unless you are a Skłodowska–Curie, a Wittgenstein or a Kahlo, we should look to extend our ideas beyond asking questions to having a tangible benefit in wider society in addition to contributing to design research knowledge. While we have the luxury of free reflection and whimsy in Lancaster, there are families within 500 metres of my home where children sleep in their clothes because they don't have sheets, blankets or pillows. We all share a responsibility here to strive for a more equitable society.

There is, though, another motivation for engaging beyond the academy of design research. As someone closer to the end of their career than the beginning, I know, when the final curtain is drawn, what I'll be proud of and what will recede into the background. It will not be the monographs, the multimillion-pound funded projects. It will be through initiatives such as activating the 'friends groups' within Lancaster. These groups of volunteers have a common cause focusing on a local park, waterway or other civic resource. In activating and improving the capacity, capability, and resilience of these groups, they have been able to apply for their own funding and also contribute to the health and well-being of their surroundings. This has resulted in helping the city to have better green spaces for its inhabitants despite a 60% austerity-led cut in funding; and the social worker who used my research to decisively change the life course of a nine-year-old orphan. It will be helping young families without internet access in lockdown to discover *discovery*, changing both their and their schools' approaches to learning and exploration.

This does not mean dumbing down or backing away from theory or ideas or generating new forms of thinking. It's entirely possible to draw on challenges and contribute to these big ideas whilst also having a practical, real-world impact: the research impacts described earlier are based on a Deleuzian inflection of deconstructive philosophy—where hierarchies are to be distrusted, not just reversed (bottom up) but to deconstruct the whole notion of binaries. Ideas, theory and abstract knowledge remain a critically important part of design research, but I'm calling for projects and proposals to push beyond the internal world of academic research and to extend these ideas properly into practice. In working with and tangibly benefitting people outside academia, we have the potential for our ingenuity to have real impacts. This could be in helping companies be more creative or enabling Syrian refugees to learn to cook the food supplied by food banks or to help parents home school when they are confined to their homes and cannot afford internet access.

Let's escape our privilege; let's stop playing with ourselves and extend our thinking and doing; let's be brave enough to develop our ideas to the point that they can be tested and impact the world outside academia. As someone who dreams of sporting a bee-fur jumpsuit, I strongly encourage design research to explore the edges of the unconventional, the radical, and sometimes the abstract, but we need to go further than self-indulgence. We should be sure. And we should try to make our interventions have a tangible, positive effect in the world. We need to get hands-on in helping everyone flourish.

Chapter 15

The shadow side

Why embracing death and decay is essential to flourishing

Laura Santamaria

This provocation argues for the need to integrate these 'shadow' aspects as an essential part of creativity and innovation processes.

The Swiss psychiatrist and psychoanalyst Carl Jung coined the term 'shadow self' in reference to parts of our personality that are buried deep within our psyche—essentially, our blind spots. He argued that we are somewhat controlled and robbed of personal autonomy by that which remains in the shadows, and it is only when we become aware of, accept, and integrate these hidden traits of our-selves that we become whole, integral human beings (Jung, 2005). This got me thinking: What is 'the shadow side' of flourishing? What lies beneath, hidden and unspoken, in innovation and growth discourses? What aspects are we neglecting that need to be integrated through design?

Let us unpack the 'flourishing' metaphor by turning towards Nature and personal development.

There is no such thing as an immortal flower

In Nature, nothing is lost; everything is transformed. A seed is planted out of sight, under the ground. Growth is the product of striving, which also reaches an optimal point that is related to the ability of the soil to keep providing the nutrients. When the peak has been reached, the flower gives way to fruit. Then, withering, death, and decay follow. The soil takes care of the decomposing, trans-muting the dead matter into rich nutrients that serve as fertilisers to nurture new growth. Yes, in its flowering state, it glowed and was admired. But its role when decomposed under the ground is no less important, and for that matter, trans-forms into the substance that facilitates the continuation of life.

Flourishing, *eudaimonia* in Greek, was the centrepiece of Aristotle's ethics. He saw it as the ultimate end, or good, of human purpose, 'the highest good' or a 'life well-lived'. The shadow side or antithesis—to wither, wilt, diminish—is well portrayed in Kafka's (1915) *Metamorphosis*, where Gregor's transformation stands as a symbol of how he has been dehumanised by his job and family: he is treated more like an insect than a human being, so he becomes an insect. His new outward form represents how he feels on the inside—unsatisfying work, burdensome responsibility, sacrifice, and isolation are the environmental

DOI: 10.4324/9781003399568-18

conditions that form his reality and cause his degradation into a lesser form, a seemingly negative transformation, or anti-flourishing.

As human beings, we all undergo transformations and mutations throughout our lives. If we turn our attention to traditional folktales, it's striking to see how many address the subject of loss. A sizable number begin with the loss of a parent, sibling, fortune, home, or identity—and rarely does that which is missing return, intact and unchanged, at the end of the story. Instead, loss is the catalyst that leads to transformation. Yet in our overoptimistic culture, we render anything associated with loss a taboo subject, missing out on the fact that for some things to come about, others—old patterns, habits and ideals—will need to 'die'. Psychological development is the process of overcoming setbacks, limitations, and conditioned behaviour; rising to challenges gives us the opportunity to reach a new level of personal freedom and maturity. We accept that some sort of death, letting go of some parts of ourselves, must happen so we can be renewed and fit for purpose.

As an emergent property of living organisms, flourishing is therefore a potentiality, a positive transformation that is only realised when the right systemic conditions are present. In design, this means paying attention to how we create the right contextual conditions, acknowledging that flourishing is just one transient state of creation.

Creation, bringing forth that which is not yet in existence, implies the acceptance of destruction. There is no such thing as an immortal flower.

In-novation needs out-novation

Transformation is not alien to organisations, which are likely to undergo necessary and beneficial periods of change. Although we are familiar with the natural cycles of flourishing and decay, life and death, it is obvious we still have some work to do in integrating the 'shadow side' when we move the discussion to the context of innovation. The negative connotations these terms carry in our culture mean these aspects often get neglected. In the words of Carl Jung, "One does not become enlightened by imagining figures of light, but by making the darkness conscious. The latter procedure, however, is disagreeable and therefore not popular" (Jung, 1967, p. 335). Perhaps a mix of misinterpreted positive psychology together with an ingrained Western view of prosperity has contributed to our prevalent, dystopian view of flourishing as the absolute panacea—a joyful, ecstatic achievement, reaching higher and higher goals, constantly driving us ever upwards.

The problem is, the sky might have no limits, but we do.

Admittedly, it is more exciting to ride the wave of anti-failure, the optimistic thrill associated with innovation and creativity, and to overlook the less appealing counterparts. Who, if given a choice, would turn the pile of compost rather than tend to the flowers? But inevitably, the better the compost, the better the flowers.

In design, we are familiar and comfortable with iteration, cyclically improving, adapting, pivoting, and morphing to suit the purpose. But how willing and capable are we to deal with death, grief, and transformation as a natural part of the process? When old things need to be shed, how do we do this by design?

The first challenge implies the elimination of what is no longer of value. The hardest, unspoken side of innovation is the discarding, discontinuing, and letting go of comfort zones. 'Dead parts' need to be identified, pruned, and mourned. What can we let go of or allow to shrink, lessen, wither, cease, languish, and decline so that we create the space and conditions for the new to grow, develop, build, ripen, improve, and increase?

Pondering these questions reminded me of the *Stages of Death and Dying*, by psychiatrist Elizabeth Kübler-Ross (1969), who found that terminally ill patients progress through five distinct states towards acceptance of their fate:

- Denial—the patient may deny that the illness is really happening to them and act as if nothing is wrong.
- Anger—the patient experiences deep emotions such as rage, frustration, and resentment, which are often directed at others.
- Bargaining—the individual acknowledges the illness but attempts to negotiate more time to engage in desired activities or to complete unfinished business. In a sense, bargaining is an attempt to delay the inevitable.
- Depression—the patient becomes melancholic, sombre, and dejected. During this time, the patient may mourn things (including relationships) that are already lost as well as things that may be lost in the future.
- Acceptance—they no longer fight the inevitable and prepare for their impending death. During this time, they also experience a sense of inner and outer peace.

Innovation is a complex process that can be fraught with obstacles and 'pain points'. Surely, there are great rewards to be gained when striving towards flourishing, but the journey of organisational and cultural change, with its manifold interdependencies, is far from a joyride. Organisations are made up of people who might not be ready to transition, to let go of what is familiar and embrace the unknown, and if we do not develop tools for navigating the inevitable tensions, the tendency is to turn a blind eye and expect magic results by planting new seeds on untreated ground. Then, it is worth asking how well we are facilitating the 'phasing out' through transition and change. Perhaps when we are called to bring about the 'new and next', we have an opportunity to consider how we facilitate transformation of those involved, especially easing the hidden, unspoken, and potentially most painful parts of the process.

Better still, how can we design for everyone's creative force to emerge from within?

'A seed grows best in broken soil'

There is nothing like a crisis to shake up inertia. The COVID-19 pandemic undoubtedly has marked the end of a certain way of being. Under the influence of external factors and forces beyond our control, we were forced to adopt the new and adapt, at a global scale and in record time, feeling like we were being moved around like pieces on a chessboard. Powerlessness is not a feeling we humans

Figure 15.1
Flourishing cycle: realisation (blossom), striving (stem), potentiality (bulb).
Photo series courtesy: Francesco Mazzarella.

relish. Yet in the striving, we found the inner resources, the will and purpose to transform. Jung poses, "recognition of the shadow, on the other hand, leads to the modesty we need in order to acknowledge imperfection" (Jung, 2005, p. 73).

The nature of Nature is that it is constantly breaking down distinctions and building them up into something new and then breaking them down again, and around and around. As an integral part of Nature, our bodies, cultures, and organisations are being ground in this existential mill, more than at any time in history as we face unprecedented social and ecological systemic collapse.

We, designers, creators of human-made systems and cultures apt for flourishing, have a central role to play in creating the right conditions for the environment and people to thrive. As we engage in designing for flourishing cultures, let us turn our fascination away from newness and towards cultivating hope and a sense of collective purpose. Let us facilitate elimination, termination, and interruption of the status quo, and let us do it in the way of Nature, where the old fertilises the ground, preparing it well for the fledgling to grow strong.

Flourishing then becomes not a destination but a constant process of tending to our garden, our health, and our wholeness. And as we reach a higher level of awareness, let us develop resilience and kindness to execute our designerly ways with grace.

Reference list

Jung, C.G. (1967) *Collected works of C.G. Jung: alchemical studies*. vol. 13. London: Routledge and Kegan Paul.

Jung, C.G. (2005) *The undiscovered self*. London and New York: Routledge. Ebook. Available at: https://fleurmach.files.wordpress.com/2016/07/jung-the-undiscovered-self-1957.pdf (Accessed: 15 June 2023)

Kafka, F. (1915) *Metamorphosis*. Leipzig: Kurt Wolff Verlag.

Kübler-Ross, E. (1969) *On death and dying*. Abingdon: Routledge.

Chapter 16

Making design research *work* by flourishing through disappearance

Joseph Lindley

From its roots, which were established in the middle of the last century, design research has grown, is alive and kicking (Rodgers and Yee, 2016), and is blossoming in design-led research centres around the world. One reason for its relevance at this moment in history is its ability to provide insightful lenses and viewpoints on challenges and issues that the dominant science-oriented paradigm struggles to make sense of. But what of the future? What should we expect of design research? What does it mean for the discipline to flourish?

But before we get to that, I want to take a moment to consider *science*.

Many would agree that science represents an astonishing set of traditions that underpin a cornucopia of human achievement. So many wonders of the world have been delivered through scientific endeavour. But science has a cousin, a concept called scien*tism*. And while science represents a rich tradition of curiosity, experimentation, and knowledge, its descendant, scientism, is the dangerously hubristic belief that the *only* way of making sense of the world is through a scientific lens. In 2022, I performed a comedy set about my research, during which I introduced the concept of scientism by musing that the 'ism' suffix has a habit of transforming concepts that people generally approve of and refiguring them as unpleasant nasties. For example, sex is generally considered to be a good and healthy thing in one's life. Sex*ism*, however, reflects the realities of millennia of female oppression. Alcohol can be delicious and is, for many, an enjoyable social lubricant. Meanwhile, alcohol*ism* is an addiction that, in countries like the United Kingdom, causes more societal damage than pretty much anything else. The same pattern, of the 'ism' suffix turning a good thing into an anathema, is also true for science and scientism. Scientism takes the spirit of open exploration characterised by science and turns it into a blinkered and closed-minded position that, although it believes itself to be championing the scientific endeavour, has a totally different and far more sinister character.

But why does scientism matter? Well, if we look closely, it turns out that scientism isn't rare. In fact, it's infused into the very core of most organisations and institutions. Scientism both tints and, arguably, taints our view of the world.

Almost every site of power, education, knowledge, and government is imbued with this tacit alignment to a worldview coloured and informed by scientism (and its underlying philosophical foundation, positivism). It is because of this deep infusion that over-simplistic sentiments such as political regimes' declarations to

DOI: 10.4324/9781003399568-19

'follow the science' seem palatable to the masses despite their intrinsic flaws. We are societally conditioned to accept, seek, and desire, the tempting certainty that scientism promises. Of course, *proving* my position would be rather difficult, and I do not suppose anyone should consider my argument to be 'true'. However, for the purposes of this chapter, please bear with me. At the very least, let's agree that it's possible that there are some places where scientism exerts influence.

In support of the validity of my line of reasoning, I can cite as evidence that I have presented this argument to several hundred scholars and professionals over the last year. The conceit that scientism, or something like it, informs the prevailing view of the world is something that my audiences have rarely contested. In isolation, you might just think this could be explained by the individuals making up the audiences being polite. However, given how forthright they have been about challenging other matters, I have taken their acceptance as adding credence to the position. I should also point out that I believe there are many circumstances in which science *does* offer the best way to make sense of a situation, for example, in establishing the efficacy of a new vaccine or proving the existence of subatomic particles. However, there are many situations where science is not the *only* pathway to making sense of the world, for example, formulating policy in response to a pandemic, making ethical, aesthetic, or moral judgements, and virtually all conundrums that involve imagining the future.

These are the thorny quandaries that science needs help with; these are the challenges that we mustn't let scientism blinker our view of; these are the issues that design researchers are perfectly placed and poised to help address. The reason that design research is so aptly paired with such tricky problems is that, by being grounded in the generative and creative act of design, design research has a natural tendency to break free from the tendrils of scientism's positivist reach. Positivist approaches strive for facts, testability, and research questions that can be shown to be true or false. In contrast, design researchers hope, expect, and embrace the fact that each time they run an experiment, they would get a different answer. This is not to say design research is devoid of evidence but rather that the evidence is of a different type and constitutes a different kind of knowing.

There is much debate and a healthy amount written about what it is 'under the hood' that makes design research work. Some examples include Frayling's categorisation of different types of design research (1993); Schön's conception of the reflective practitioner (1983); Deweyan pragmatism as a foundational epistemological framework (Dixon, 2019); not to mention a cornucopia of models, methods, theories, and diagrams that pop up in specialist publications, conferences, and journal articles. Through the work I've done with *Design Research Works*,[1] I've been exposed to many of these ways of looking, and they're great! But there's a subtle irony that cuts through these attempts to formalise design research in a scholarly manner. Almost all these disciplinary accoutrements tend towards a kind of certainty and surefootedness that seems reminiscent of the positivistic outlooks that the kernel of design research rejects. This, in my view, is the biggest current challenge for the world of design research. Theories, models, and methods are needed to make the practice accessible; however, over-theorisation that doesn't allow for emergence and draconianly methodical methods undermine the very nature of design research's value proposition. Finding a sweet spot will pay dividends. The ideal balance will allow design research to be widely taught, shared, and applied, but all the while sustaining the emergence, dynamism, and flexibility that offers a productive counterpoint to science. This is the challenge that I and my team aspire to tackle.

I estimate that, in the short term, design research centres will continue to grow. Alongside the rhetorical argument for design research's relevance I've presented in this chapter, the *impact* of the kind of research we do is even more compelling, and those impacts will continue to attract partners and investment. We're already seeing that design research is more frequently the lead discipline in large multidisciplinary research schemes. Historically, it was often a supporting act to more established disciplines, but these days, it can be the linchpin at the centre. In the medium term, in part driven by the climate emergency, the unsustainability of capitalism, and an increasing awareness of the need to 'defuture'[2] (a concept that rejects the assumption that the future simply 'is'), I think the dominance of positivism and scientism will gradually wane. The existential necessity to meaningfully engage with the wicked problems of the 21st century depends on this rebalancing of our knowledge ecosystem. The space that the rebalancing will create will be filled by practices like design research. In the slightly longer term, as design research truly flourishes, perhaps it will start to disappear. By this, I don't mean cease to exist but rather cease to be so visible, cease to be an exception, and cease to be confined to specialist centres. The ways of seeing, knowing, and exploring that specialist design researchers operationalise may, one day, become a significant tenet of that day's presiding knowledge paradigm. With this potential in mind, the case is put; design research will truly flourish through its own disappearance (Lindley and Green, 2021).

When he was chief executive of the Royal Society for the Encouragement of Arts, Manufactures, and Commerce, Matthew Taylor introduced the strapline '21st-century Enlightenment' (2010). The concept resonates here. The original Enlightenment was a time when ideas, thoughts, and cataclysmic shifts in understanding took place. The ripples of these shifts still bounce around our culture and society today. Right now, however, we live among new sources of agitation— e.g., the climate crisis, huge geopolitical shifts, the advent of the Internet and artificial intelligence—and these require new modes of response. We are being forced to live differently, and to live differently is to *think* differently. In Taylor's words, "As the architects of the Enlightenment understood this means being able to see our world and ourselves from a new perspective" (2010, p. 9). I hope, and I believe it is possible, that in some version of the future, on the other side of a 21st-century Enlightenment, our descendants will look back on a time *before* design research flourished and disappeared. If they did that, they might wonder what it was like to live in a world under the spell of scientism. They might muse on how the pioneering work coming from the design research discipline helped disrupt the status quo. If any of them happened to research this question, then there's a chance they would find a copy of this book, and if they did, then I would say, "*Hello from the past!*"

Notes

1   See https://designresearch.works
2   See www.youtube.com/watch?v=mpFhpuK3vlc

Reference list

Dixon, B. (2019) 'Experiments in experience: towards an alignment of research through design and John Dewey's pragmatism', *Design Issues*, 35(2), pp. 5–16.

Frayling, C. (1993) 'Research in art and design', *Royal College of Art Research Papers*, 1(1), pp. 1–9.

Lindley, J. and Green, D.P. (2021) 'The ultimate measure of success for speculative design is to disappear completely', *Interaction Design and Architecture(s)*, 51, pp. 32–51. https://doi.org/10.55612/s-5002-051-002

Rodgers, P.A. and Yee, J.S.R. (2016) 'Design research is alive and kicking', *Design research society conference*.

Schön, D. (1983) *The reflective practitioner: how professionals think in action*. New York: Basic Books.

Taylor, M. (2010) *Twenty-first century enlightenment*. Available at: www.thersa. org/globalassets/pdfs/reports/rsa_21centuryenlightenment_essay1_mat thewtaylor.pdf (Accessed: 14 March 2023).

Chapter 17

Working at the junction

Reconciling numbers and vulnerabilities

Marzia Mortati

It is now common rhetoric to say that we are undergoing massive change. We live in an era in which, for instance, the notion of prosperity is undergoing great transformations. As reported in the preface of the Global Competitiveness Index released by the World Economic Forum in 2018:

> With the Fourth Industrial Revolution (4IR), humanity has entered a new phase. The 4IR has become the lived reality for millions of people around the world, and is creating new opportunities for business, government, and individuals. Yet it also threatens a new divergence and polarization within and between economies and societies. [. . .] Combined with a background of growing inequality and geopolitical flashpoints, this has fuelled citizens' concerns about globalization and polarized the political debate. [. . .] The 4IR and the consequences of the Great Recession are redefining the pathways to prosperity and, indeed, the very notion of prosperity, with profound implications for policymaking. Concerned leaders are grappling for answers and solutions, aiming to go beyond short-term, reactionary measures.
>
> (Schwab, 2018, p. v)

The traditional notions of competitiveness, growth, prosperity, well-being, and even innovation do not seem to apply well to the future. For example, addressing innovation challenges now means adopting a global perspective while also considering environmental/sustainable challenges and the rapid pace of technological advancement. The business and national strategies for growth needed to accommodate these issues require complex interventions negotiated between different socio-economic actors (companies, institutions, citizens etc.) and working in teams of multi-experts. In this scenario, the old, siloed approaches to development no longer apply. Considering recent disruptions (beginning with the financial crisis of 2008 until the more recent global spread of the COVID pandemic), theories have come to the fore proposing how—if they are to thrive—businesses and organisations can no longer solely rely on the traditional numerical points of view. Instead, they need to reconcile the human perspective with numbers, one that can better comprehend culture and vulnerabilities, thus telling stories out of situated and local observations.

DOI: 10.4324/9781003399568-20

In a recent article in the *Financial Times*, award-winning journalist Gillian Tett pointedly explains why development in the future, whether regarding business, finance or technology, needs to be blended more decisively with human and qualitative insights, looking at the deep 'reasons why' of people and society:

> The real issue at stake is tunnel vision. Today most professions encourage their adherents to adopt intellectual tools that are at best neatly bound or at worst one-dimensional. Economic models, by definition, are defined by their inputs, and everything else is deemed an 'externality' (which was how climate change issues used to be perceived). Corporate accountants are trained to relegate things not directly linked to profits and losses (such as gender ratios) into the footnotes of company accounts. Political pollsters or consumer surveys often operate with pre-determined questions. These tools are often very useful, if not indispensable. But they have a flaw: if the wider context outside that economic model, company, political poll or Big Data set is changing, that bounded tool and neat quantitative analysis might not work.
> (Tett, 2021a)

The point made by Tett is crucial: context and culture matter. It is at the crossroads between numerical analysis and contextual insights that we should look for the answers to the most relevant alternative models for development, reconciling the cold understanding of quantitative math with the fuzzy logic of qualitative discovery. However, the availability, centrality, and use of data are currently steering the way forward and occupying decision-makers' minds.

Examining the current digital transformation and the increased centrality of numbers, Italian philosopher Maurizio Ferraris (2021) argues that the real difference between digital and analogic is in the recording, which regulates and traces each interaction, choice or sentiment. Recording feeds the uncontrolled growth of data, (ab)using the unintentional traces of human activity, thus realising a dream in the fashion of Jules Verne: everything is data, and data is faith. This recording includes numbers, letters, sounds, images, and behaviours, thus creating the false homology between the mechanics of the human mind and the artificial intelligence fed by the data. In Ferraris's argumentation, recording is, therefore, the fundamental force that is disrupting the world and that is making data central to both economy and society. Data (and the algorithms that manipulate it) is already affecting how people live, consume and dream through forecasting, predictions and recommendations. However, largely skewed data sets also produce skewed applications that, together with other flaws (i.e., the idea that data is objective), shows how data is not sufficient to forecast or counteract undesired events. Furthermore, reading data is not a neutral act. As Alkhatib (2021), director of the Centre of Applied Data Ethics, describes, machine learning systems do not perform analysis based on particular reasons. They provide patterns without reasons, as any data set still portrays the biases, shadows and faults of human history. Data sets—to feed algorithms—are manipulated, skewed, flattened, filtered, and interpreted; they always lack the depth that only lived experiences can provide. Thus, the author concludes that algorithms create a world devoid of meaning, where humans are rewarded or punished according to the extent to which they fit into the model that sits at the core of the algorithm.

Consequently, looking at the dominant logic in economy and innovation, we should ask: Is data enough to guide the flourishing of humans, organisations, and the planet? And, if yes, what data?

Here lies one of the main contributions design can make: helping to frame numerical approaches less centrally in the current debate. Design is not a discipline and practice that has been particularly concerned with data, neither framing methodologies for collection nor discussing data in general. As a discipline, it has partially discussed how it analyses data while counting on its ability to empathise with people. Building on this, design has been popularised as a discipline that can put people at the centre of innovation processes (Elsbach and Stigliani, 2018; Mortati, 2015), capturing desires and needs. Throughout this process, the designer mainly collects qualitative data by studying current phenomena, contexts and trends and by using direct observation methods. This way of examining and understanding an innovation problem leads designers to collect at least 15 different types of qualitative data, including for instance user observations, direct interviews, the information provided by clients (e.g., mission, vision, strategic objectives, company culture, and so on), and others. This data, which expresses a deep knowledge of people, motivations, contexts, and stories, is referred to in ethnography as Thick Data (Geertz, 1973; Wang, 2017), describing people's wants, needs, and desires. Having a qualitative nature, it cannot be quantified and is a source of great inspiration for creatives. However, this is not the dominant logic that organisations follow in order to flourish; typically, economic models follow the laws of numbers, caring little about understanding why people buy a particular object or pay for a service. Consequently, this has often left design hidden in the process of innovation and has relegated the human dimension to a few specific best practices (e.g., the history of several small Italian companies that have become well known as 'design-driven companies', like Alessi, Kartell, and others) and theories (e.g., Piore and Sabel, 1984; Verganti, 2009; Tett, 2021b).

This junction, where the dominant logics of quantitative analysis are blended with qualitative and thick knowledge, is where intriguing new directions for research and practice can be found. Quantitative analysis can provide extensive knowledge of the behaviour and evolutionary trajectories of society. In contrast, qualitative knowledge can offer a situated understanding of culture and individual behaviours, thus reaching a deeper and more nuanced understanding of situations.

However, the panoramic overviews calculated through quantitative analysis and the stories told by qualitative observations still struggle to converge in the design process. In their typical search for the hidden reasons behind people's behaviours, designers look mainly for the human side of data and struggle to engage with quantitative data sets. This has both positive and negative consequences. Looking at the negative side, it will be increasingly difficult for designers to impact the shaping of society and economy if they don't learn to dialogue with the widely accepted quantitative perspective. Looking at the positive side, designers refuse to give data the responsibility to dictate people's futures—to decide who will be hired or fired, those to be admitted to school or that are worthy of credit, these being the direction of several current applications of algorithmic decision-making. For designers, all data must become thick. Creatives engage with data through thickening them, that is, giving them depth and context. Thus, they strip data and algorithms of their fake veil of objectivity to shape them into vulnerabilities and dense representations. In so doing, they also reorient the value of data while bringing human fragilities back to the centre of prosperity.

The study of the process that might happen at the junction between quantitative and qualitative and how this could transform design practice opens relevant research areas, for instance, by asking: How can designers meaningfully include different types of data in their creative process? What skills and competencies do they need to work effectively with mixed data sets? And how can the explorative and qualitative nature of design research be connected to the quantitative nature of digitally sourced data and algorithmic processes of analysis without losing its identity? What new design practices can we explore that can guide a reconciliation of perspectives?

This junction might represent one of the most relevant transitions for design in the 21st century, after a long process of development started in the 1960s. Since then, the interests of the discipline have been constantly growing and bringing the design research community to theorise Four Orders of Design challenges (Buchanan, 2001). Notably, Richard Buchanan describes this evolution, arguing that design started—after the first industrial revolution—by focusing on communication, symbols, and images. It then progressed to artefacts getting closer to engineering and architecture while adopting the principles of mass production. Finally, in the 20th century, design moved toward devising more than physical outputs for industrial production; that is, it focused on outputs that were at the same time tangible and intangible, from processes to services and interfaces, mainly devising how people relate to other people or objects. A further evolution for Buchanan (2001) is designing the environments and systems within which all the previous objects and activities live: understanding how these systems work, what interactions, exchanges and relationships hold them together, what ideas and values sit at their core is for the author a fourth-order problem of design. Arguably, design may now be entering fifth-order challenges (Mortati, 2022) as it begins to look at complex socio-technical systems, data feedback loops and pathways to transformation. These deserve not only to be problem-solved but to be interpreted under the lens of a more sustainable notion of prosperity. Several scholars describe these new frontiers in research and practice, referring to the necessity of including a 'more-than-human' dimension when designing. On the one hand, the increasing dominance of algorithms requires the renovation of the ethical principles of designing and the active inclusion of these agents in the creative process (Giaccardi and Redström, 2020). On the other, the necessity to include other species, micro-organisms and nature in a design endeavour opens wide the concerns of design (Oxman, 2016; Tsing, 2015). These two positions are both cogent for designers of the 21st century to reconcile the needs of humans, their organisations and the planet.

Finally, this debate also supports the idea that to help organisations flourish and prosper in the future, diversity and the multi-layered essence of each creature will have increasing importance. This includes contradictions, complexities and the dazzling variety of cultures and points at a diversity that can be valued only by working 'at the junction', that is, the boundary spaces between disciplines, approaches, and areas of knowledge.

Reference list

Alkhatib, A. (2021) 'To live in their Utopia: why algorithmic systems create absurd outcomes', *Proceedings of the 2021 CHI conference on human factors in computing systems*, pp. 1–9.

Buchanan, R. (2001) 'Design research and the new learning', *Design Issues*, 17(4), pp. 3–23.

Elsbach, K.D. and Stigliani, I. (2018) 'Design thinking and organizational culture: a review and framework for future research', *Journal of Management*, 44, pp. 2274–2306.

Ferraris, M. (2021) *Documanità. Filosofia del mondo nuovo*. Milano: Editori Laterza.

Geertz, C. (1973) *The interpretations of cultures*. New York: Basic Books.

Giaccardi, E. and Redström, J. (2020) 'Technology and more-than-human design', *Design Issues*, 36(4), pp. 33–44.

Mortati, M. (2015) 'A framework for design innovation: present and future discussions', *Design Issues*, 31(4), pp. 4–16.

Mortati, M. (2022) 'New design knowledge and the fifth order of design', *Design Issues*, 39(2), pp. 21–34.

Oxman, N. (2016) 'Age of entanglement', *Journal of Design and Science*. https://doi.org/10.21428/7e0583ad

Piore, M.J. and Sabel, C.F. (1984) *The second industrial divide*. New York: Basic Books.

Schwab, K. (2018) 'The global competitiveness report 2018', *World economic forum*. Available at: http://www3.weforum.org/docs/GCR2018/05FullReport/TheGlobalCompetitivenessReport2018.pdf (Accessed: 26 June 2021).

Tett, G. (2021a) 'The human factor—why data is not enough to understand the world', *The Financial Times*, 28 May. Available at: https://amp-ft-com.cdn.ampproject.org/c/s/amp.ft.com/content/4f00469c-75da-4e29-baf3-b7bec470732c (Accessed: 26 June 2021).

Tett, G. (2021b) *Anthro-vision. How anthropology can explain business and life*. London: Penguin Books.

Tsing, A.L. (2015) *The mushroom at the end of the world: on the possibility of life in capitalist ruins*. Princeton: Princeton University Press.

Verganti, R. (2009) *Design-driven innovation: changing the rules of competition by radically innovating what things mean*. Boston, MA: Harvard Business Press.

Wang, T. (2017) 'The human insights missing from big data', *TEDTalk*. Available at: www.youtube.com/watch?v=pk35J2u8KqY (Accessed: 20 September 2020).

Chapter 18

Public value by design

Toward a flourishing design culture in public services

Louise Mullagh and Jez Bebbington

In recent years, the established disciplines of service design and policy design have proved the compatibility of design practices and principles with the pursuit of public value (Bason, 2016). Here, we reflect on the increasing levels of collaboration and integration from the dual perspectives of the design researcher and the public manager. We contend that public services can flourish by moving beyond the deployment of design methods as 'tools' or 'instruments' toward a deeply embedded culture in which the natural role of the public servant is lived out through ongoing, participatory design and redesign at all levels of operations, management and strategy.

This chapter explores the concept of 'flourishing', defined by the Oxford English Dictionary (2021) as to "grow or develop in a healthy or vigorous way, especially as a result of a particularly congenial environment". Whilst we eagerly await literary contributions on how design may achieve the alternative definition of the word—"wave [something] about to attract attention" (OED, 2021)—in this chapter, we consider how design principles and practices can contribute to 'flourishing' public services and, as such, how design can itself 'flourish' in the 'congenial environment' of the public sphere. We argue that an organisation's 'flourishing' should be evaluated based on its 'fruitfulness' and, as such, that the flourishing public organisation should be measured in terms of its creation of tangible public-value outcomes.

Our ongoing collaborative work pursues two primary objectives. First, the creation of 'public value'; that is, the environmentally, socially, and economically beneficial outcomes that will have a positive impact on the lives of citizens. Second, the development of the skills, capabilities, and ways of working that will enable public servants to embed design and participation into their everyday, 'native' practice.

Collaboration between designers and public services in Lancaster, UK, has recently flourished. Co-design projects such as Leapfrog: Transforming Public Sector Engagement by Design (Lancaster University, 2018), and the comprehensive 'Beyond Imagination Life Survey' of residents (Lancaster University, 2022), have showcased the possibilities for better public services and policies to be created through a design-enabled, outcome-focused methodology. While this dynamic has existed for many decades in liberal democracies, there has been

DOI: 10.4324/9781003399568-21

a shift during the 21st century toward engaging citizens not only in the lengthy cycles of the democratic process but in ongoing participation in the design and delivery of public services and policies. Governments today must tackle complex and often wicked problems, such as the climate emergency, public health, and economic challenges. Policymakers at all scales are operating within resource constraints while being under pressure to deliver services. Add to this the convergence of global priorities, connections, and technologies, and it is clear that the role of the public manager must evolve from 'management' toward 'orchestration', as described by Crosby, Hart and Torfing (2016).

We find that design's emphasis on understanding, visualising, and ultimately navigating complexity is well suited to enabling public organisations in harmonising public 'problem-solving' (such as preventing health hazards and supporting local economic development) with the more aspirational imagining of futures (such as enabling the decarbonised, connected, inclusive places of the future).

Public value and design

From the perspective of the public manager, if the flourishing public organisation is to be measured by its fruitfulness in terms of public value creation, then the quality of its fruit can only be evaluated by those who experience that value in a tangible way: i.e., the citizens who exchange a degree of social freedom, and of course taxation, for positive and valued public outcomes.

Design, and particularly co-design or participatory design, appears to be ideally suited to support this dynamic. Bringing stakeholders from across public, business, and community sectors directly into the design of public services and policies provides an opportunity not just to optimise the services and policies themselves but to unlock resources and creativity far beyond the capability and capacity of the public organisation itself.

How, then, can design be successfully integrated into all corners of public management in which it can effectively contribute? How can we create the 'congenial environment' in which both public value and design are able to mutually flourish?

Our experience of collaborating on design-enabled public projects has shown us that while a clear opportunity exists to create a 'native' public-service design culture, substantial development work is required before we can claim success.

For example, a recent consultation and engagement project around social housing provided excellent opportunities for co-design to be built into the process. The project used co-design to engage with residents of a housing estate in order to understand how improvements might be made. The public managers involved were enthusiastic about the possibility of a design-led approach, and the designers similarly embraced the project's context and requirements. Despite this willingness to collaborate and co-design, a number of barriers hindered the true flourishing of both public value and design throughout the project. First, both public officials and designers were unclear of their respective roles in the project: was this consultancy, project delivery or something else? Second, the mutual benefits to public managers and design researchers required some navigation: how could the project be designed and delivered in a way that created both public value and quality research outcomes? Third, matters of resourcing and decision-making were continuously evolving: how should the public organisation integrate rigorous co-design principles with democratic accountability and decision processes?

None of these questions were unanswerable, but the pressurised nature and time scales of public projects created sticking points that would be far more readily navigated within a 'native' public-service design culture, in which the 'co-design consultation and engagement process' becomes simply the 'consultation and engagement process' with co-design principles being implicit yet fundamental.

Design and public policy

As design researchers working with local government, it has become clear, through exploration of literature and carrying out design research, that there is perhaps a lack of understanding of what, on the one hand, design might offer to public policy and, on the other, what we as researchers need to know to work with policymakers.

Literature relating to the relatively new area of 'design for policy' often situates the role of design and of the designer as a mode through which problems can be solved (Bason, 2014). Policies, or more specifically policy areas, are therefore considered to be 'the problem'. While acknowledging that design does play a role in the solving of problems, it can also offer opportunities for flourishing and provide valuable transformation that can bring about far more benefits for both organisations and communities. However, to achieve this, we must consider key challenges.

A recent project carried out in collaboration by both authors, P-PITEE (Participatory Policies for Internet of Things (at the edge) Ethics), explored how we can design ethical policies for IoT (Internet of Things) devices in public places with local government (Mullagh, 2021). The project explored how local governments need to account for practical, technical, and ethical considerations when using Internet of Things sensors and 'edge technology' (where processing happens on the devices rather than on a central computer) in public spaces and when managing proposals for installation and use of these technologies by other organisations or people. The project used a design method (design fiction) to develop new policies for transparent and ethical deployment of secure IoT sensors in public spaces. The use of design fiction is of particular value because this approach is used "not to show how things will be but to open up a space for discussion" (Dunne and Raby, 2014, p. 15). The intention of using design in this context was to enable participants (council officers) to have conversations as they encountered the signs and the objects while walking through the city. The design fictions consisted of signs placed on both made-up and real objects in the city, some of which had IoT devices embedded and some of which did not (waste bin, parking meter, CCTV cameras). The signs suggested additional functionalities, for example, a smart bin that might identify contents as well as weight or an audio and video CCTV monitor in the town centre that carried out gait analysis as well as recording people's voices.

A key reflection from the project is that we need to think about a possible mode of design that is embedded in the processes of policymaking that becomes less 'othered', where designers are brought in to solve problems. As designers and researchers, we are often parachuted in to carry out projects that benefit us in terms of gaining insights and developing useful tools or methods and that *might* benefit the council and wider stakeholders through the provision of such tools. We often decide on a specific 'problem' to be solved, such as how to design a new service that can bring about greater efficiencies or to develop methods of policymaking that engage wider communities and stakeholders. However, problem-solving is not flourishing. Flourishing, as identified earlier, should be a vision for local policymakers to think about alternative futures in which their communities can thrive. This is seemingly a utopian vision in our complex times, where public managers and politicians must wrestle with complex, wicked problems while simultaneously delivering services within constrained resources and demands from their citizens.

Furthermore, we should think about design that is 'everyday' and commonplace within public policy, where tools and methods can be picked up by public managers or politicians and become so embedded they are no longer defined as specifically 'design' methods. Furthermore, it is vital, as highlighted earlier, that designers, public managers, and politicians can understand not only the roles they play but also the complex environment in which they are exploring design.

Opportunities for flourishing

Through a range of design-enabled public projects, we have found that public value and participation are enhanced by the design approach. But we have also found that the process required to 'bring design to the table' is not always smooth, swift or conducive to agile, fluid project delivery. The requirements of public servants to acclimatise to the unfamiliar ideas of design and of designers to engage with the context and complexity of public service can create barriers to the effective deployment of design. We believe that a considered, deliberate approach to embedding a new, 'native' design culture within public organisations can overcome these challenges and provide a 'congenial environment' for creating public value by design. We are convinced that flourishing can truly be achieved when design happens not as an 'other' activity, unfamiliar and outside the remit of the 'day job', but when design becomes the day job itself.

While design experts and researchers have a truly significant role to play in creating a design culture for public services, we believe that the culture itself should come to rely less on 'others'—the exotic, unfamiliar methods, tools, and interactions brought in from outside by 'designers'—and that design principles and practices should be deeply embedded as part of the everyday 'flow' of public management. In this culture, public managers do not go out of their way to source design principles and methods externally to their organisation but are equipped with the role-definition, skills, tools, behaviours, and relationships to design continuously and effectively at operational, managerial, and strategic levels.

Our next substantial collaboration will explore opportunities for co-designing climate-related policy from a place-based perspective. We aim to harness high levels of engagement around the climate emergency across public, business, and community sectors and translate this into co-owned policies and interventions that will enable local stakeholders to contribute effectively to creating a climate-neutral future place. Considering questions of roles, objectives, and decision-making from the outset, alongside a deliberate goal of embedding co-design principles and capabilities with all those who participate in the process, will enable further progress in creating public value through a native public-service design culture.

Reference list

Bason, C. (ed.) (2014) *Design for policy*. Farnham: Gower Publishing.

Bason, C. (2016) *Design for policy*. Farnham: Gower Publishing.

Crosby, B.C., Hart, P. and Torfing, J. (2016) 'Public value creation through collaborative innovation', *Public Management Review*, 19(5), pp. 655–669.

Dunne, A. and Raby, F. (2014) *Speculative everything: design, fiction and social dreaming*. Cambridge, MA: MIT Press.

Lancaster University (2018) *Leapfrog: transforming public sector engagement by design*. Available at: https://imagination.lancaster.ac.uk/leapfrog-tools/ (Accessed: 14 July 2023).

Lancaster University (2022) *Beyond imagination life survey findings*. Available at: https://imagination.lancaster.ac.uk/update/life-survey-findings/ (Accessed: 7 March 2023).

Mullagh, L. (2021) *P-PITEE project description*. Available at: https://imagination.lancaster.ac.uk/update/p-pitee-launch/ (Accessed: 7 March 2023).

Oxford Languages (2021) *Flourish*. Available at: www.google.com/search?q=flourish+definition&rlz=1C1AVFC_enGB816GB825&oq=flourish&aqs=chrome.1.69i57j69i59j0i131i433i512l2j46i175i199i512j0i3j0i131i433i512j46i175i199i512j0i131i433j46i175i199i512.2485j0j7&sourceid=chrome&ie=UTF-8 (Accessed: 12 July 2021).

Chapter 19

What schools do we need?

Ana Rute Costa

The relationship between users and learning environments can be seen as an ecology. Attending school is not only about teaching and learning but is also about growing human beings. While social learning helps shape personality, relating to others and being better citizens, these social dimensions are often underestimated and forgotten under pressures of final grades and curriculum delivery. More than schools, we need learning organisations to equip students with knowledge and skills necessary to succeed in an uncertain and constantly changing environment, bringing the learning community together for a better and enhanced learning experience. This chapter investigates the key role design research can play in this flourishing process and re-imagining schools as part of a wide ecosystem that enables innovative pedagogies and practices. By bringing school communities, industry, policymakers, designers, and researchers together, design research can manage expectations and promote an aspirational dialogue towards better future learning environments.

How does design research shape physical learning environments and help schools to flourish as learning organisations?

Literacy levels across the world have risen drastically in the last couple of centuries (Roser and Ortiz-Ospina, 2016). If you are reading this text right now, you have probably attended more than one school in your lifetime and experienced different learning environments. What do you remember from those schools? Have you any particular memory of a learning environment? What was the impact of the school's spaces on your school's organisation?

In most cases, we associate the physical learning environments with activities we've performed, specific moments and particular people (Costa, 2015). Research evidence (Barrett *et al.*, 2015) shows that physical learning environments play a key role in student engagement and attainment, and according to Sir Ken Robinson's *Planning Learning Spaces* (2020), we should provide learning environments in which children want to learn and discover their true passion naturally. Therefore, the way we conceive physical learning environments plays an essential role in achieving this. But what type of schools do we need? How can we learn from previous experience and have schools that meet the demands of our current and future society?

Over the last 25 years, governments around the world, e.g., Britain (Building Schools for the Future); Australia (Building the Education Revolution); and Portugal

DOI: 10.4324/9781003399568-22

(Parque Escolar), have invested huge amounts of money in their school buildings. In some cases, they have focused mainly on building conditions and technical interventions (Duthilleul, Woolner and Whelan, 2021) by improving the quality, comfort, and performance of the buildings but not necessarily promoting an update on teaching and learning spaces and practices.

In other cases, the interventions provided a transition from traditional school buildings to innovative learning spaces (Imms and Kvan, 2021) and accommodated innovative teaching and learning approaches. However, not every school has been able to adjust their practices to the new innovative learning environments immediately.

There were several projects developed across the world to support this transition and adjust learning spaces and practices, for example, the Innovative Learning Environments and Teacher Change (ILETC) project led by the Learning Environments Applied Research Network (LEaRN) at The University of Melbourne. This project has explored an unprecedented collaboration with industries and education departments across four countries and produced some insightful outcomes, e.g., the impact of different spatial school layouts on student learning (creativity, critical thinking, communication, collaboration, and problem-solving) (Byers, Marian Mahat and Imms, 2018). The ILETC project highlighted the importance of having transdisciplinary approaches that adjust physical learning environments alongside the introduction of new teaching and learning practices.

Nevertheless, upgrading the physical learning environments in alignment with aspiring teaching and learning practices seems not to be enough. According to OECD-UNICEF, "schools should be reconceptualised as 'learning organisations that can react more quickly to changing external environments, embrace innovations in internal organisation, and ultimately improve student outcomes" (OECD, 2016, p. Introduction). More than schools, we need learning organisations that are capable of equipping students with the knowledge and skills they will need to succeed in an uncertain and constantly changing environment and bring the learning community together for a better and enhanced learning experience.

As part of the large-scale school improvement reform in Wales, the government implemented the 'schools as learning organisations' policy. The resulting report (OECD, 2018) shows that developing schools as learning organisations requires concerted efforts and means where the school community needs to expand their skills and learn new ones.

Kools and Stoll (2016) present what makes a school a learning organisation. The dimensions and underlying key characteristics provide practical guidance on how schools can transform themselves into learning organisations and ultimately enhance student outcomes. The seven overarching 'action-oriented' dimensions are:

- Developing and sharing a vision centred on the learning of all students.
- Creating and supporting continuous learning opportunities for all staff.
- Promoting team learning and collaboration among staff.
- Establishing a culture of inquiry, innovation, and exploration.

- Establishing embedded systems for collecting and exchanging knowledge and learning.
- Learning with and from the external environment and larger learning system.
- Modelling and growing learning leadership.

To support schools to flourish as learning organisations, we need to analyse the physical learning environments and the teaching and learning practices in which these organisational changes take place. Taking into consideration what makes a school a learning organisation, design research can support the translation of these organisational characteristics into spatial requirements and inform future interventions.

If we have a school with enclosed classrooms with desks facing the teaching wall, we will be promoting an instructionist teaching approach (behaviourism) in which it is difficult to establish a culture of inquiry, innovation, and exploration. To do that, we need to create spaces for experiential learning (cognitive constructivism) in which students and staff are able to explore and test different theories and practices. We need to create spaces in which we promote collaborative learning (social constructivism) and generate peer learning opportunities between student/student and staff/staff and staff/student. The physical learning spaces should promote networked learning (connectivism), in which we can bring people together in a welcoming and stimulating physical environment and at the same time provide space for individual and group activities.

On the one hand, if we have a school with independent staff offices and classrooms, teachers and students will be isolated and won't interact with each other. On the other hand, if we don't have dedicated spaces for teachers to work while not teaching and spaces for students to learn while not attending a scheduled teaching and learning activity, they could go home and not interact with each other. Shared spaces and common physical learning spaces are essential to generate team learning and collaboration. However, these should be provided alongside spaces that allow different levels of privacy and interaction.

While conceiving, appropriating and improving the physical learning environments, more than considering the building condition and technical interventions, we need to understand the specific context of each school. Solar orientation, design features, and relationship between interior/exterior are some of the factors that affect teaching, learning, and organisational practices. Symbolic features, classroom décor, finishing materials/colour, ownership, flexibility, and furniture all influence student learning and achievement (Barrett *et al.*, 2015; Cheryan *et al.*, 2014) and have a significant impact on how teaching, learning, and organisational practices are delivered. There are good examples of new schools that provide these types of learning environments, e.g., with soft seating areas, experiential rooms, flexible table arrangements (Byers and Imms, 2016), and schools that have been refurbished and redesigned into spaces that are flexible, supporting a wide array of teaching and learning possibilities (French, Imms and Mahat, 2019). In this sense, how can design research add a new dimension to these exemplary designs?

Design research can help schools to flourish as learning organisations by considering the physical learning spaces, the teaching and learning practices and the organisational activities from an integrated perspective and by proposing articulated and complementary adjustments. The changes promoted in the physical learning environments need to be planned in parallel with the changes to the teaching and learning practices and designed to meet the organisational aspirations.

Imagine a school in which a 'learning atmosphere', 'learning culture' and/or 'learning climate' is nurtured and in which 'learning to learn' is essential for everyone involved. Design research can push the physical and pedagogical boundaries of schools and craft learning environments that promote collaboration and encourage creativity.

What schools do we need? We need schools that combine the physical learning environments with teaching and learning practices and organisational aspirations towards an integrated and complementary approach. We need schools that enable us to educate children and young people as ambitious, capable, lifelong learners, enterprising, creative, informed citizens and confident and resilient individuals.

Design research can uphold a transdisciplinary approach and support the conception and promotion of the organisational learning experience at schools. By understanding the use and improving physical learning environments, we can better implement innovative teaching, learning and organisational practices.

Design research can help schools to flourish as learning organisations and consider the physical learning environments and teaching and learning practices at three different stages:

1. **Design research for conception of physical learning environments:** consider the teaching, learning and organisational aspirational practices and provide guidance and references to shape the ideal design brief.
2. **Design research for use of physical learning environments:** consider the teaching, learning and organisational aspirational practices and provide guidance to occupy, use and appropriate the physical learning environments.
3. **Design research for improvement of physical learning environments:** monitor school occupation, use, and appropriation. Analyse the current teaching, learning, and organisational practices and provide guidance to adjust the occupation, use, and appropriation of the physical learning environments and/ or re-design the existing physical learning environments.

Design research can play a key role in this flourishing process and re-imagine schools as part of a wide learning network that enables innovative pedagogies and practices. By bringing school communities, industry, policymakers, designers, and research together, design research can manage expectations and promote an aspirational dialogue towards better future learning environments and, ultimately, enhance student outcomes.

Reference list

Barrett, P. *et al.* (2015) 'The impact of classroom design on pupils' learning: final results of a holistic, multi-level analysis', *Building and Environment*, (89), pp. 118–133. https://doi.org/10.1016/j.buildenv.2015.02.013

Byers, T. and Imms, W. (2016) *Does the space make the difference? An empirical retrospective of the impact of the physical learning environment on teaching and learning evaluated by the new generation learning spaces project.* Brisbane: Anglican Church Grammar School.

Byers, T., Marian Mahat, K.L. and Imms, A.K. (2018) *A systematic review of the effects of learning environments on student learning outcomes.* Melbourne: The University of Melbourne.

Cheryan, S. *et al.* (2014) 'Designing classrooms to maximize student achievement', *Policy Insights from the Behavioral and Brain Sciences*, 1(1), pp. 4–12. https://doi.org/10.1177/2372732214548677

Costa, A. (2015) *Diálogos e perspetivas de jovens sobre o ambiente construído da escola, uma etnografia da relação dos jovens com os espaços educativos.* Porto: University of Porto.

Duthilleul, Y., Woolner, P. and Whelan, A. (2021) *Constructing education: an opportunity not to be missed.* Thematic Reviews Series. Paris: Council of Europe Development Bank.

French, R., Imms, W. and Mahat, M. (2019) 'Case studies on the transition from traditional classrooms to innovative learning environments: emerging strategies for success', *Improving Schools*, pp. 175–189. https://doi.org/10.1177/1365480219894408

Imms, W. and Kvan, T. (2021) *Teacher transition into innovative learning environments—a global perspective.* Singapore: Springer. https://doi.org/10.1007/978-981-15-pp.7497–9

Kools, M. and Stoll, L. (2016) *What makes a school a learning organisation?* Paris: OECD Publishing. https://doi.org/10.1787/5jlwm62b3bvh-en

OECD (2016) *What makes a school a learning organisation? A guide for policy makers, school leaders and teachers. Policy advice and implementation support.* Paris: OECD Publishing.

OECD (2018) 'Assessment and recommendations', in OECD Publishing (ed.) *Developing schools as learning organisations in Wales.* https://doi.org/10.1787/9789264307193-en

Robinson, S.K. (2020) *Planning learning spaces.* Edited by M. Hudson and T. White. London: Laurence King Publishing.

Roser, M. and Ortiz-Ospina, E. (2016) *Literacy.* Our World in Data. Available at: https://ourworldindata.org/literacy (Accessed: 23 March 2023).

Chapter 20

Evolutionary change of organisations and its flourishment over the design paradigms

Kun-Pyo Lee

The nature of paradigm shift

It is tempting to consider change within design paradigms as a discreet and defined movement, where one paradigm is set aside as another is taken up. But change is constant. What we identify as a paradigm is not a unified, cohesive structure but a series of inter-dependent facets: tools and techniques, methods and media, communication structures, social factors, economic conditions, and more.

Each of these elements experiences its own growth and development—as though each is a ball bearing whose rotation allows a larger bearing to move. The trends accumulate, the movements combine and the paradigm shifts.

Across it all, there are two major forces at work driving this change: technology and culture. Again, these are not entirely separate factors, but they exist in symbiosis—where technical innovation shapes our social and economic development, while the shifting cultural environment creates the demand for new tools and approaches. And just as these two forces have shaped eras of human development, they have produced a succession of design paradigms.

Design through the ages

We can chart these paradigm shifts through the ages of human civilisation, from pre-industrial society to the industrial revolution, into the digital age and finally with the post-digital age emerging today.

Before the advent of heavy industrial technology, to design was to make by hand. This was crafting, turning clay into crockery or wood into furniture—creating artefacts out of raw materials.

With the industrial revolution of the late 18th and early 19th centuries, this process of handmaking was disrupted by the ingenuity of machines. Design turned from crafting into drawing—plans, drafts, and blueprints. The designer's role was not construction but instruction. Manufacture moved from the workshop into the factory.

With another revolution came the next paradigm shift. Digital technologies ushered in an age of AutoCAD and Photoshop. Alongside these design tools, we developed new design techniques—design thinking and user-centred design.

DOI: 10.4324/9781003399568-23
107

	Designer	Methods	Question	Work	Education	Users
	craftsman	inherited skills	how	solo	over the shoulder	without/neighbour
	stylist	drawing	how	in-house	studio	to/mass
	midwife	UCD D-thinking	what	consultancy	interactive workshop	for/with segmented
	enabler	empowering	why	networked collectives	online/virtual	by/crowd

Figure 20.1
Technological forces driving paradigm shifts.
Source: Diagram by the author.

Today, we are in the midst of another shift. Artificial intelligence and big data are replacing some of those core competencies of the digital age. Where does this leave the designer? If we are leaving behind those tools and techniques, what will our role be in the future? We are only just beginning to find that out.

Methods, motivations, and outcomes

To understand what today's paradigm means for designers, we can look to how the role has evolved from paradigm to paradigm in the past—their tools and training, their methods, and their output.

The craftsmen used their hands, practising a skill passed from generation to generation. It was a solo craft, learned at the elbow of the previous generation—an apprentice watching the master. And the result was an object made for someone living locally.

Moving into the industrial age, the designer became a stylist—drawing or painting plans for others to execute in factories. They worked as part of large in-house teams, using methods developed in a studio. This process produced a mass-manufactured product for an increasingly global market. For both the craftsman and the stylist, the challenge was centred on how: how to create, how to draw.

The digital age then cast the designer as midwife. The computer and the Post-it replaced the brush, while user-centred design and design thinking replaced drawing. Working in design consultancies, employing skills developed in interactive workshops, designers created artefacts for tightly defined market segments. The central challenge of the role also moved on—from how to create to what to create.

Now, in our post-digital era, the role of design is that of enabler. Designers use a network to empower the crowd, harnessing design skills learned through online or virtual experiences. Today, the challenge is not how or what to create but why.

While the craftsman worked to create a complete, finished object, today's designers increasingly create something resembling the idea of a 'non-finito' product. Italian for 'incomplete', this intentionally unfinished product fosters the creativity of the end user's experience. Instead of crafting something to be handed over, to design is to enable creation.

For instance, if you look at Netflix today, you'll see something different to what your neighbour, your spouse or anyone else sees. The interface has been created to allow the user—via data processed by algorithms—to design their own version of the application. As the streaming service's communications director said, there are "33 million versions of Netflix" (Carr, 2013). It is not the complete design but a product that facilitates each user in creating their own experience.

Organisational development and K-pop

This evolution in the way we work is not limited to the individual. The shifting methods, tools and outputs of our paradigm are all mirrored by the changing nature of collaboration—in the structure of our relationships and the models of leadership.

At the start, organisation was minimal—a solo effort or that of a very small team. As teams grew, organisations adopted rigid hierarchies to provide a clear framework of leadership. This changed with the matrix approach, in which the 'team' is a temporary construct for a specific task or project. Today's organisations are looser still, with fluid structures bound by shared purpose rather than formal links.

This has dramatically altered the function of the leader. In the craftsperson model, a leader offered guidance and direction—as a parent to a child. Within the strictures of hierarchy, the leader was a general commanding his soldiers. Then, as the structure dissolved into collaborative working, the leader became more of a mentor and colleague.

Now the leader facilitates a community. Within this conceptual organisation, they do not dictate action but inspire it. Which means it can be argued that K-pop megastars BTS offer a prime example of modern leadership. While 'pop' groups have always been defined by their 'popularity', this modern model of mass fandom is different. Their community, known as the ARMY (Adorable Representative M.C. for Youth) is not a planned organisation; its membership is not up to BTS. It is not homogenous or structured but a constantly evolving, fluid community.

But the power of this fandom has given BTS greater celebrity and a potent platform. The ARMY will take on social and political causes, mobilising through a range of social media campaigns—from sabotaging a Donald Trump rally and

	Designer	Tools	Process	Discipline	Value
	objects	hands	no process	no discipline	possessable/ physical
	appearance	brush	trial & error	art	pleasurable/ emotional
	experience	computer Post-it	prescriptive/ iterative	multi-discipline	usable/ cognitive
	ecosystem	network	incomplete	trans-discipline	plattformable/ social, ecological

Figure 20.2
Cultural forces driving paradigm shifts.
Source: **Diagram by the author.**

blocking a police surveillance app to adopting wildlife and raising funds for charities. These activities were not directed or even suggested by BTS but are deemed to reflect the band's values and are hence done in the band's name.

What it means to flourish

In this environment of inspired collaboration and fluid structure, what does flourishment mean today? Traditionally, success is measured on a straight line: more is better. More output, more productivity, more money. Organisations and individuals seek out the shortest possible distance between the resources invested and the product produced. But this quantitative mindset is not sustainable.

Now, we are beginning to recognise that flourishing does not always mean more. Our model has pushed beyond that idea. Instead, our perception of 'good' can mean good enough.

In Korea, there is an expression—소확행—which translates to "small but certain happiness". This reflects a focus on self-fulfilment without grand ambition for the unobtainable. As Daniel Kahneman and Nobel Laureate Angus Deaton suggested in their research, an individual's life evaluation will increase along with their income. But beyond a threshold of around $75,000 a year, further increases in income do not offer the same lift in emotional or 'hedonic' well-being (2010, p. 16489).

But what about the organisation? How does it flourish? This is the question for the designer in today's paradigm. The organisations are out there among the billions of stars—constellations to be linked, communities waiting to be nurtured, formed and reformed via the medium of those non-finito products. This is the future of the designer: one who enables ever-fluid organisations to foster their creativity and sustainable flourishment.

Reference list

Carr, D. (2013) 'Giving viewers what they want', *New York Times*. Available at: www.nytimes.com/2013/02/25/business/media/for-house-of-cards-using-big-data-to-guarantee-its-popularity.html (Accessed: 23 March 2023).

Kahneman, D. and Deaton, A. (2010) 'High income improves evaluation of life but not emotional well-being', *Proceedings of the National Academy of Sciences*, 107(38), pp. 16489–16493. https://doi.org/10.1073/pnas.1011492107 (Accessed: 21 September 2010).

Chapter 21

It is time for radical co-design

David Perez

The world is facing an era of social transformation from capitalist systems to more inclusive and sustainable ways of living. This is a call for action to rethink how we use design within organisations, shifting its focus from profit maximisation to sustainability, collaboration, inclusion, and engagement. De-centring the role of design as a profit maximiser for the capitalist economy and focusing it on creating social and environmental value is crucial to overcoming the social and environmental challenges we are facing.

Historically, design has been related to creating new products and services that generate new demands, and the impact of this approach has been enormous. Private corporations have increased their wealth by creating beautifully designed products and services. Everything seems over-advertised and over-designed, leading consumers to buy more and more. Every day, designers are actively involved in creating new products, services, and content that grab people's attention. Through carefully designed seamless interactions, websites, apps, social media, and digital devices collect private personal information and influence people's behaviours, decisions, and desires. To diversify the offer and make services and systems more inclusive, designers advocate their capacity to empathise with communities. The human-centredness characteristic of design has positioned designers as agents of change by creating products and services that fulfil people's needs. However, can we really say that designers fully understand people's needs to develop the right products and services? Can a human-centred approach genuinely bear in mind the actual needs of communities and the planet? Moreover, can we really do this when the objective of organisations is to maximise shareholders' revenues? Design has had the luxury to stimulate consumerism without much ethical trepidation (Boylston, 2019). But it is time to wake up, rethink our actions, and focus on what really matters.

Design is about change. As Herbert Simon said, we design when we want to change a particular thing or situation into a preferred one. So what if we design to improve our society and environment? We have good examples of design used for this purpose. Over recent decades, we have seen an increasing interest in social design as a design-based practice toward social and collective, rather than commercial, ends (Armstrong *et al.*, 2014). For example, the Design for Social Innovation and Sustainability Network (DESIS) brings together higher education institutions worldwide to find valuable ways to use design knowledge to create

DOI: 10.4324/9781003399568-24

social changes fostering meaningful collaborations with stakeholders. In this way, the magic happens when design is put at the service of social rather than economic issues.

Participatory and collaborative design practices such as co-design and participatory design have returned the power to people, repurposing their role in society from mere consumers to active collaborators in developing a more prosperous future. For example, between 2015 and 2019, ImaginationLancaster's project, Leapfrog: Transforming Public Sector Engagement by Design (Lancaster University, 2018), aimed to equip people with creative engagement tools by co-designing off-the-shelf toolkits that could help people connect and interact differently with their communities. Hundreds of tools were co-designed to facilitate conversations in the public and third sectors. The tools have been widely used by public-sector organisations, museums, libraries, and people with lived experience in food poverty, to name a few. These materials enable people to have conversations that otherwise would not happen. And these tools have helped them connect groups with different backgrounds, make organisations work more creatively and collaboratively, and support people with lived experiences to advocate and campaign about their circumstances. In addition, local authorities have been using collaborative approaches to decide what to do with social and public spaces. For example, during the pandemic, we used co-design methods to bring about a difficult conversation between the local city council and residents of a social housing community about what to do with the estate (Lancaster City Council, 2022). We used these methods to spark people's creativity to think about the places they would like to live in the future. Co-design can build bridges between communities and policymakers by understanding each other's agendas and collaboratively designing solutions that meet citizens' expectations.

We know of examples of collaborative design in the public and the third sectors, but what about private corporations? Some models have shown the potential to become relevant in the ways we re-imagine our futures. For instance, B Corporations and social entrepreneurs seek to generate profits by addressing social needs or working side by side with communities. B Corporations is a network of organisations that have agreed to standards and certifications to transform the global economy to benefit people, communities and the planet. Social entrepreneurs apply their business expertise to achieve positive social change throughout their organisations, and their ways of working are not only focused on the maximisation of profits but also on the generation of positive environmental and social impact. This is a fertile ground focusing co-design to understand what people need, what they have, and what they want to achieve, and to collectively design a harmonious future that does away with the toxic relationships between consumers and producers.

To propagate the benefits of these approaches, we, as a society, need to come up with a new mindset that reframes human relationships from transactions of goods and money to meaningful collaborations. In this new mindset, those who create, produce, and consume will work together towards sustainable and meaningful ways of living. The role of design will also shift towards fostering collaboration, social and environmental awareness, and action. In this new paradigm, design must be aligned with social and environmental flourishing by fostering meaningful relationships across different sectors of society. For this, we need radical co-design.

Radical co-design is a new form of looking at design as a collaborative practice which seeks radical changes that cherish inclusion, diversity, respect for the environment, and different ways of perceiving and inhabiting the world. It is neither a bottom-up nor top-down approach but a side-by-side way of working. This new model requires a design approach centred not just on the people's understanding as an empathetic exercise but as a model in which people collaborate, bringing their experiences, resources, and capabilities to the conversation. To transition to more sustainable ways of living, we will have to consider local communities' particularities, diversity, and context in developing solutions. Therefore, radical co-design is a community-led rather than a designer-led process. It aims to open more opportunities for design *with* or *by* people rather than *at* people. This approach requires the development of ways of designing that don't rely on designers being at the centre of these processes. The ontological design shift is thinking of design not as a servant of a capitalist system but as a natural way of working across communities and organisations. By radically shifting design processes into co-design processes, we will see organisations and communities with aligned motivations to build a better and more just society—a more inclusive society in which everyone is accountable.

In this model, organisations will play an essential institutional role in systemic change. New organisations, such as B Corporations and social entrepreneurs, will act as catalysts for community cohesion and development by actively collaborating with local communities and policymakers to identify, design, and produce products and services that satisfy real needs in socially and environmentally responsible ways. Similarly, they will work with policymakers on a new agenda that goes beyond the measurement of the gross domestic product as a growth indicator toward long-term societal and environmental goals.

What can designers do? In this space, designers will not be responsible for interpreting people's needs but for providing scaffolds and collaboration tools, and they will play an essential role in creating the conditions for these transitions. Designers will engage with communities, organisations, and policymakers, building trust and aligning visions for better futures. Designers will also enable communities to work collaboratively by exchanging knowledge and practices to create new sustainable ways of living.

It is time to take responsibility for the impact of design on our planet and society. Design has much more to offer by radically shifting its role in the economic system. Design can be the catalyst for a prosperous future, and we need to design collaboratively and inclusively. We need radical co-design for a better world.

Reference list

Armstrong, L., Bailey, J., Julier, G. and Kimbell, L. (2014) *Social design futures: HEI research and the AHRC.* Brighton: University of Brighton, p. 84.

Boylston, S. (2019) *Designing with society: a capabilities approach to design, systems thinking and social innovation.* New York: Taylor & Francis Group.

Lancaster City Council (2022) *My Mainway update.* Available at: https://keepconnected.lancaster.gov.uk/my-mainway-lancaster (Accessed: 14 March 2023).

Lancaster University (2018) *Leapfrog: transforming public sector engagement by design.* Available at: https://imagination.lancaster.ac.uk/leapfrog-tools/ (Accessed: 14 July 2023).

Chapter 22

Design after things

Chris Speed

Ecologies are interesting imaginaries; the term evokes either an image of a biological community of interacting organisms within a natural environment or one adopted from the start-up cultures of Silicon Valley. If we were to be generous and imagine something between the two, a term that may be useful in helping us navigate our way toward 'blossoming ecologies' is the concept of co-creation, the interactive formation of value through the interactions between parties within a constellation (Ramírez, 1999; Vargo and Lusch, 2004). The contemporary generation of design researchers is highly sensitised to enabling multiple stakeholders within an ecosystem to find voice and agency. With a wide variety of participatory methods at their disposal, designers are slowly flattening the hierarchical research cultures that would have previously placed them above a community with a tendency to impose research challenges and extract data to support their assumptions. These days, approaches are much closer to those of a social science for design that identifies our positionality within social and environmental ecosystems, supported by strong ethical guidelines that allow us to protect participants and researchers.

Nevertheless, while our methods and languages are becoming more sophisticated toward a co-creative culture, we should pause to ask if our compulsions to design 'some-thing' have evolved. Cultivated and perpetuated by art and design school education in which design remains wedded to the teleological assumption that design students are there to fulfil projects that make a positive difference to a community, it is worth asking what the 'thing' is that we think we are co-creating. Co-creation literature will assert that it is value, but much of the literature assumes a service-dominant logic in order to make this claim (Vargo and Lusch, 2008), and in doing so, it dismantles the object as the 'thing'—supplanting it with services.

In her 2003 essay 'Posthumanist Performativity: Toward an Understanding of How Matter Comes to Matter', Barad reminds us of the tendency for humans toward 'thingification' as a way of organising and separating our relationships within complex systems:

DOI: 10.4324/9781003399568-25

Thingification—the turning of relations into 'things,' 'entities,' 'relata'—infects much of the way we understand the world and our relationship to it. Why do we think that the existence of relations requires relata? Does the persistent distrust of nature, materiality, and the body that pervades much of contemporary theorizing and a sizable amount of the history of Western thought feed off of this cultural proclivity?

(2003, p. 812)

While it may be a little ambitious to suggest that service design is a practice extending from agential realist theory, certainly, we see significant hope in design as it turns away from the compulsion to engineer objects that will solve problems within a community and instead looks toward fostering entanglements between people, objects, and systems—even if this results in developing an understanding of value destruction.

However, as a community, we are spread far apart in place and culture, and how we do design remains distributed and uneven according to our histories and imaginaries. To exemplify these differences, I offer three summaries of personal imaginaries that 'thingify' relationships to a greater or lesser extent. The intention of the passages is to find personal identification and perhaps see through the lens of someone else within our ecosystem.

If you were born in the 20th century, please read Part A.

If you were born in the 21st century, please read Part B.

If you are more than human, please read Part C.

Part A

You and I were born within an epoch that has defined the course of many people's futures. The globalisation project that defined the 20th century placed us on a path whose consequences are going to prove difficult to escape.

One might argue that central to the challenges we face are the imaginaries that were socially, economically, and environmentally constructed with us through our childhood and formative years. It is hard to escape them, as they have defined our lifestyles and practices. They have provided us with a narrative in which we value the things we own and how we should acquire and keep them. We enjoy the experiences that our favourite products lead us to, and we understand how they represent gateways to see our friends, experience different cultures and visit different places.

We also work hard to mitigate against the impact of our practices on society and the environment. We believe in fairness and justice, and we care for institutions that reflect these values. We also like how things end. We were brought up on stories that have endings, and we seek endings to help us define our lifestyles, although these days, we're getting used to stories that don't end the way we want them to.

Figure 22.1
Source:
Photograph by
the author.

Part B

You know something that I don't know. You have a way of doing things that doesn't make sense to me. But my guess is that you know about networks and about how people and data are connected in such a way as to make experiences that place you within them, part of them. You are highly tuned to the implications of this, and you moderate your behaviour within them because any inappropriate act can expose you to hundreds or thousands of others. You are also aware that they can be bad for your health because these networks demand a lot of you, and you have to work hard to calibrate your identity, your sense of self.

But these experiences are more than products, more than artefacts you would dream of owning. They are experiences and communities that you care to be part of or to distance yourself from. You are able to use the services that underpin these experiences to understand how something is valued by different people. You use the networks to understand the tangling of values that shape how something appears and disappears in the world. You are even capable of working with others to make something grow or go away.

For you the network is never ending, the service never stops, it keeps unfolding and behind every turn is a new way of seeing events, images, friends, and yourself. Nothing is ever the same, and being within the network is the only way to watch things unfold and become more or less meaningful.

Figure 22.2
Source:
Photograph by the author.

Part C

To us, you are the data that passes through the router, you are the coffee, you are the chair, you are the cat, you are the tree and mountain. But you don't much care for calling yourself anything, and you certainly don't care what we call you. For how we separate you from the world according to a product or a service has no bearing on your experience. But you do experience. And you watch and grow and come and go.

You interact with many 'things', but where they stop and where you start is not interesting or important to you. In fact, you find it hard to understand yourself as separate from everything, and why humans do this is constantly confounding to you.

You are material and you are active; you have agency through your interactions with others, but you are not alone. Doing it alone isn't a language that you know. You are always immanent.

You don't vote, you don't buy things, you don't own anything, and yet your interactions with others produce the world as we know it. Some interactions just involve more energy than others.

Figure 22.3
Source:
**Photograph by
Gemma Coupe.**

The role of design in supporting the 'flourishing of futures for organisations' is one in which it doesn't differentiate between things according to their identity as a product or a distinguishable object that plays a role in delivering a service. Existing models of design are convenient in separating out the 'things' in order to promise a win, win, win. But they rarely reveal the intrinsic loss to ecosystems. More likely, design will become sensitised to an assemblage of interactions that support just, fair, and sustainable experiences—experiences that according to every 'thing' [sic] within the network do not result in a loss, an extraction, or an exploitation, but in the exchange of agency.

Design research will continue to practise with distributed and uneven imaginaries about its purpose, but let's hope that it understands the histories of people who grew up in Part A alongside those that are producing new cultures in Part B within everything that takes the 'hit' in Part C.

Reference list

Barad, K. (2003) 'Posthumanist performativity: toward an understanding of how matter comes to matter', *Signs*, 28(3), pp. 801–831. https://doi.org/10.1086/345321

Ramírez, R. (1999) 'Value co-production: intellectual origins and implications for practice and research', *Strategic Management Journal*, 20(4), pp. 49–65.

Vargo, S.L. and Lusch, R.F. (2004) 'Evolving to a new dominant logic for marketing', *Journal of Marketing*, 68(1), pp. 1–17.

Vargo, S.L. and Lusch, R.F. (2008) 'Service-dominant logic: continuing the evolution', *Journal of the Academy of Marketing Science*, 36(1), pp. 1–10.

Part 3

Flourishing in the world

Chapter 23

Flourishing in the world

Deyan Sudjic

If we can understand the history of design practice as a continuing struggle between William Morris and Raymond Loewy, that is to say, between a sense of social purpose and testosterone-fuelled shape making, then Morris's legacy is currently in the ascendant. It has been a long time since designers saw their role as persuading us to buy more stuff that we don't really need at a price that we can't really afford, or at least since they admitted to it. But even as designers work on autonomous electric-powered people movers, self-administered HIV tests, plant-based plastics, biodegradable pregnancy kits, and contributions to policymaking, they face a growing pushback. Well-meaning practice may not be enough.

Designers are, by temperament, optimists with a touching conviction that design really can make the world a better place. And that is what made the violence of Victor Papanek's assault on them in his incendiary book *Design for the Real World* (Papanek, 2019) so provocative. Designers saw themselves as part of the solution rather than as an aspect of the problem.

I'm not sure if Papanek would have much liked Michael Bierut's cover for the new edition. The original 1971 version with its prologue that suggested that "there are professions more harmful than industrial design but only a few" looked carefully artless, in fact almost deliberately un-designed. It was like a conspicuous announcement that Papanek wasn't trying to sell us anything. Bierut repackaged the book in 2019 with sophisticated typography and colour, as if to distract us from Papanek's enthusiasm for amateurish cardboard children's car seats and tin-can radios.

In the half century between the two editions, Papanek's reputation has gone through a remarkable roller-coaster ride. First, he went from radical visionary to irrelevant naïf and then became a pioneering inspiration. That *Design for the Real World is* still read 70 years after Papanek wrote it reflects his continuing relevance for those who question a system that floods the world with single-use plastic containers, unnecessary air travel, and a diet based on red meat.

Papanek is not the only figure from the 1960s to have been rediscovered. Ivan Illich, the Jesuit priest who wrote *Tools for Conviviality* and blamed conventional medicine and education for most of society's ills, Christopher Alexander, author of *The Pattern Language* (Alexander, 1977), and Ralph Nader, born in the same generation as Papanek, have all become startlingly relevant to the current debate.

DOI: 10.4324/9781003399568-27

Half a lifetime since Nader published *Unsafe at Any Speed* (Nader, 1965), a devastating investigation of the American car industry in general, and GM's flawed, rear-engined Chevrolet Corvair in particular, Samya Stumo, the 24-year-old daughter of Nader's niece, and 156 others were killed when Ethiopian Airlines flight 302, a Boeing 737 Max 8, crashed shortly after takeoff from Addis Ababa airport. Nader has helped to overturn Boeing's attempts to blame inadequately trained foreign pilots for the tragedy. The discussion has been reframed into an exploration of how the fight for market share with Airbus made Boeing circumvent the design-and-development process needed to build a fuel-efficient new airliner and, instead, to push an ancient 737 template beyond the point of airworthiness.

Papanek took the view not that almost all relationships between design and commerce were unacceptable but that any kind of formal design language was essentially manipulative and dishonest. It is a prejudice that informs the world-view of the co-designers and the theorists whose version of design research takes it ever further from the world of material culture into a new territory.

This prejudice is, in part, a response to the issues that face us all and in part a cyclical response as a new generation supplants its predecessors. But it can also be understood as another manifestation of the disdain for the utilitarian described by Thorstein Veblen in his book, *The Theory of the Leisure Class*, as long ago as 1899. Veblen astutely showed how we have come to value the 'useless' above the 'useful' for the status that it confers (Veblen, 1965). The philosophy, politics, and economics course at Oxford, for example, is still regarded as an easier path to becoming prime minister than studying engineering in Manchester. And for much the same reason, Henry Cole's original vision of the Victoria and Albert Museum as a place to inspire and educate manufacturers and designers and put to use what they saw was abandoned. It became a museum of the admittedly exquisite decorative arts unburdened by the embarrassment of utility.

Following the triumph of the Great Exhibition of 1851, Cole set about reform-ing the national network of Government Schools of Design established after 1837. He argued that the schools had diverged from their founding principles, which he suggested were,

> to provide for the architect, the upholsterer, the weaver, the printer, the pot-ter and all manufacturers, artisans better educated to originate and execute their respective wares, and to invest them with greater symmetry of form, with greater harmony of colour, and with greater fitness of decoration to ren-der manufactures not less useful by ornamenting them, but more beautiful, and therefore more useful.
>
> (Great Britain Department of Practical Art, 1853, p. 55)

He appeared to blame the students as much as their professors for the fail-ure of the schools to do so.

> Students did not exist sufficiently qualified by previous art education to enter them, but had to be trained not merely to understand and practise the

principles of design but to learn the very elements of drawing. Indeed principles of design were hardly admitted to exist. . . . Instead of being a school for teaching the principles and practice of applied art, circumstances had necessitated that they teach the basics of drawing and they were under the obligation of teaching little else than the mere ABC of art.

(Great Britain Department of Practical Art, 1853, p. 55)

In today's language, Cole was suggesting that the design schools were forced to concentrate too much on basic design skills and not enough on applying design in the world.

According to some contemporary practitioners, design education has produced a parallel world of design research, which is increasingly detached from the practice of design. It suggests a privileging of research over practice. For an extraordinary figure such as Cole, who did not go to university but was nevertheless able to flourish as an administrator, a curator, an educator, a theorist, and, under the name of Felix Summerly, work as a practising designer, these distinctions did not matter. But in the world of the academy, they have mattered a great deal.

Design is a vital part of the cultural landscape because its concerns and ideas have continually recalibrated and adjusted as the world has been reconfigured by technological and social change. The idea of critical design has its roots in William Morris's questioning of society from the perspective of a convinced socialist. His antipathy to the machine ensured that his ideal of having "nothing in your home that you do not know to be useful, and believe to be beautiful" (Mackail, 1899, pp. 62–63) was beyond the means of the workers whose cause he championed. But that did not stop him from designing for the world as he believed it should be rather than as it actually was.

The contribution of Ettore Sottsass and Enzo Mari was to explore the emotional and ideological as well as the practical and utilitarian aspects of design. Sottsass in particular was able to work simultaneously on industrial projects and on personal poetry.

In 1959, when Sottsass worked for Adriano Olivetti on the first Italian mainframe computer, the Elea 9003, alongside the engineer Mario Tchou, he began by asking himself "What should a computer look like?" (Sudjic, 2015). He answered his question himself in a note in his sketchbook: "Not like a washing machine". He was suggesting that there were aspects of the identity of an object as potentially as momentous in its powers as a thinking machine that needed to be acknowledged in its form. That realisation did not prevent him from commissioning ergonomists from the Ulm Hochschule to work on the layout of the keyboard.

Tony Dunne and Fiona Raby have pioneered a speculative approach to design that convinced their students that asking questions is as important as trying to answer them. Some years ago, they turned their attention to the nature of design education, a project which casts a revealing light on the rapidly evolving understanding of what design can be, not so much a matter of technique but as a way of understanding.

> Today we visited a new school of design developed specifically to meet the challenges and conditions of the 21st century. It offers only one degree, an MA in Constructed Realities. . . . There are no disciplines in the conventional sense; instead, students study bundles of subjects. Some that caught our attention were "Rhetoric, Ethics, and Critical Theory" combined with "Impossible Architecture"; "Scenario Making and Worldbuilding" mixed with "Ideology and Found Realities"; and "CGI and Simulation Techniques" taught alongside "The History of Propaganda, Conspiracy Theories, Hoaxes, and Advertising".
>
> (Maharam.com, 2016)

Clearly, they were teasing the Eindhoven Design Academy, which established its reputation by abolishing traditional-skills-based definitions of design. Rather than teaching industrial design or furniture design, graphics, or interior design, as design schools once did, just as a previous generation had departments of leather, metal, ceramics, glass, or textiles categories that, incidentally, were also once used to define departments in museums, it offers programmes in contextual design, social design, and design curating. In some ways, this is a response to the accelerating pace of change triggered by the digital explosion. As the emphasis has shifted from material objects to the immaterial, design education has been reconfigured. Yet the more that world dematerialises, the more we value tactile, physical qualities and skills.

Design research, which was once understood as the theoretical study of design, has turned into a form of practice but one which is increasingly distanced from the discipline with which it has emerged.

At the Eindhoven Design Academy, the newest department is named GEO-DESIGN and was established in 2020 by Andrea Trimarchi and Simone Farresin, two designers who have attracted considerable attention with their own studio, Formafantasma. Italian born and Eindhoven-educated, they have read Papanek. They combine pessimism about the way that overconsumption is threatening the survival of the planet with a willingness to work for traditional design-conscious clients. They remain cautious about what they take on. You get asked some very old-fashioned questions, like "Can you design a sofa?"

They call GEO-DESIGN a platform to explore the social, economic, territorial, and geopolitical forces shaping design. They acknowledge "the legacy of industrial production as the fundamental source for the designer's expertise and agency in contemporary society, while problematising and addressing its historic contribution to environmental and social instability and its incompatibility with models of sustainable or even survivable futures" (formafantasma.com, 2020).

They offer a tool to develop an investigative practice and as an instrument to facilitate change.

"As a department, GEO-DESIGN will grow like an octopus, with a complex central consciousness and individual far-reaching tentacles. Students will build up new methodologies combining hands-on material techniques with innovative media formats, historical philosophy with urgent critical discourse, transparent collaboration with tactical subversion" (formafantasma.com, 2020).

Trimarchi and Farresin have addressed such themes with their own work. *Botanica*[1] was about the world as it could be without plastics. *Ore Streams*[2] was a sophisticated research project that made an elegant, unsparing analysis of technological waste over three years. *Cambio*,[3] which was shown at the Serpentine Gallery in 2020, is about the timber industry.

Design is a way of looking at the world from multiple perspectives. It is based on understanding people and their behaviours, on the application of technology and the use of systems. It's a powerful way to understand the potential for unintended consequences. Henry Ford thought he was designing the first mass-produced car. It turned out that he had invented the traffic jam. Steve Jobs and Jony Ive made the first smartphone and discovered that it was more than a device to surf the internet with a built-in music player and phone. They changed everything from the nature of modern politics to sex.

Design remains a duality. Morris and Loewy may be one axis of that duality. The other axis could be represented by a scale that moves from the analogue to the digital or from the city to the individual. We must hope that there are still ways in which we can use our resources and the insights offered by design to avert our worst fears of a world in danger of being cooked and drowned.

Notes

1   *Botanic*. See https://formafantasma.com/work/botanica
2   *Ore Streams*. See www.orestreams.com
3   *Cambio*. See www.serpentinegalleries.org/whats-on/formafantasma-cambio/

Reference list

Alexander, C. (1977) *A pattern language*. Oxford: Oxford University Press.

formafantasma.com (2020) *GEO-design—FormaFantasma* [online]. Available at: https://formafantasma.com/work/geodesign (Accessed: 17 March 2023).

Great Britain Department of Practical Art (1853) *First report of the department of practical art: presented to both houses of parliament by command of her majesty*. London: H.M. Stationery Office.

Mackail, J.W. (1899) *The life of William Morris*. vol. 2. London, New York, and Bombay: Longmans, Green & Co.

Maharam.com (2016) *The school of constructed realities* [online]. Available at: www.maharam.com/stories/raby_the-school-of-constructed-realities (Accessed: 16 March 2023).

Nader, R. (1965) *Unsafe at any speed*. New York: Grossman.

Papanek, V. (2019) *Design for the real world*. 3rd edn. London: Thames and Hudson Ltd.

Sudjic, D. (2015) *Ettore Sottsass and the poetry of things*. London: Phaidon Press Limited.

Veblen T. (1965) *The theory of the leisure class [1899]*. New York: Augustus M Kelley Publishers.

Chapter 24

Making a difference by design

Sevra Davis

A new remit

In May 2021, the 17th International Architecture Exhibition at the Venice Biennale of Architecture opened. Postponed from its original 2020 run due to the universal COVID-19 pandemic, the global showcase opened with 61 national pavilion exhibitions and 112 participants from 46 countries in the main exhibition. The central question of the Biennale in 2021 'How will we live together?' was first asked by the Biennale's curator, Hashim Sarkis in 2018.

By posing this question as the central theme for a global architecture exhibition, it is clear that what we deem to be the remit of architecture and design has changed and continues to change. From the not-so-distant past that celebrated the 'starchitect' and singular statement buildings, there is now an increasing emphasis on social, economic, and environmental responsibility and a celebration of more modest, locally relevant, and socially engaged work. Sarkis's own curatorial statement called upon architects to contribute to a new spatial contract in the context of widening political divides and growing economic inequalities. He declared that "We can no longer wait for politicians to propose a path towards a better future. As politics continue to divide and isolate, we can offer alternative ways of living together through architecture" (*Statement by Hashim Sarkis*, 2020).

As the Commissioner of the British Pavilion, I worked closely with a curatorial team and a more extensive team of architects and designers to deliver an exhibition that attempted to answer Sarkis's question through the single lens of privatised public space. Particularly prevalent in London and the rest of the UK, the number of privatised public spaces is also growing around the world, and the 2021 British Pavilion exhibition challenges the polarisation of private and public as a tool for creating divisions in society. Titled *The Garden of Privatised Delights*, it asked how architects can work with the public to invent new frameworks to improve use, access and ownership of Britain's public spaces. While conceived, designed and delivered by a team of architects, designers, researchers, and writers, the exhibition touched on issues of governance, politics, and social action in a direct response to Sarkis.

But not everyone agrees that this new remit for architecture is a good thing. In his review of the Biennale, *Guardian* critic Oliver Wainwright wrote that "there is very little in the way of concrete spatial proposals addressing how our cities and habitats might be rethought for a more equitable future. Instead, we are offered

DOI: 10.4324/9781003399568-28

a series of projects that use global crises as the inspiration for installation art (or what architects like to call 'research')" (Wainwright, 2021).

Wainwright's critique demonstrates the dilemma that faces many architects and designers: damned if you do [attempt to tackle wicked global challenges] and damned if you don't. So is there a role for architecture and design in helping us flourish, and if so, what is it?

#NewNormal

The word 'flourish' conjures up different ideas and meanings for different people, but one thing most agree on is that we aren't flourishing at the moment. We are living in and through what is increasingly called the 'New Normal' in the shadow of the COVID-19 pandemic in which a plurality of issues, sometimes collectively called the 'VUCA world' (volatility, uncertainty, complexity, and ambiguity), has created and continues to create sweeping societal and environmental change. Many feel that life will get worse for most people as greater inequality, rising authoritarianism and rampant misinformation take hold.

We know that our current systems are not fit for purpose, and we know that there is now an urgent need for creativity and creative solutions—more so than ever before—and that we must commit to re-skilling and lifelong learning. In the face of the 'New Normal' there is then, understandably, a wariness surrounding the other post-pandemic soundbite 'Build Back Better', with many arguing that we shouldn't build back better, but rather build forward differently. We can't rely on the way we've done things before and simply try to do them better. We need a fundamental shift in how we organise ourselves, our values, our priorities, and our systems. And we are back to the question of how: how do we design for people and planet to prosper, now and in the future?

The UN Sustainable Development Goals (SDGs) provide a useful framework for the future that we want to see particularly as they have global relevance and are widely adopted by organisations, communities, and governments around the world. I have found the SDGs a useful foundation for my own work, and I strive to pin all the programmes I develop and deliver on them as a way of sense-checking direction and impact. That said, the SDGs don't tell us how to get to where we want to be, only what we hope things will be when we get there.

We must think differently about the role of these creative fields in our lives. The pandemic has shown that our work—including arts, culture, and design—is interconnected with public health. The relationship between cultural organisations, such as museums and theatres, and public health is going to be more important than ever as we move forward. And design must play a role in how we do this.

And so we are back to trying to understand the role of architecture and design as facilitators, guides and actors toward and in the future we want to see. But in recent years, there has been much talk about design's need to engage in systemic thinking, and we've seen the creation of new fields such as system design (building on service design and design for social innovation). While efforts to encourage design—and designers—to think bigger have been welcomed by many, this has also drawn attention, in some cases, to design's unpreparedness to tackle larger issues and to balance competing priorities. There are now some big questions for designers about their readiness to tackle large global challenges and how design will help us flourish.

Beyond the diagram

While it is discussed endlessly, the field of design still seems to confound many, including some designers themselves. There has been a general shift to ensure that 'design' is meant to cover everything including the output (the final 'design') and the action (one often hears that we mean both the noun and the verb), and increasingly, it also encompasses design thinking, widely understood to mean a deliberate process of designing.

> With design thinking, [perhaps now the most widely 'sold' aspect of design], the difficulty is less with the 'design' part than with the 'thinking'. Thinking is a conscious, deliberate activity involving analysis and the development of general, context-free rules and principles that are then 'applied' to practice. The principles turn out to be good intentions and desirable outcomes. They use what are called 'achievement verbs' like discover, define, develop and deliver and they sound like actions but are really achievements.
>
> (Hurst, 2016)

Sadly, much of what is practised under the guise of design thinking seems to comprise little more than running structured workshops. The process can now sound technocratic and feel meaningless, and we move further away from the action and the 'doing' of design and spend more time analysing the process.

Design thinking initially gained traction because a successful design process achieves elegance, sensorial acceptance and emotional appeal for the solution (whether a product, service or campaign). In a new era for design and design research, I think we must reassert the value of the design that goes beyond traditional technocratic and top-down solutions. Design research has the power to reassert design ethics—how design decisions impact the world around us. I hope we see more of that.

We need a rethink about what we mean when we talk about the role of design in helping us to flourish. Design, now so often equated with design thinking and design-thinking diagrams that describe how 'design' comes about, doesn't actually demonstrate how design can make change or help us to flourish.

Making change

How do we actually make change, and what is the role of design in it? The answer surely lies in design that results in tangible action, and sometimes that action, that 'doing', can be slow. In this sense, there is perhaps some value in, ironically, slowing down so that we can accelerate change. We need to slow down to build movements and use human connection and the power of knowledge, exchange and dialogue.

At the British Council, my role is to work with designers around the world to build connections, build trust, and then build knowledge. This is a slow process, but it is integral to the way forward and perhaps represents a shift from a focus on the quickfire thinking and processes we've become accustomed to equating with design. Nevertheless, I think slowing down is key if we are to build movements and deliver change.

Within the Architecture Design and Fashion team at the British Council, we run a programme called Making Matters. Making Matters aims to foster a global dialogue around the topic of circular design. The multi-disciplinary programme explores how principles of the circular economy can be a catalyst for creativity, collaboration, and regenerative thinking within architecture, design, and fashion practice. The programme aims to provide a space for an international exchange of knowledge and expertise, exploring how design and making can respond to global environmental challenges to support restorative and alternative futures.

Making Matters acts as a framework for a range of projects—both digital and physical—focusing on four strands of engagement: convening, participatory learning, co-creation and, finally, developing new lexicons. The programme is slow, deliberate, and much more focused on the journey than the outcome.

As part of the 'lexicons' strand, we have been building a Material Atlas (*Material Atlas*, 2020). While at first glance this, may seem like 'just a website' that acts as a materials library, we have strived to make it much more a living map of materials, language, landscapes, and material practices. Material Atlas begins to decolonise the language around materials and goes beyond the current dominant universal understanding of what materials are, where they come from, and who gets to use them.

The medium of expression is not just language or imagery but also sound, science, and storytelling. Doing something in this way, however, takes time, but the website serves to build a community and make change by creating spaces for new dialogues and reflection and very slowly tackling some of the big challenges we face, from decolonisation to climate action; and in this, we need to take a long-term approach.

But how . . . ?

To make a difference by design, we must build connection and knowledge and movements. We must experiment (and we must apply design research to this to do it well). We must be resilient and be patient, and we need to try. And that is perhaps the most important point: the trying, the doing, the action. There will always be those who feel that architects and designers are overstepping their boundaries by tackling the big global challenges of the day, but our shared flourishing future will be our collective reward. We must focus less on the achievements and more on the action. We must be patient.

Reference list

Hurst, D. (2016) *Re: saving design thinking from itself*, 15 May [Blog comment]. Available at: www.thersa.org/blog/2015/12/saving-design-thinking-from-itself (Accessed: 28 February 2023).

Material Atlas (2020) Available at: https://materialatlas.world (Accessed: 27 February 2023).

Statement by Hashim Sarkis (2021) Available at: www.labiennale.org/en/architec ture/2021/statement-hashim-sarkis (Accessed: 27 February 2023).

Wainwright, O. (2021) *Venice architecture Biennale 2021 review—a pick'n'mix of conceptual posturing*. Available at: www.theguardian.com/artanddesign/ 2021/may/21/venice-architecture-biennale-2021-review-how-will-we-live-together (Accessed: 27 February 2023).

Chapter 25

Transdisciplinary design

Next-generation bio-inspired building materials

Jenny Sabin

Imperatives for change

According to the World Green Building Council, building and construction account for 39% of annual global carbon emissions. Heating, lighting, and cooling account for 28% of that figure, with the remaining 11% coming from embodied emissions, i.e., the carbon associated with the materials, construction, and building processes throughout the building's life cycle (World Green Building Council, 2019).

In order to meet the Paris Climate Agreement's ambitions—limiting global warming to 1.5°C above pre-industrial levels—the world's building sector must cut the energy intensity per square metre by an average of 30%. And this isn't the only challenge facing the sector. The COVID-19 pandemic not only provoked a raft of new products and stretched supply chains to breaking point, it also abruptly forced us to reconsider the spaces we occupy in our day-to-day lives, from our homes and workspaces to our schools and retail and recreational spaces.

Both these crises have accelerated and highlighted a range of systemic issues around the inequality of access and inclusion, amplifying ongoing entanglements of systemic racism and persistent issues impacting diversity and equity—globally and locally.

To meet these issues, we need radical new models of design research and cross-disciplinary collaboration. One such model brings science and design together, with the hybridisation of labs and studios. With this transdisciplinary design model in place, putting professionals from different worlds into one shared space, we can force new perspectives, explore new inspirations and provoke new ways of thinking about our own fields. By fostering innovation and ingenuity in this way, we can look forward to next-generation materials and structures that are adaptive, inclusive, resilient, efficient, and smart.

Dynamic by nature

At our research lab-studio, we cultivate trans-disciplinary collaboration by coupling architectural designers with engineers and biologists, which helps us develop new ways of working, seeing, and thinking in each of our fields. In this setting, design can enable a range of possibilities for combatting the crises of the future and developing a fairer, healthier and safer built environment.

DOI: 10.4324/9781003399568-29

Figure 25.1
Compilation of design research conducted at the Sabin Design Lab, College of Architecture, Art, and Planning, Cornell University.
Source: **Image compilation courtesy Jenny Sabin and the Sabin Design Lab, Cornell University.**

Together, we investigate how architecture can respond to pressing issues of ecology and sustainability by drawing inspiration from nature. We ask: How might buildings behave more like organisms? How might these buildings interact with their environment? How could they adapt and evolve with changing conditions? And what role will the inhabitants play; how will we respond to our buildings, and how will our buildings respond to us?

To answer these questions, we are creating new adaptive materials that are more than simply elements, things or objects within buildings. We are seeking to transform static and unyielding environments into dynamic and immersive spaces that interact with humans, adapting to our needs. From physical surroundings, we can craft social and emotional experiences.

Like cells within the human body, sensors and materials in the not-too-distant future will learn and adapt to a range of stimuli, not only making buildings smarter—connected and efficient—but also healthier, aware and sensing.

However, to make this evolution of our buildings and their materials possible and to reduce carbon emissions and better serve people and the planet, we must step away from the anthropocentric paradigm. We must shift away from resource consumption to resource renewal, turning our attention to circular economies, adaptive reuse and a focus on resiliency.

To that end, we have harnessed this radical model of design research to develop the tools for creating that future: integrating bio-inspired design processes and the dynamics of light and energy to create responsive, non-standard photovoltaic building skins, developing a range of bio-inspired bricks and tiles and creating sentient spaces powered by AI.

Project One: sustainable architecture and aesthetics

Working in partnership with Mariana Bertoni, associate professor at the School of Electrical, Computer and Energy Engineering at Arizona State University, we investigated the role of design and aesthetics in sustainable architecture. Could a bio-inspired approach, matched with high-performance engineering systems, help us address issues of optimisation and drive the widespread adoption of alternative energy—especially active power systems such as photovoltaic panels for the residential and industrial sectors?

This collaboration fuelled innovation in the design and engineering of building-integrated photovoltaic systems, using biomimicry techniques and concepts to

Figure 25.2
Archive wall, Sabin Design Lab, Cornell University. A collection of 3D prints, material experiments, and prototypes.
Source: **Photo by William Staffeld, Cornell College of Architecture, Art, and Planning.**

maximise energy conversion while integrating aesthetics. Harnessing computational design and 3D printing, we created an architectural pavilion prototype to demonstrate how bio-inspired design can deliver in terms of both form and function.

The project centred around the development of a highly customisable and site-specific assembly of panels and filters, with a non-conventional layout which borrowed a series of ideas from nature. Inspired by the heliotropic mechanisms of sunflowers, orienting their petals toward the sun throughout the day, we developed an array configured to maximise energy capture across the sun's arc without the need for mechanical elements.

Next, we looked to the light-scattering structure of lithops (or 'living stone' plants) by integrating a series of filters and reflectors throughout the structure to provide a more even distribution of the sun's energy across panels, even under

Figure 25.3
Early prototype for Sustainable Architecture and Aesthetics, a collaborative project between the Sabin Design Lab at Cornell College of Architecture, Art, and Planning and the DEfECT Lab at Arizona State University.
Source: **Image courtesy Jenny Sabin and Mariana Bertoni. This research project is generously funded by the National Academy of Engineering Frontiers of Engineering Program and the Grainger Foundation.**

varied light conditions. This light-scattering effect is a vital cooling mechanism for the lithop plants and also serves to maximise the utility of our structure, with the combination of solar panels and crops below, known as agrivoltaics. This has the double benefit of creating more efficient conditions for both elements: while the plants below keep the panels cooler (hence more effective), the panels provide partial shade and diffusion for the plants beneath, which can increase crop yield and carbon absorption while reducing evaporation (and therefore additional water usage).

Finally, we drew inspiration from cellular packing and modular morphology to determine the physical formation of the panels. Much like cellular arrangements, these configurations can be unique to their surroundings, with a modular flexibility that allows us to create site-specific structures through computational design. As such, we can vary the formations to suit local conditions, providing more cooling ventilation in warmer climates or more densely packed arrangements in cooler environments.

Focusing purely on productivity, this biomimicry-led approach offers a higher efficiency of energy conversion through more effective positioning and efficiency as well as providing potentially fruitful conditions for plants or crops under the structure. However, this also delivers from an aesthetic perspective. Traditionally, photovoltaic panels have not been considered as design elements—whether they are bolted on or integrated into a building, the first and only consideration is utility. With bio-inspired design and advanced digital fabrication techniques, we have developed a more productive function as well as a beautiful and compelling form.

Figure 25.4
Rendering of the Agrivoltaic Pavilion for Sustainable Architecture and Aesthetics, a collaborative project between the Sabin Design Lab at Cornell College of Architecture, Art, and Planning and the DEfECT Lab at Arizona State University.
Source: Image courtesy Sabin Design Lab. This research project is generously funded by the National Academy of Engineering Frontiers of Engineering Program and the Grainger Foundation.

Project Two: PolyBrick and PolyTile

We have also conducted a series of material investigations, asking: How might we rethink building materials through 3D printing and biologically informed design?

We have interrogated the potential of rapid manufacture of full-scale 3D-printed parts for large architectural assemblies by developing a range of non-standard components. These bio-inspired materials offer the promise of low-cost, on-demand fabrication with components that allow buildings to react to environmental conditions and respond to its human inhabitants.

In collaboration with the Luo Labs at Cornell University, we have examined the potential of designing with light and energy. Our PolyBrick[1] investigates the possibilities of living building tiles and bricks through the integration of DNA and living programmable materials with non-standard clay components. These advanced ceramic biotiles demonstrate how 3D printing, offering speed and scale of manufacture, could harness programmable bio-functionality.

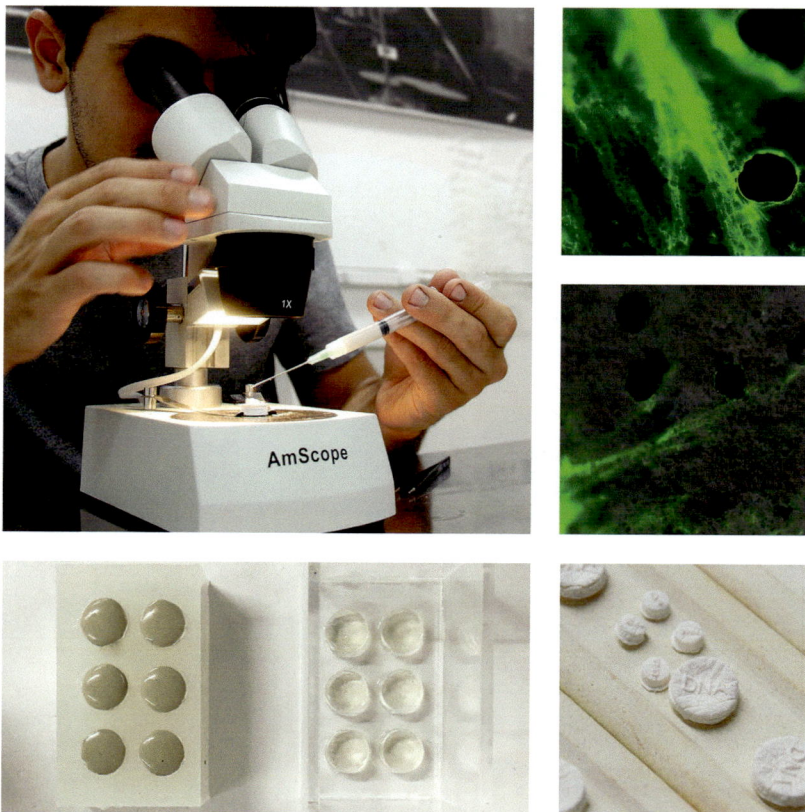

Figure 25.5
PolyTile and PolyBrick 3.0, a collaboration between the Sabin Design Lab and Luo Labs at Cornell University.
Source: **Images courtesy Sabin Design Lab and Luo Labs.**

Much like the traditional stamped brands, names or symbols used in historical brick manufacture, this project's 3D-printed patterning techniques used a bio-engineered hydrogel glaze on the surface as a unique signature. This can then respond or adapt to environmental conditions—whether at micro or macro scale.

In the first phase, we used these gels to create a unique live signature that would fluoresce in the clay, with a glowing C for Cornell. Could this become a glowing warning or indicator in a residential or industrial setting, signifying issues with air quality or a concentration of a particular contaminant?

Building on this reactive functionality, the second phase will look to a future in which these tiles and bricks interact and influence the environment around them—bonding with proteins or breaking down particulate matter. In this sense, your walls could clean your air, reducing harmful pollution. Put simply, these components could create a built environment designed to protect your health and well-being.

DNA nanotechnology will open up a range of possibilities in this area, for creating nano- to macro-scale materials and architectural elements which dynamically respond to environmental cues and biochemical stimuli, including ourselves and how we engage with our immediate built environment.

Project Three: Ada

The spaces we inhabit, the places we live and work in, are huge parts of our life. They influence how we feel and act and, therefore, are central to our physical and emotional well-being. With this project, we investigated how bio-architecture with integrated artificial intelligence can personalise our rooms and buildings. By harnessing big data and a network of sensors, can our building materials be made more responsive to our needs—not only reacting to human behaviour but supporting our health?

Affectionately titled Ada, the project was based in Microsoft Research's building on their Redmond Campus in Washington State. Working with researchers at the campus, including Daniel McDuff, we created an architectural pavilion with responsive materials—powered by AI and driven by individual and collective sentiment data, giving it the capacity to promote and ultimately increase users' well-being.

The pavilion is a lightweight construction of data-driven and responsive tubular and cellular textile components, held in continuous tension by a semi-rigid 3D-printed exoskeleton. Within this structure is an integrated lighting system, together with a network of cameras and microphones. This cyber-physical architecture, developed in collaboration with the researchers at Microsoft Research, is designed to observe, collect, analyse, and identify users' sentiments—responding to facial patterns and voice data with algorithms transmitted as light and colour.

A central aim for the project is to expand and inspire engagement with humans. Here, users are not only observing but directly influencing the architecture around them. While AI powers the interaction through its precise narrowing and statistical averaging of the data, gathered from individual and collective facial

Figure 25.6
Ada by Jenny Sabin Studio for Microsoft Research Artist in Residence (AIR) 2018–2019.
Source: **Image by Jake Knapp, courtesy of Microsoft.**

Figure 25.7
Ada by Jenny Sabin Studio for Microsoft Research Artist in Residence (AIR) 2018–2019. Opening night at Microsoft Research in Redmond, Washington, USA.
Source: **Image by Jake Knapp, courtesy of Microsoft.**

Figure 25.8
Ada by Jenny Sabin Studio for Microsoft Research Artist in Residence (AIR) 2018–2019. View from above with reflection.
Source: **Image by John Brecher, courtesy of Microsoft.**

patterns and voice tones, the architecture of Ada augments emotion through the aesthetic experience.

As such, this broadens the possibilities for possible emotional engagement with our physical environment and, in turn, opens new pathways to new avenues for research into the use of AI. This may include issues of ethics, privacy, and consent—even if a building can improve your well-being, where do the boundaries lie in gathering data on your mood or analysing your physical health?

This also offers new opportunities for greater understanding of the correlation between human emotion and our physical environment. Personalised architecture has the power to sense subtle changes in its inhabitants' emotions and therefore responds in ways that protect, promote and, hopefully, improve their health. With the integration of responsive materials and emerging technologies, Ada offers an interface for making architecture more human and reflexive.

Ada shows how we can expand human emotional engagement with the physical environment through beauty and materiality, harnessing that engagement as a vehicle for improving our mental and emotional well-being.

Learning from nature

Turning these innovative models and concepts into broad practical applications is a process that may be measured in decades. This is likely to be as much about the process of rethinking methods, building collaboration, and shaping design research practice as it is about mass-manufacturing a tile, for instance.

What these examples also show is that drawing inspiration from nature allows us to consider sustainability and aesthetics side by side. Nature is not efficient or optimised, but it is resilient. As such, we need not treat function and form as separate aims. Looking beyond pure performance—to resilient, integrated and non-standard models that touch on issues of aesthetic beauty—offers real value in gaining community buy-in or prompting positive sentiments around adopting new sustainable models.

In this sense, these three projects demonstrate the enormous potential of our radical new models of transdisciplinary collaboration, offering optimistic visions of what design research can achieve when working in tandem with scientists and engineers. By opening our doors to other disciplines and perspectives, we can meet some of our most urgent global challenges.

Note
1   PolyBrick. See www.sabinlab.com/polybrick-2

Reference list

World Green Building Council (2019) *Bringing embodied carbon upfront*. Available at: https://worldgbc.org/article/bringing-embodied-carbon-upfront/ (Accessed: 7 March 2023).

Chapter 26

Can design heal a city?

Ravi Naidoo

Advancing the practical power of design

For more than 25 years, Design Indaba has been inspiring and empowering people to create a better future through design and creativity. We are not simply a think tank, but rather a 'do tank'. After all, to paraphrase the proverb, design without action is a daydream—so ours is a practical movement focused on achieving tangible outcomes.

We recognise the incredible power of design to convene, coordinate, and focus great minds. As designers, we have the opportunity to take this power out of the studio and onto the high street, into the public square—reshaping spaces and improving services. Serving people, not brands. Putting quality of life over quality of product.

Indaba in action

We have been prolific over the last quarter of a century, launching over 200 impact-led projects locally and abroad. Across those projects, we have explored and expanded the limits of what design can do.

Can you design for dignity? We designed a series of terraced houses to replace ramshackle shacks in informal settlements, stepping as far away from the ivory towers of design studios as we could imagine. These gave the residents the opportunity to live in healthier, more stable and more dignified conditions. We achieved this by drawing expertise from across the globe—corralling the best of the best—and bringing them together with South African architects for intellectual transfer. The homes were then built for real people in local settlements, but the impact didn't end there. We then open-sourced the designs to governments across the continent contributing to the African knowledge commons regarding the design of low-cost housing, and as a result, many more were built beyond South Africa, including in Ghana.

Can design fight gender-based violence? We created a huge installation on a major road through Cape Town in support of an NGO called Violence Prevention through Urban Upgrade. This came in the form of a mural, by local artist Faith47, and integrated lighting from the interaction design team Thinking studio. This powerful piece highlighted the plight of women in a particular Cape Town township, called Monwabisi, by linking the installation

DOI: 10.4324/9781003399568-30
143

with a crowdfunding campaign to bring streetlights to the township. Every time a light was funded, another was added to the mural—not only charting progress but also provoking interaction, raising awareness, and promoting participation.

Can design enhance democracy? On his 86th birthday, Archbishop Desmond Tutu said that those who wanted to support him or protect his legacy should support and protect South Africa's constitution. We created a sculpture to do just that—dubbed an Arch for an Arch, placed on the country's oldest avenue between the Parliament and St George's cathedral. Created in collaboration with international architectural practice Snøhetta and Johannesburg-based Local Studio, the sculpture draws its inspiration from the constitution, with 14 interweaving arches representing its 14 chapters and 14 lines of preamble. This was created amidst a massive communications campaign to promote the vital role of the constitution as democracy's last line of defence.

Across all of our projects, our model has been to use our platform's power to foster collaboration as a means of bringing design out onto the high street and into the community, making an impact in the real world.

South Africa's social time bomb

South Africa is far from flourishing. The halcyon days of post-apartheid optimism are gone. The hope and ambition—of hosting the World Cup, of sending the first African to space, of looking to the future—have given way to decades of decline, with our abundance of natural, human, and institutional wealth wasted. The country is languishing.

Inequality ranks among the world's worst: the top 0.01% own more than the bottom 90% in housing, asset wealth, and pensions. There is huge unemployment: almost two-thirds of 15- to 24-year-olds and two-fifths of 25- to 34-year-olds are out of work. And the education system is failing the vast majority of pupils, with yet more inequality: children in the top 200 schools achieve more distinctions in maths than the next 6,600 schools combined.

The intersection of inequality, unemployment, and failing education has produced 3.4 million NEETs (not in employment, education, or training) (Quarterly Labour Force Survey, 2021)—millions of chances destroyed. This litany of depressing statistics shows a generation falling by the wayside: the dividends of democracy have not served South Africa's children well. Instead, today's crisis is exacerbating the issues left behind by apartheid, driving an underclass deeper. To survive, the youth turn to an 'informal' economy or resort to illicit activities. This is the government's purview. Yet the municipalities that should address these issues are blighted by cronyism and corruption, eroding competence and driving out the professionals. This dysfunction damages service delivery, breeds distrust of all government and further escalates the issues.

Without intervention, this generational crisis will engulf South Africa. What can we do to step into this breach?

Treating dead spaces with urban acupuncture

In seeking opportunities for design to address these issues, we can look to the wasteful, empty, and overlooked spaces across our cities. These are not simply the result of poor urban planning, but also represent a deeper cultural issue—the spatial legacy of segregation and land use.

This leaves our cities with an exceptionally unproductive urban form of dead space: between residential areas and commercial spaces, between transport nodes and the buildings they serve, between public buildings and in the vast parking areas that surround major buildings. These are interstitial—between use, between function, between value. Devoid of economic or social activity, with no vitality or vibrancy, featureless and joyless, they sever the connections of daily life, presenting an obstacle to cohesion and mobility—physically and socially.

Where people live matters a great deal. If we can re-imagine the routine functioning and economic performance of everyday collective spaces, we can open up one avenue for profound social transformation. It is in these spaces that design can act as a lever for socio-economic growth—creating the sparks that may help our cities heal and flourish. With considered interventions, we can release pain and pressure in the fabric of our cities.

> I believe that some medicinal 'magic' can and should be applied to cities, as many are sick and some nearly terminal. As with the medicine needed in the interaction between doctor and patient, in urban planning it is also necessary to make the city react.
>
> (Urban Planner Jaime Lerner, 2023)
> former mayor of Curitiba and governor of Paraná

Lerner characterised these targeted design interventions as urban acupuncture— "precise pinpricks of change that can heal whole districts or even cities". So, in treating what he called the "living organism that is city life", could we provide equitable access to services, mobility or housing? Promote health and wellness? Support entrepreneurship?

Qommune

Inspired by Lerner's concept, we established Qommune: a therapeutic treatment to revive creative optimism. This was based on our own doorstep, in the city of our annual Design Indaba conference. The Strand Street quarry is the country's oldest quarry and is said to be the foundation of the city, as slate from the site was used in the building of the Castle of Good Hope. In recent times, the abandoned quarry has become a known site for littering, vagrancy, and crime. For our intervention, we lobbied the city to allow us to reimagine the space. Could we propose a solution to nourish this space of historical significance and future potential?

Qommune is our attempt to resuscitate the creative, social, communal, and economic heartbeat of the city—to reclaim this space for entrepreneurs and artists, re-energising the hospitality and service industries. To fill the spaces and spark activity, we turned to our 'do tank', harnessing the creative talent and enterprising attitude of the speakers at Design Indaba, restoring the site's legacy as a catalyst for growth.

An assembly of inspiration

Working with South African architects and urban planners, together with international partners, like LOLA Landscape Architects in Rotterdam, we envisioned a place that would inspire and entertain people. This would include a theatre, forum, and market hall—placing a hive of activity in the underused space. Qommune offers a canvas for various ideas offering different forms of impact.

We also propose to base Qommune around **Africa's first cross-laminated timber (CLT) building**, as it's not only the building's form and purpose that offer an impact but also its construction and fabric. CLT is a strong, natural material that provides a much lower level of embodied carbon when compared to the usual steel and concrete. It also makes the construction faster and could be locally produced, supporting local skills and business development.

This CLT could even be made from the invasive species of trees from nearby Table Mountain, including Australian Blue Gum. These have not only presented a wildfire risk but have put significant pressure on the region's water resources; ridding the area of these species and restoring the ecosystem would save a million litres of water a month, effectively freeing up one of the seven dams serving the city.

With all these elements, the collective impact of Qommune supports what we might call our 'ultimate design manifesto'—the UN Sustainable Development Goals. In seeking to bring purpose and life to some of Cape Town's dead spaces, we can support seven of these goals—from climate action and life on land to decent work and economic growth and sustainable cities and communities.

Sub-City

Sub-City explores the city of Johannesburg's provisional infrastructure through the lens of underutilised city spaces. Uncovered during our search, electrical substations present wonderful opportunities. They were originally built to support the technical hardware of the time, but rapid technological advancements over recent decades have resulted in more compact and space-saving hardware. This has meant that space allocated to the hardware will eventually not match the area needed for their function. Substations will therefore be left as unoccupied structures within the city landscape, usually with new electrical processors housed in a small steel sub-box just to the side. Herein lies an opportunity to flourish.

Exploring the transformation of brick-and-mortar substations into cross-laminated timber mixed-use towers for local communities, Sub-City's pilot project is centrally located in Eldorado Park, Johannesburg. The substation backs onto an archetypal social-housing courtyard between two blocks and will catalyse transformation of this courtyard into a sustainable community space. Sub-City will service the immediate community of the housing blocks as well as the adjacent primary school. Due to the needs of the surrounding residents, the repurposed mixed-used space will function as a library, observation tower, and event space.

Designing change

> We are more likely to see change come from culture than politics, as culture enjoys more trust now than politics.
>
> (Olafur Eliasson, 2017)

In the past, we could argue that design was a narrower, more mercantile practice. Today, we can see that it is far more expansive and socially conscious. To be a designer is to be an optimist, dreamer, thinker, researcher, instigator, provocateur, demonstrator, visualiser, storyteller, educator, changemaker, activist, reformer, and humanitarian. Now, we recognise that we can—and should—look beyond our own walled garden to bring design skills to bear on social issues.

There are, of course, limits to our influence; designers do not have all the answers. But all these abilities share a common thread—of bringing others together, of creating collaborations, just as Indaba has. We can assume the role of a fulcrum by listening and canvassing, drawing others together in a common cause. The power of design thinking lies in uniting people across civil society, academia, government, and business to create genuinely useful, effective, sustainable interventions for the world's issues.

Reference list

Eliasson, O. (2017) 'We chat to awe-inspiring artist Olafur Eliasson', *Design Indaba*. Available at: www.designindaba.com/articles/interviews/we-chat-awe-inspiring-artist-olafur-eliasson (Accessed: 25 March 2023).

Quarterly Labour Force Survey (2021) *Department Statistics South Africa*. Q2:2021. Available at: www.statssa.gov.za/publications/P0211/Presentation%20QLFS%20Q2_2021.pdf (Accessed: 23 March 2023).

Urban Planner Jaime Lerner, Curitiba, Brasil—Thomas Eugster (2023) Available at: www.thomaseugster.com/portfolio/urban-planner-jaime-lerner-curitiba-brasil/ (Accessed: 23 March 2023).

Chapter 27

The idea of 'agency' in design today

Camilla Buchanan

This chapter looks at the question of 'agency' in today's design work. It is written from my perspective of design, which mostly comes from using it outside the design world, with policymakers in government and social sectors. I argue that the concept of 'agency' (who is doing vs. who is being done to) has been foundational to definitions of design. But design needs to get to grips with a legacy of individualism by asking whose experiences and ingenuity are not being adequately represented in design as whole. And ideas about design could be bolstered—could flourish—with more expansive and plural concepts of agency.

Ideas of 'agency' in design theory

The idea of 'agency' is essential to foundational definitions of design. One of the most resonant of these comes from John Christopher Jones, figurehead of the design methods movement. It took him a lifetime of revisions to get to it, and his final attempt is like a small poem. For Jones, design is:

> thoughts and actions
> intended to change
> thoughts and actions.

(2002)

Possibly the most famous theoretical definition of design, "courses of action aimed at changing existing situations into preferred ones" (1998), developed by Herbert Simon in the late 1960s, also emphasises agency—conscious and knowing intervention—in its reference to both intention and desire. Simon is clear in associating design with the 'artificial' and with everydayness. Victor Margolin had a similarly active and quotidian notion of design and its products. He thought that designing was about the conception and planning of the "human-made material and immaterial objects, activities, and services, and complex systems or environments that constitute the domain of the artificial" (1995, p. 122). In these theories, design is about thinking and doing, which impacts ways of thinking and doing in the material world. It is both intentional and practical.

DOI: 10.4324/9781003399568-31

I find many of the foundational definitions of design beautiful in their own way. But they are each decades old, concerned with getting to the essence of a thing rather than the reality of how it is being enacted and who by. Because these ideas are so encompassing, they miss important questions that might be more obvious to ask today, like: Who gets to design, and who gets changed by design? Who is doing and who is being done to?

The legacy of individualism in design

Although many of the core theories of design emphasise 'everydayness', the powerhouse of mainstream professional design has done very little to reinforce it as a common act, available to us all.

Almost everyone will be familiar with the comic, even infamous, stereotype of the designer as a lone wolf. The omnipotent *auteur* with a vision so singular and transformational that mainstream society simply hasn't yet cottoned on to its significance. This is *The Fountainhead*'s Howard Roark in fiction (Rand, 1943) and people like the fashion industry's (Roy) Halston[1] in reality. While these historic figures are sometimes outcasts and can be from more marginalised groups, they are almost always male, white and either have or gain agency.

The singular designer is an outmoded trope—and there are far more nuanced recent examples of this like the trailblazing Virgil Abloh,[2] who brought streetwear to high fashion—but it has been disproportionately influential in characterising design and designers. And it is true that design has been incredibly good at both elevating individuals and designing for the needs of some—through soothing interfaces, artefacts, and interactions—whilst marginalising others.

Participation, co-design, and engagement

Fortunately, there are alternatives to this dogma of individualism and designer-led agency. Towards the latter part of the 20th century, the involvement of non-designers in design work became a common feature of design, and sub-fields such as participatory design, user-centred design, and co-design were increasingly recognised as part of design as a whole—although there is considerable diversity among them (Sanders and Stappers, 2008). While each of these approaches can be critiqued, depending on context, for being extractive or falling short of true collaboration, the emergence of participation in design represented a shift in agency from designers 'doing to' towards 'doing with'.

Nowadays, designers working in some of the newer areas of design are often responsible for involving or representing the experiences of non-designers in decision-making. For example, in my area of work, 'policy or strategic design' (Buchanan, 2020), designers are now engaging extensively with different groups—from empowered people like elected officials to more vulnerable individuals and citizens whose voices are rarely amplified—as part of participatory design processes. This gives designers an important curatorial role in deciding who should be part of the design process and how the information and experiences they share should be interpreted and represented. But it also means that, more and more, designers are empowering and enabling non-designers to take part in design.

We see this in our work at the UK Policy Lab,[3] where in the last eight years, we have completed over 200 projects inside the UK government and occasionally beyond. In many of these, we have been commissioned to understand the experiences of people who are not well represented in policymaking, and much of our work draws on participatory and co-design methods as well as more fledgling approaches like collective intelligence.[4] For example, during the COVID-19 pandemic, people who generously gave time to our work included adults who were shielding and those living with disabilities in the UK (2021), all of whom were experiencing the pandemic differently and in challenging ways that were not immediately visible to policymakers. Other published examples of our participatory work include ethnographically led research with members of the Windrush Generation (2020) and with parents and guardians experiencing the children's social care system (2022).

In such contexts, the work of contributing to the design process and generating design products becomes more distributed, meaning that some of the agency that designers have is shared around through the involvement of many more people in designing.

There are divergent and even opposed pathways in design today. Some corners of the design sector are still wedded to producing design outputs which privilege and elevate or exclude specific groups of people. We see this in the 'founder obsession' that has become such a prominent part of business culture and where design has been an ingredient in the success of many start-up organisations. But there are also newer and increasingly powerful voices in design calling for different understandings of how it is being made and by whom. These ideas about design require a broader understanding of agency.

More expansive ways of designing

In her article, *Made in Patriarchy II: Researching (or Re-Searching) Women and Design* (2020), Cheryl Buckley revisits an argument she made more than 30 years ago: that design history had hidden the role of women and instead privileged 'heroic', usually male individuals and their intentions; as a result, what was considered to be within and outside design was often predicated on gender. Buckley looks again at this argument in light of growing awareness of intersectionality and identity politics to understand whether she still finds it valid. She argues that:

> perhaps we are still failing to recognise not only that design is polysemic, but also that the work of design makers, producers, and assemblers can be ordinary and everyday—part of routine, mundane lives—and it is this capacity that makes design so potent.
>
> (p. 21)

Buckley finds that in different ways around the world, small-scale and domestic design activity taking place in the intimate spaces of everyday life remains at the periphery of what today is thought of as design. What she asks is for this design activity—making/production/assembling—to be considered as part of a "continuum" that is design as a whole (p. 27). For example, recognised acts of design should include the re-interpretation of high fashion on the domestic scale by individuals remodelling and wearing outfits made from garments accumulated in their wardrobes over time or the design of services in the home which are required to keep a household or family running (pp. 24–25). Certainly, in referring to some of the foundational definitions of design and its connections to everyday-ness, expressed by Herbert Simon and others, these private and intimate activities count as design.

The idea that non-professional design is part of design practice is now relatively well accepted. Ezio Manzini is well known for discussing this in his book *Design, When Everybody Designs* (2016). He sets out the idea of "emerging design", which represents a major departure from the expert-led industrial design of the 20th century (p. 53). He also argues that the increasing availability of design tools, combined with widespread social transformations, means that more people are now being forced to redesign the circumstances of their own lives. Here, the role of the professional designer is increasingly as a facilitator and enabler of 'lay design' activities by non-designers (2015, 2016).

While Manzini clearly challenges the idea that design is solely the realm of professionals, Buckley seems to be going further by taking professional design out of the picture altogether—in contexts like domestic environments—and recognising intimate, small-scale acts as part of design in their own right. Although the focus of Buckley's argument is gender representation in design, it is important that this is expanded to other facets and intersections of identity—including heritage, economic circumstances and geographical location. What she offers is a heterogeneous and "polysemic" idea of designing and design products (p. 21).

I think we miss a lot if we do not consider these private acts and design work undertaken by a wide range of people as part of design's products and potential. Buckley's perspective offers a kind of blueprint for us to think about agency in design in more expansive ways.

Design ethics and agency

I am also convinced that the issue of agency in design is linked to its values and ethics and that for design to 'flourish', designers need to address questions about who is being given agency in design head-on. There will never be a one-size-fits-all set of principles in design—it is too expansive—but in recent years, design has grown so rapidly in new sectors that perhaps more emphasis has been placed on getting a foot in the door than it has on expressing an explicit ethical stance or ethos. For example, design activity inside government agencies has typically lacked an activist or agitating position in favour of being accepted as part of the *status quo*. This is partly because it is difficult for designers to simultaneously be part of and challengers to any given system. However, there is a role for the wider design community to establish a clearer position about who design intends to serve and empower in the rapidly growing area of public sector design.

This is already happening in parts of the design sector. Examples include the UK Design Council's recent initiative Design for Planet,[5] which intends to galvanise the design sector around the climate crisis, an effort that must include designers' consideration of non-human agents as part of design. Other initiatives work to decolonise design by challenging Anglocentric/Eurocentric ways of seeing and conventional systems of power and oppression in design (Tunstall, 2023). The book *Designs for the Pluriverse* (Escobar, 2018) fuses both of these themes together in its exploration of the possibilities for design practice which is deeply grounded in nature and collective social movements, taking communities in Colombia as its point of reference and inspiration.

The more initiatives and ideas such as these flourish, the more designers will find the support and language they need to consider and explain who is being given agency and who is being impacted by their work. As Buckley notes in reference to a provocation developed for a research summit "design cannot change anything before it changes itself" (2020, p. 19).

Conclusion

This chapter has looked at the idea of 'agency' in design: who is designing, who is participating in the design process and whose designs get to be seen as part of design. The practicalities of how design can be deeply attentive to, representative of and inclusive to new types of agency still needs so much thought and work. But I am excited and hopeful about a design field that questions deeply who is being included and excluded by design, that looks beyond the world of professional design for inspiration and that is insightful enough to consider below-the-radar forms of designing—like domestic service design—as part of its practice. Design is a brilliantly plural, nosy way of working and thinking. The more expansive designers can be about whose agency counts in design processes, the richer and more ingenious design will become.

Notes

1 Halston. *Fashion designer*. See wikipedia.org/wiki/Halston
2 Abloh. *Fashion designer*. See https://en.wikipedia.org/wiki/Virgil_Abloh
3 Policy Lab. See openpolicy.blog.gov.uk
4 Collective Intelligence Lab at Policy Lab. See openpolicy.blog.gov.uk/2021/11/04/crowd sourcing-policy-how-can-collective-intelligence-improve-policymaking/
5 Design for Planet. www.designforplanet.org

Reference list

Buchanan, C. (2020) *What is strategic design?* Lancaster University Press. Available at: https://eprints.lancs.ac.uk/id/eprint/148558/1/2020_Buchanan_PhD.pdf (Accessed: 22 March 2023).
Buckley, C. (2020) 'Made in patriarchy II: researching (or re-searching) women and design', *Design Issues*, 36(1), pp. 19–29.

Cabinet Office, Disability Unit (2021) *Exploring the everyday lives of disabled people* [online report]. Available at: www.gov.uk/government/publications/exploring-the-everyday-lives-of-disabled-people (Accessed: 22 March 2023).

Escobar, A. (2018) *Design for the pluriverse: radical interdependence, autonomy, and the making of worlds*. Durham and London: Duke University Press.

The Independent Review of Children's Social Care (2022) *Experiencing children's social care: the perspective of parents* [online ethnographic research summary]. Available at: https://openpolicy.blog.gov.uk/2022/06/09/an-independent-review-of-childrens-social-care-appreciating-the-wider-family-context/ (Accessed: 22 March 2023).

Independent Windrush Lessons Learned Review (2020) [Policy Lab, ethnographically-led films]. Available at: www.youtube.com/watch?v=xEJksQpWkaE (Accessed: 22 March 2023).

Jones, J.C. (2002) *What is designing?* Available at: www.publicwriting.net/2.2/digital_diary_02.07.14.html (Accessed: 22 March 2023).

Manzini, E. (2015) *Design, when everybody designs*. Cambridge, MA: MIT Press.

Manzini, E. (2016) 'Design culture and dialogic design', *Design Issues*, 32(1), pp. 52–59.

Margolin, V. (1995) 'The product milieu and social action', in Buchanan, R. and Margolin, V. (eds.) *Discovering design: explorations in design studies*. Chicago, IL: University of Chicago Press.

Rand, A. (1943) *The Fountainhead*. London: Penguin Books.

Sanders, E. and Stappers, J.P. (2008) 'Co-creation and the new landscapes of design', *Codesign*, 4(1), pp. 5–18.

Simon, H. (1998) *The sciences of the artificial*. 3rd edn. Cambridge, MA: MIT Press.

Tunstall, E.D. (2023) *Decolonizing design: a cultural justice guidebook*. Cambridge, MA: MIT Press.

Chapter 28

The Anthropocene warrants a new standard time

Rupert Griffiths

Time and the Anthropocene

The Anthropocene is a proposed epoch (Crutzen and Stoermer, 2000) wherein human activity profoundly affects earth systems and ecologies to the extent that it is clearly written into the geological record of the earth. The term brings into view the interdependencies between the atmosphere, oceans, ecologies, societies, and individuals, and highlights the many timescales over which the processes that underpin these interdependencies play out—from the geological timescales of many millions of years to the timescales of daily life. We can, for example, draw a clear line from the demise of the dinosaurs to our weekly trip to the supermarket. The Cretaceous–Paleogene mass extinction created the oil and coal that have driven the social and economic development of the modern age and which, today, fuels the car that releases carbon dioxide into the atmosphere as we drive there.

The unfolding ecological crisis makes it clear that the socioeconomic cycles of extraction, production and consumption that sustain human societies and the cycles that more broadly sustain life on earth are misaligned. The increase in atmospheric carbon dioxide driven by two centuries of carbon-based human activity is driving global changes in temperature and climate. This is, in turn, creating asynchronies in ecological cycles due to uneven changes in migration, reproduction, and predation between species of flora and fauna. This disrupts the finely balanced choreographies between species and environments that have emerged over evolutionary timescales, with the potential to cause the collapse of ecosystems.

Aligning the global with the planetary

For human societies across the globe, a key tool for choreographing activity is Universal Coordinated Time (UTC). Global time standards, such as UTC, emerged from the smoke of the industrial revolution and modern capitalism to facilitate the synchronised movement of workers, raw materials and commodities between regions, nations, and continents. UTC is unique to human beings and is not shared or accessible to any other species, although, through our activities, it profoundly affects their lives and environments.

How can we realign human and non-human forms of timekeeping? Here, a prototype timepiece (Griffiths, 2021) is proposed, which provides an alternative to UTC that combines both human and non-human forms of timekeeping. This is

DOI: 10.4324/9781003399568-32

in line with calls for a critical horology (Bastian, 2017; Pschetz and Bastian, 2018) and imaginative clocking practices whereby "clocks do not need to be produced in only one form, but could be remade to respond to temporal challenges in new ways" (Bastian, 2017, p. 11). As such, the timepiece demonstrates how creative methods employing design practice can be used to critically consider how we situate ourselves more equitably, as individuals and as a species, in relation to the wider systems and ecologies within which we are held.

Marking a new time standard

UTC is a linear abstraction of time that is not shared by any other species, and it places the human at the centre of our worldview. In contrast, the natural cycle of light and dark is a biological cue that entrains the circadian rhythms of most living organisms (Schmal, Herzel and Myung, 2020). It is shared by humans and non-humans alike and has regulated life on earth for billions of years.

The prototype timepiece takes these daily changes in natural light as a basis for timekeeping that is shared by most life on earth. Furthermore, it situates those daily rhythms of light into longer seasonal and annual rhythms and their relation to the movement of the earth around the sun and where one is physically situated on the earth.

The timepiece (see Figure 28.1) is thus designed to immediately situate the viewer in local, planetary, and celestial scales. The foot of the clock is specific to its location, angling the clockface in accordance with the local latitude. In this way, when the foot of the base is aligned with magnetic north and the viewer looks directly into the glass, the pole star will be directly behind the viewer's head— their line of sight parallel to the earth's axis with the heavens slowly rotating around them. Meanwhile, a light sensor (see Figure 28.2) detects the colour and luminosity of the sky, recording a single pixel of colour—what might be thought of as a one-pixel photograph—and sending it to a server via the Internet.

The timepiece picks up this one-pixel photograph and displays it as a fleck of colour dancing around the most northerly position of the display. Earlier flecks of light trail behind, a trace of the earth's rotation. As dusk unfolds, an arc will slowly appear, moving from daylight hues to deep blues (referred to by photographers as the blue hour) and into the umber of the urban night. Each rotation of the earth is traced as a circle of light and dark. These circles of light join into a continuous spiral (see Figure 28.3), with previous days recursively nestled inside the current day. The spiral builds over weeks and months, making the changing lengths of the day and night visible as the sun's arc above the horizon changes over the seasons. The spiral is in fact a perspectival view of a helix (see Figure 28.4), which the user can move in virtual three-dimensional space. This traces out one's position on earth as a helix that corresponds to the rotation of the earth as it orbits the sun.

A new standard offers new perspectives

In simple terms, the timepiece describes the changes in environmental light that falls on a sensor over time. By situating each timepiece in its local environment,

Figure 28.1
Timepiece showing 24-hour changes in ambient environmental light over a period of approximately 30 days.
Source: **Photograph by the author.**

Figure 28.2
Light sensors collecting ambient environmental light.
Source: **Photograph by the author.**

Figure 28.3
Detail of clock showing dabs of colour and spiral form. This shows the weeks after the vernal equinox, with the days slowly growing longer than the nights.
Source: **Photograph by the author.**

it challenges the anthropocentric and universalising tendencies of UTC (that time is the same everywhere). It challenges the tendency of UTC to abstract time into a repeating sequence of numbers that acts as an index and datum for the daily life of humans but which does not refer to any observable or shared quality of the environment.

In contrast to our clocks and watches, the proposed timepiece is situated in both its immediate environment and the planetary context of that environment, referring directly to light and how it changes—from the present moment to days, months, seasons, and years—due to the rotation and movement of the planet. Furthermore, by providing a referent (ambient light) and showing how this changes from moment to moment over long periods of time, it also brings memory, experience, and anticipation together (memory of the past, experience of the present, and anticipation of the future) in a way that is congruent with the way that other species of flora and fauna respond to the passage of time as it unfolds through environmental variables such as light and temperature. In this

Figure 28.4
View showing the spiral to be perspectival view of a helix. This image shows about 40 days of light data.
Source: **Photograph by the author.**

way, it emphasises an important function of the circadian clocks that regulate the biologies and behaviours of organisms: to give organisms survival advantages by allowing them to anticipate rather than simply respond to environmental and ecological events. Measuring time in this way—through environmental observation—challenges anthropocentric understandings of time and foregrounds the cyclical diurnal intensities of light that entrain the circadian rhythms of flora and fauna. This situates the viewer in a temporal commons shared with our environment and non-human companions.

The term 'Anthropocene' alludes to many processes and timescales that, in turn, affect the processes and timing of life cycles across ecologies and environments. Human time standards tend to obscure this and, in doing so, can create a sense of humans as a sovereign species that stands outside of and dominates the environment rather than being inexorably entwined in it. The unfolding ecological and climate crises drive home how fundamentally flawed such a view is and how vital it is that we seek ways to collaborate with rather than dominate our environments. The timepiece described here offers a measure of time that foregrounds an environmental cue that we not only share with life on earth but that is foundational for all life. It makes visible the daily rhythms of light and dark as well as our planet's movement around our star—a process that brings into view periods that range from days, months, and years to millennia and aeons.

Further considering our place in the world

Future work will continue to develop such time-based methods for bringing our environments and ecologies into view. One aim is to develop a platform whereby such measures of time will be made more widely available through a global network of sensors. One question underpins this work and will drive it forward: How can we make our environment meaningfully legible as a more-than-human ecology? (Griffiths, 2020).

Design has an important role to play in answering this question by helping to develop new methods and methodologies that give voice and presence to the many agents and forces we rely on, often unknowingly. Scholars have grappled with how we might conceptualise and develop the capacity for such attentiveness (e.g., Stengers, 2011; Hinchliffe *et al.*, 2005; Latour, 2014; Haraway, 2016). Developing the capacity to hear these non-human voices is a necessary first step towards developing a more-than-human approach to urban design. Such an approach would treat the urban environment as a more-than-human ecology and urban development as a collaborative process that requires us to be attentive not only to human needs but also to the many non-human lives and processes through which urban environments emerge.

The value of creative methods for both doing and disseminating research is increasingly acknowledged in field-based disciplines, such as cultural geography (Hawkins, 2020), archaeology (Griffiths and Wei, 2017), and anthropology (Gunn and Donovan, 2016). In recent years, such methods have also started to appear in traditionally theory-based disciplines, such as philosophy, with *field philosophy* (Frodeman, Briggle and Holbrook, 2012) being an emerging area of inquiry.

Drawing together design and fieldwork-based disciplines, such as geography and field philosophy, may facilitate experimental collaborations between humans, non-humans, and the environment—an area of collaboration that will become increasingly important as we attempt to find more equitable ways to inhabit the planet and mitigate the adverse effects of human exceptionalism that are unfolding around us.

Reference list

Bastian, M. (2017) 'Liberating clocks: developing a critical horology to rethink the potential of clock time', *New Formations*, 92, pp. 41–55.

Crutzen, P.J. and Stoermer, E.F. (2000) 'The "Anthropocene" ', *The Global Change Newsletter*, 41, pp. 17–18.

Frodeman, R., Briggle, A. and Holbrook, J.B. (2012) 'Philosophy in the age of neo-liberalism', *Social Epistemology*, 26(3–4), pp. 311–330.

Griffiths, R. (2020) 'Design practice as fieldwork: describing the nocturnal biome through light and sound', *Proceedings of the 4th international congress on ambiances, alloaesthesia: senses, inventions, worlds*. vol. 1. Réseau International Ambiances, pp. 108–113.

Griffiths, R. (2021) 'The circadian clock [artwork]', *Online gallery for material life of time conference*, University of Edinburgh.

Griffiths, R. and Wei, L. (2017) 'Reverse archaeology: experiments in carving and casting space', *Journal of Contemporary Archaeology*, 4(2), pp. 95–213.

Gunn, W. and Donovan, J. (eds.) (2016) *Design and anthropology*. London: Routledge.

Haraway, D. (2016) *Staying with the trouble: making kin in the Chthulucene*. Durham: Duke University Press.

Hawkins, H. (2020) *Geography, art, research: artistic research in the GeoHumanities*. London: Routledge.

Hinchliffe, S. *et al.* (2005) 'Urban wild things: a cosmopolitical experiment. *Environment and Planning D: Society and Space*, 23(5), pp. 643–658.

Latour, B. (2014) 'Agency at the time of the Anthropocene', *New Literary History*, 45(1), pp. 1–18.

Pschetz, L. and Bastian, M. (2018) 'Temporal design: rethinking time in design', *Design Studies*, 56, pp. 169–184.

Schmal, C., Herzel, H. and Myung, J. (2020) 'Clocks in the wild: entrainment to natural light', *Frontiers in Physiology*, 11, p. 272.

Stengers, I. (2011) *Cosmopolitics II*. Translated by R. Bononno. Minneapolis; London: University of Minnesota Press.

Chapter 29

Just toys? From material sustainability to co-design and degrowth

Katherine Ellsworth-Krebs

A month before a friend had a baby, she told me if I planned to send a gift, they only wanted books. What a relief: to be told what would be appreciated and used. To not have to walk the blue and pink segregated aisles of a Toys 'R' Us and wonder how the parents would respond to being gifted a doll for their son or a tractor for their daughter. I've found picking out appropriate toys for my five young nephews to be a sustainability minefield. I don't want to encourage violence with Transformers covered in rockets, but what if they think it's boring because it's not their favourite character and it just gets thrown away?

These anxieties are an occupational hazard. I'm a sustainability scholar in a design research centre, and it's hard to put down the critic's hat when it comes to the climate emergency. Yet if you go by what's in the news, I apparently worry about this more than most people. In contrast to increasing headlines about climate change, plastic pollution and fast fashion, toys are fairly absent from any public debate around sustainability. Yet toys are important facilitators of education and societal values, and their roles have long been discussed in relation to career choices and perceived gender norms. Less often, though, is it acknowledged how toys carry implicit messages about environmental sustainability or social justice. Like how it wasn't until 2019 that Barbie included someone in a wheelchair, six different body types, and nine skin tones. What does that (un)intentionally teach children about acceptable ways of being in society?

One of the few examples of toy sustainability reaching UK headlines was also in 2019, thanks to seven- and nine-year-old Ella and Catlin, who complained to their parents about the waste from free toys from fast food chains and successfully lobbied them so that several newspapers ran with the headline "Burger King ditches free toys". I'm all for reducing the amount of unwanted, fast toys (ones designed for 5 minutes of play life), but it feels like another example of how sustainability is too narrowly defined. Too often, the responsibility to create change is placed on children. Too often, environmental sustainability is understood only as an issue of materiality and pollution.

Toys appear to follow these problematic framings. For example, in 2020, Lego announced a $400 million investment to drive a low-carbon transition. Their focus: alternative materials. Certainly, 90% of the global toy market is made from virgin plastics, and plastic production is intimately linked to fossil fuel refineries, and thus it's a contributor and political interest that stands in the way of

DOI: 10.4324/9781003399568-33

decarbonisation plans. But using "more sustainable materials" is actually a tech-nological-fix; it is not about reducing production or consumption overall.

In contrast, the recognition of the importance of degrowth or 'sufficiency policies' has recently been acknowledged by the Intergovernmental Panel on Climate Change (IPCC) in their latest report on Mitigation. Here, the IPCC defines sufficiency policies as "a set of measures and daily practices that avoid demand for energy, materials, land and water while delivering human well-being for all within planetary boundaries" (2022, p. 31), and the report suggests that on a global scale, this sort of degrowth intervention will provide similar carbon reductions (10%) as investment in renewable energy generation (9%).

Here, the mention of human well-being and flourishing is significant because it signals a move away from using only economic measures of progress. Indeed, this IPCC report included "Literature on degrowth, post growth, and post development [that] questions the sustainability and imperative of more growth especially in already industrialised countries and argues that prosperity and the 'Good Life' are not immutably tied to economic growth" (p. 178). This is because "Vital dimensions of well-being correlate with consumption, but only up to a threshold" (p. 514), and this is what growth-critical scholars call the saturation hypothesis, which implies that reducing income per capita in rich countries (one of the implications of degrowth) will not reduce quality of life if income levels do not fall below a certain level.

Economist Tim Jackson, renowned author of *Prosperity without Growth*, explains this as the double dividend: "If the consumer way of life is both ecologically damaging and psychologically flawed, then the possibility remains that we could live better by consuming less and reduce our impact on the environment at the same time" (Jackson, 2005, p. 11).

Relating this back to the subject of toys, children in high-income house-holds arguably consume more toys than 'needed' for their well-being. If you need something to play with and you suddenly get access to a toy, you're happy. If you get a second toy, you'll perhaps still be happy but not as much as the first time. If you get 20 toys, you won't bother using some because you already have two. If you get a hundred more toys, you may actually be annoyed because you won't know where to put them all. At a certain threshold, the well-being you derive from them will saturate. This common sense we can see in our everyday lives is true for a country as a whole. Past a certain threshold of gross domestic product per capita, further economic growth will not improve well-being. This idea of a satiation threshold divides consumption in two kinds: one below the threshold that should be increased and one above it that we can afford to decrease.

My nephews' homes are certainly saturated with toys, some well loved and others hardly touched before my siblings pilfer them away to donate to local charity shops. While it's common to suggest people could better manage the toys or items they purchase so things aren't wasteful, I prefer to look for collective solutions that go beyond putting responsibility for climate action on individuals. With this in mind, one potential degrowth response to the concerns of material (over) consumption of toys is an old idea: libraries.

When I think about libraries, it always reminds me of a scene from *Matilda*. When Matilda reaches the age of four, she discovers the local library and starts pulling wagon-loads of books the ten blocks home after the librarian has told her, "You know you can have your very own library card and you could take books home. . . . You could take as many as you like". In a voice filled with quiet, lisping awe, she responds "That would be wonderful" (Davito, 1996).

I can imagine the same wonder and appreciation children and families could and do gain from being members of a public toy library. Access to libraries can teach us about collective action and civic pride, and they can be an economic leveller ensuring that basic needs and well-being are accessible to everyone. But it's also a good formative time to introduce the idea of temporary possession and things not having to be new to be desirable. This sort of solution is admittedly more complicated than each toy manufacturer—like Lego's $400 million investment— or company that sells or gives away toys—like Burger King and other fast-food chains—making their own business model more sustainable because it requires many stakeholders to work together for the public good. And this is where designers and design research can play a key role.

Designers excel at bridging ontologies, bringing together different stakeholders, creating community and translating ideas into action with policymakers and local government. Co-design is a method for creatively engaging citizens and stakeholders to find solutions to complex problems, and it means thinking beyond simple material substitution to collaborative problem-framing and -solving. What design research has to offer these sorts of degrowth interventions is this form of holistic intervention, looking beyond the design of the toy and its materiality to wider systems in which toys are acquired, used, and disposed of.

The next time someone applauds themselves for finding a sustainable toy because it's made from wood (I am completely guilty of this), see if you can gently expand the conversation beyond environmentally friendly materials to how we reimagine toys as a service rather than a commodity. Or the messages they carry about (over)consumption and needing more and more to be satisfied. Finding out what sort of toys or children's gifts will be valued by your friends of family members is an obvious start to avoiding them going quickly to landfill or a charity shop. But even more than that, toy sustainability means opening up conversations with toy manufacturers, designers, parents, teachers, children, local government, and academics to reimagine the values and skills 21st-century toys should embody.

Reference list

Davito, D. (1996) *Matilda*. Surrey: TriStar Pictures.

IPCC (2022) 'Climate change 2022: mitigation of climate change', in Shukla, P.R. *et al.* (eds.) *Contribution of working group III to the sixth assessment report of the intergovernmental panel on climate change*. Cambridge, UK and New York, NY, USA: Cambridge University Press. https://doi.org/10.1017/9781009157926

Jackson, T. (2005) 'Motivating sustainable consumption', *Sustainable Development Research Network*, 29(1), pp. 30–40.

Chapter 30

Legacy and sustainability in design research

A global dialogue

Emmanuel Tsekleves

A few years ago, I was fortunate enough to participate in a durbar—community meeting—in Ghana.

As colleagues from my institution were going around asking elders in the community to voice the challenges they saw as important for their community and what they wanted from them (the researchers) that would be of real help, I noticed the old gentleman sitting beside me. He was very quiet yet in deep contemplation.

I asked him, "What about you, what do you want?" He turned to me and said: "I just want one thing. . . . I want you to come back. So many researchers have come here before, got what they wanted and then left. I just want you to come back after the project is over."

Creating a legacy after the project ends is a challenge for any research project, but it is one that poses a greater challenge for Global North researchers working in the Global South. On the one hand, many Global South research institutions still lack the capacity to self-sufficiently undertake research to translate findings into impact and policy (Bradley, 2007; Olivier, Hunt and Ridde, 2016; Franzen *et al.*, 2017). On the other hand, there have been far too many research projects that use practices of 'mosquito' or 'parachuting' researchers into Global South countries. These projects perform research work and fly the data out—with the results being learned only on publication (Edejer, 1999). With more design researchers engaging in international projects addressing global challenges in the Global South, this becomes a major consideration. How do we ensure that as design researchers operating in the Global South, we embed legacy and sustainability in our research project? How do we ensure that we 'come back' after the project and funding have finished?

In fact, dissemination oriented towards international journals and conferences rather than local knowledge translation not only diminishes local communities' trust in Global North–led/funded projects but also impedes local dissemination and impact (Godoy-Ruiz *et al.*, 2016). Indeed, our academic delivery of results is often unusable for the research participants. A larger and more difficult challenge is to involve the communities themselves in the research questions and to link the research to their own development (Bhutta, 2002). Could design research methods such as storytelling and co-design be the answer to sharing knowledge with communities and giving back to them?

DOI: 10.4324/9781003399568-34

There are three points and recommendations I would like us to consider regarding this.

First, it has become clear that unless the model of North–South collaboration changes, the unintended detrimental consequences on local research will continue to subvert efforts to apply research effectively. Could building local capacity and training local Champions be an answer to this? Equitability is also absolutely critical in a successful and productive partnership, and building capacity will eventually put the South on an equal footing with its Northern partners (Edejer, 1999). Capacity-building opportunities for Northern and Southern researchers and institutions are an essential aspect of many if not most partnerships. Although, historically, the assumption was that Southern researchers have the most to gain from North–South partnerships, it is often the Northern researchers whose capacity is most significantly enhanced through partnership exercises (Bradley, 2007). This is because Northern partners learn from their Southern colleagues how to navigate different cultural contexts and how to adapt research methodologies to suit diverse conditions in the field.

Hence, in order to nurture true equitability amongst North and South partners, equitable capacity building should also be in place, as previously discussed. Nurturing local scientific and design research leadership and research capacity is key to capacity building in the Global South (Atkins et al., 2016). This can be achieved through the meaningful involvement of all partners in the field research planning and implementation (Casale, Flicker and Nixon, 2011) and by running short capacity-building and training courses at the start of the project aimed, on the one hand, at local research staff and on the other, at Global North research staff in order to develop better contextual research understanding.

Second, we are in need of a new knowledge-transfer paradigm to make change that is sustainable and that reaches beyond adults. Preliminary evidence from projects in several developing countries suggests that working through schools has a double advantage: children take in what they are taught and also take these messages home, where they influence their families; the teachers themselves are also influenced.

Building capacity of potential change agents forms a key education practice that can address sustainability development within the community. In selecting research participants, projects should therefore also consider the potential of actors in engaging in future actions and experiments, and the process should provide them with opportunities to learn, build capacities, and access resources (Silvestri et al., 2018). The model of change agents can also be applied in the school environment. Particularly in contexts in which there are no effective government/state change agents, community-level change agents—such as community leaders and school teachers—are critical to sustainable development services in communities, and thus resources should be made available to support them (Tyndale-Biscoe, Crawford and Bailey, 2020).

Hence, should design research explore children's potency as agents of change in the home and the community? And how can we best be actively empowering schoolchildren as agents of change?

The literature suggests that asymmetry between partners remains the principal obstacle to productive research collaboration. The '90/10' gap refers to the phenomenon in which 90% of the health research is done in countries with 10% of the world's health problems and in a mismatch between the disease burden and the technical and human capacity for research in developing countries (Atkins *et al.*, 2016; Edejer, 1999). Colonialist mentalities in research partnerships are another serious concern. Especially as there is a movement in design research towards decolonising the design syllabus, there is a clear need for this to also be extended into practice. We therefore have a unique opportunity to put our money where our mouths are!

It is, therefore, clear that as researchers, and especially as design researchers, we have the social responsibility and duty to do so. The era of colonialism is over, and this should apply in the way we conduct research. Next time you get a chance to do research in the Global South, ask yourself "How can I 'come back' to the communities, research beneficiaries and other stakeholders my research has engaged with?"

For those who have travel or financial restrictions, remember that coming back need not only be achieved via physical presence. More importantly, it is our actions throughout the research that serve communities long after the project has finished, and digital advances in communications now provide opportunities for doing this remotely.

It has now been five years since my meeting with the wise old gentleman in Ghana. His words, "I just want you to come back", echo loudly each time I engage in research. These words have had a profound impact on me . . . and I hope that you take inspiration from them too!

Reference list

Atkins, S. *et al*. (2016) 'North—south collaboration and capacity development in global health research in low-and middle-income countries–the ARCADE projects', *Global Health Action*, 9(1), p. 30524.

Bhutta, Z.A. (2002) 'Ethics in international health research: a perspective from the developing world', *Bulletin of the World Health Organization*, 80, pp. 114–120.

Bradley, M. (2007) 'North—south research partnerships: challenges, responses and trends; a literature review and annotated bibliography', *Canadian partnerships working paper*. Available at: https://idl-bnc-idrc.dspacedirect.org/handle/10625/36539

Casale, M.A., Flicker, S. and Nixon, S.A. (2011) 'Fieldwork challenges: lessons learned from a north–south public health research partnership', *Health Promotion Practice*, 12(5), pp. 734–743.

Edejer, T.T. (1999) 'North—south research partnerships: the ethics of carrying out research in developing countries', *BMJ*, 319(7207), pp. 438–441.

Franzen, S.R. *et al*. (2017) 'Strategies for developing sustainable health research capacity in low and middle-income countries: a prospective, qualitative study investigating the barriers and enablers to locally led clinical trial conduct in Ethiopia, Cameroon and Sri Lanka', *BMJ Open*, 7(10), p. e017246.

Godoy-Ruiz, P. *et al.* (2016) 'Developing collaborative approaches to international research: perspectives of new global health researchers', *Global Public Health*, 11(3), pp. 253–275.

Olivier, C., Hunt, M.R. and Ridde, V. (2016) 'NGO—researcher partnerships in global health research: benefits, challenges, and approaches that promote success', *Development in Practice*, 26(4), pp. 444–455.

Silvestri, G. *et al.* (2018) 'Transition management for improving the sustainability of WASH services in informal settlements in Sub-Saharan Africa—An exploration', *Sustainability*, 10(11), p. 4052.

Tyndale-Biscoe, P., Crawford, P. and Bailey, B. (2020) 'Engaging with the WASH enabling environment', *Journal of Water, Sanitation and Hygiene for Development*, 10(1), pp. 124–135.

Chapter 31

Falling UP and caring for better

Louise Valentine

Prefix

I think designing and design research are innately concerned with becoming 'healthier' as a species. Designing as flourishing is a marathon rather than a sprint, part of a place-based ecosystem rather than a generic system. How you learn from life and mindfully apply these lessons is the flourishing way. Flourishing has reverberations that can be sensed at the time of occurrence. Still, the sagacious outcomes cannot be seen or felt clearly until after the event, *and* only if you invest in understanding the lessons learned. This writing is a short descriptive story about observing the extraordinary powers of the human mind and spirit, an example of flourishing as a reciprocal arrangement.

Introduction

From the wicked torment of psychosis and the brink of suicide came an unwelcome need to accept, or not, the complexity and trauma of mental illness.

Following three years of tremendous suffering with no diagnosis and medication, Drew was diagnosed in 2009 with obsessive-compulsive disorder {ICD 10 F42.2} and autism spectrum disorder (Asperger Syndrome) {ICD 10 F84.5}. Following this, his journey of 'Falling UP to recovery' began from the inside out and the outside in.

'Falling UP' is Scottish artist Drew Walker's concept and process. It is conceived and practised to re-configure an idea of the self with a sense of purpose that is personally meaningful. It is a negotiated and renegotiated set of values, practices, theories, histories, conflicts, and traumas. It is also a research study: an original investigation to understand the change in how society perceives and understands mental illness to design a better care system. The observations in this short story are made from involvement in this research and from the dual perspective of a design researcher and research supervisor.

In 2017, Drew invited me to be his primary doctoral supervisor. My knowledge of design for health studies and my experience supervising practice-based research were part of his reason for asking me. Temperament, character, and values are equal contributors. This crafted mixture of ingredients was carefully

DOI: 10.4324/9781003399568-35

blended through time, a responsibility that is not unusual when building a doctoral advisory team. First, let me offer a short context for the research before presenting a summary of 'Falling UP' as a flourishing with its implications and insights for everyone to learn.

Falling as experience: four perspectives
Drew

I am Drew, but for a time, I wasn't. . . . One day in September 2007, I felt too different. . . . With little warning, everything fundamentally changed . . . inside my head, and I didn't know what was wrong. . . . I began to suffer from mental illness. . . . Every day visual triggers of ordinary things caused me intense, unbearable anxiety. . . . I would suffer daily bombardments of terrifying stimuli. Reacting to anxiety through constant rumination caused extreme stress. I could never escape unwanted thoughts. I was locked into a vicious cycle of constant checking. It was an unremitting personal horror. My family [was in] a nightmare limbo, but I [couldn't] care about them. I was often suicidal. My visual triggers took over my life. It was a danger going out. It was equally a danger to stay at home. Films, TV, books, newspapers, magazines, graphic novels, [and] even toy figures and statues at home all transformed into devices of fear. My psychosis meant that I suffered delusions. I had no understanding of what was [happening] inside my mind, and no one could tell me what would happen next. No one's words can ever do justice in translating what it is like to experience serious mental illness [because all] those consecutive moments of loss and pain add up to greater and greater strains on living, trapped inside a moment of psychic fixations. The essence of failing and falling into a wild alternative mindset was that everyday things induced a drop in the chest, a tingling in nerve-ends, [that] led to a fury of disturbing thoughts.

Drugs stabilised me, but Cognitive Behavioural Therapy and Exposure Response Prevention enabled me to understand and rationalise my mind-functions during anxiety-provoking situations. . . . Family was a strong support framework. Mum stopped teaching [to care] for me when I fell ill, becoming the dayshift. My Dad became the sole earner, taking the nightshift. . . . I could only feel calm and at peace when no people were around, and therefore no visual triggers to corrupt and contaminate my damaged mind. . . . Although I hid from the real world, my family managed an outdoor recovery pattern that extended beyond being trapped in my bedroom.

Drew's Dad

What's happening to us? I still don't know. Drew has no medicine, no diagnosis. We're fucking fucked. It's so dire, I've just promised Drew that if he isn't any better by Christmas, we'll both go up to the Lost Valley, we'll lay down in the snow, and we'll die together in our sleep (Drew's Dad's diary, 22 October 2007).

Drew's Mum

Who is Drew? Has he 'become' different since his descent into Hell aged 19, when not just his but my world changed forever? His life is full in many ways since returning to college, a successful education, degrees, studying, finding 'Gugging', 'Falling UP' collaborators, etc. . . . All good. But it's not life as a man in the sense of fulfilment of a relationship, responsibility, independence, freedom, and a desire to explore. He is missing out on a lot, in my opinion, but is that a valid statement? Is he happy? Does he have 'joy'? Ambition? I feel sad for him, angry at the world, genetics, my genes, or my inability to come to terms with the 'hand' that life has flung at him (15 March 2019).

Drew's Brother

I got a phone call from my brother Drew saying he wanted to kill himself. It was so irrational and crazy that I couldn't believe it. I thought mental illness was made up by people until that point and for weeks after. I stayed on the phone for an hour, angry that I couldn't leave him for fear he would do it and angry that nothing I said could help (9 September 2019).

Falling UP as research

[The focus] is on art, mental illness, and recovery within the innovative model of therapeutic healthcare in the Gugging House of Artists, a small-scale psychiatric facility in Austria. . . . [It investigates] Gugging's capacity to destigmatise mental illness through art, treatment, and community; how the creativity-relationship played a role in residents' recovery through the renegotiation of self; the significance of place to operational mutuality; and the researcher's perceptions arising from investigating these.

Primary research deployed artistic practice, ethnography, interpretive autoethnography, duoethnography, art collaboration, and action research. . . . [Why?] . . . Scotland's reductionist position towards artistic and psychological therapeutic care of mentally ill patients does not offer the scope, efficacy, or ambition of Gugging's system. Therefore, my research thesis concludes by proposing recommendations for change to Scotland's system of mental health treatments.

(Walker, 2021, p. 10)

Falling UP as flourishing

I interpret 'Falling-UP' as a search for meaning when faced with the uncompromising impacts of severe and multiple mental conditions. A pursuit of salvation. A practice-based body of research on the artistic and psychological process between patient-artist and artist-doctor, how to destigmatise mental illness through creativity, and how to renegotiate the sense of self. It is a socially innovative model of therapeutic healthcare for mental illness, a pragmatic review of service delivery that focuses on nurturing mutually supportive relationships for everyone involved.

Standing beside the theoretical and objective viewpoints demanded by doctoral research, Drew's 'Falling UP' is a story of supreme spirit and awe-inspiring, unconditional parental love: learning to flourish in wild circumstances. How one young man, his community, network, intelligence, temperament, and family did not concede: together, and in their own ways, foraged for paths to keep moving forward. His research is driven by a social necessity to improve the service and mental healthcare experience. An intense search for an alternative to the current healthcare model because the existing standard has been experienced and perceived as a life-diminishing service that fails to recognise the interconnected nature of living with multiple acute mental illnesses. And therefore, it fails to substantively help people and their families living with it during times of chronic need.

This example of design for flourishing is an unfolding dialogue of a transformation process. It is open-ended, and the holistic nature of creative thinking is central to everything. Family is a cornerstone. The lived experience of family members is shared through first-person accounts of their darkest hours of caring. The work is imbued with unconditional parental love. It is perpetual, living metaphorically and silently on the side, sharing the day shifts and night shifts that come with critical care for mental illness.

It is a journey to a recovery lifestyle focusing on well-being. *It re-imagines* how to care for people with acute and multiple mental illnesses. *It focuses on collaboration*, social ecologies, inter-country learning, connections between people, art, the act of making and being together, a disconnect with culture and connecting with nature.

As an example of Thackara's eye-to-eye (rather than one-to-one) connected design model, 'Falling-UP' does not promise significant future health breakthroughs for people with mental illness or a wealthy return on the enormous emotional investment (2015, p. 123). Instead, if there is a game-changing element of 'Falling UP', it lies in its potential as the development of a new collaborative, socially driven culture of equality in mental illness healthcare. This example has implications for us to learn from as a society and as a design community. And it has propositions for next-generation design research supervision with its propensity for attracting a broad spectrum of neurodiverse people to educate, study, and practise design in traditional, contemporary, and collaborative ways.

My privilege was being Drew's research supervisor.

Over four years of regular, intense conversations, he indirectly asked and reminded and, perhaps most fully, taught me *only* and *always* to give the highest form of research supervision when supervising:

- Be fully present to the circumstances and the surroundings of each moment in time.
- Recognise that there are no limits on human emotions and capacity, only those a person imposes on themselves.

- A state of discombobulation is never invited; it can arrive on a whim and stay for an unknown amount of time, i.e., no one is in control at this moment, and this energy is natural, albeit unsettling. Stay with it.
- The most accurate form of teaching is acceptance and gentleness.
- Allow yourself to be as you are, always.
- Learn to relinquish all false expectations, such as fulfilling an objective when the environment has wildly changed.
- Please do not give a diluted version of yourself when it matters to a person or people you give 100% to *now*. Doing this for an unexpected, prolonged period is not easy; it is hard won through a commitment to valuing human nature's diversity.

In one way or another, I've come to appreciate the simplicity of designing as a quest to be and do better. It is a creatively strategic search for improving how we make stuff connect with life in a sustainably responsible manner. It is energy, ideas, repercussions, revelations, transactions, and transformations. On a primitive level, it is an activity undertaken by animals, machines, nature, people, and a mixture of them all. Design researching is a framework for understanding why we need to improve the act of designing. It is about how design and its communities can reassess its values and develop new behaviours, knowledge and skills to improve how designers and their collaborators understand what 'better' is in a specific context.

In doing so, teachings (in life and of design research education) are shared to offer an example of the profoundly intimate journey that flourishing can be and the positively transformative capabilities one individual and one family can have on the lives of others. Here, I present 'Falling UP' as an example of John Thackara's design concept of social and embodied eye-to-eye "connectedness that sustains healthy communities" (2015, p. 123). On one level, it is an investigation that seeks to create more compassionate policies and services that embrace the complexity of living with mental illness, one that champions mutually supportive relationships between people and local environments. On another level, it is a steelily ferocious, honest, sympathetic, and profoundly courageous account of one person's journey to self-actualisation.

Note

In 2021, Drew and Rab Walker set up a charity called 'Falling UP together' (SCIO) SC051447. In January 2022, it was awarded £80,000 from the Scottish government to create and deliver its version of the Austrian Gugging Atelier as a model of peer-to-peer health with very high levels of care and emotional support. In addition, they are developing a book called *A Gugging Odyssey* and a film about Gugging, and are planning for a public exhibition of the Gugging Artists in the Scottish Parliament, Edinburgh.

Reference list

Thackara, J. (2015) *How to thrive in the next economy: designing tomorrow's world today.* New York, NY: Thames & Hudson.

Walker, D. (2021) *The importance of place: a practice-led investigation into the liminal space between artist-doctor and patient-artist, in the process of making art and recovery in the house of artists and the Gugging Atelier at Maria Gugging in Austria.* Doctoral Thesis. The University of Dundee. Available at: https://discovery.dundee.ac.uk/en/studentTheses/the-importance-of-place (Accessed: 7 March 2023).

Chapter 32

Sustainability

Designing for a technological utopia or dystopia?

Michael Stead

Designing for sustainability is all about the future. As a discipline, design is rightly concerned with bringing about positive change for the long-term flourishing of the planet. From atomic bomb fallouts to shampoo microplastics, the Earth's environmental woes are indelibly linked to modern society's overconsumption of resources and the mass waste that this creates, particularly in Global North countries across Europe and North America. In an effort to curb their impacts, many of these countries' governments signed the Paris Agreement in 2015 with the collective goal of keeping global temperature increases to a maximum of 1.5°C as well as pledging to meet ambitious net-zero carbon emission reduction targets by the year 2050.

Despite this growing consensus, how we collectively go about instigating the vital societal, economic, and technological transformations needed to move beyond the current Anthropocene remains a contentious issue. Consequently, the dialogues that surround sustainability—both broadly and within the field of design—can often deviate into two opposing silos: one which frames 'the future' as a sustainable utopia and the other as an unsustainable dystopia. Given their long-standing power and influence in shaping the modern world, technologies sit at the heart of this dichotomy.

Taking a solutionist stance, a number of scholars believe that advanced technologies will ameliorate most of society's environmental problems in the future. They argue that until then, we should 'learn to love our monsters' and embrace the Frankenstein-like consequences that modern technologies have wrought upon the planet. In contrast, other practitioners foresee an ecological non-future on the horizon. Looking through a rear-view mirror, they contend that in order to avoid climate collapse, we should eschew technological progress and readopt pre-industrial cultures and values.

This dichotomy in sustainable narratives is persistent and persuasive. It can lead to inertia amongst policymakers and publics in regard to the best ways to redress unsustainable processes and practices. It can create tensions amongst designers who are aware of their discipline's often-lamentable environmental record but who also want to innovate novel strategies for restabilising our biosphere. It is therefore time to move away from the reductive binary of utopias and dystopias. These narrow and dogmatic visions of the future are not inspiring the

DOI: 10.4324/9781003399568-36

Figure 32.1
Electronic waste.
Source: **Photograph by damrong—Stock.Adobe.com.**

type or level of sustainable change needed. The propensity of some to promote idealistic and overly solutionist futures should be seen as 'postalgia'. Similarly, hagiographic interpretations of the past contain elaborations and constructions which can distort history as well as conceal its flaws.

A more useful way to look at the issue of global unsustainability is to view it as a hyperobject (Morton, 2013); it is massive in scale and continually evolving. Maintaining some form of sustainable equilibrium is a 'wicked problem' (Rittel and Webber, 1973) which is becoming increasingly difficult to redress. Escobar's (2018) concept of the pluriverse reinforces this complexity. We live in a deeply heterogeneous world in which 'sustainability' means different things to different people in different contexts. One person's vision of a sustainable utopia might be another person's idea of an unsustainable dystopia. The earth may be one, but the world is not.

To develop new approaches for tackling unsustainability, we must directly engage with its complexity, its relationality, and its uncertainty, and it is here that design research can come to the fore. Rather than retreating to the safety of the edges, through design research, we can explore, expand, and explain the 'messy' grey areas in between. By working with communities and industry to apply future-oriented approaches such as speculative design and more-than-human–centred design, practitioners can begin to envision and consider a plurality of possible sustainable futures as well as start to critically evaluate the environmental trade-offs and unintended consequences that new technological developments may come to pose.

Figure 32.2
Repair Shop 2049 workshop at The Making Rooms in Blackburn, UK.
Source: **Photograph by Mark Gillow.**

Figure 32.3
Edge game players at the V&A Digital Design Weekend 2022.
Source: **Photograph © Hydar Dewachi.**

For example, research with ImaginationLancaster colleagues has demonstrated that by negating means for repair, upgrade, and recycling, the design of most so-called 'smart' devices—often referred to as Internet of Things devices—is unsustainable. This technological paradigm is increasingly contributing to global material scarcity issues, electronic waste streams, and pollution—such as through the illegal dumping of redundant devices in Global South countries like Ghana and Nigeria. Yet because of their innate connectivity, future, smarter devices could potentially have longer and more durable lifecycles through the incorporation of modular componentry which can be globally tracked, easily substituted, and efficiently recycled (Stead and Coulton, 2022). Emergent, related innovations like predictive maintenance and digital twins add further currency to these proposals.

However, our research has also highlighted that there is an additional caveat that comes with adopting data-driven technologies like the Internet of Things: these systems are themselves having a growing planetary impact. Invisible to the naked eye, data is often considered to be immaterial and innocuous. In reality, our billions of daily interactions with smart devices and digital services are collectively creating zettabytes of data every year. One zettabyte is 1,000,000,000,000,000,000,000 bytes—equivalent to 323 trillion copies of Leo Tolstoy's *War and Peace* or storage for 2 billion years of music. The generation, processing, and storage of this data across vast networks like the cloud (a proxy for millions of globally dispersed data centres) and mediated via systems like artificial intelligence is consuming fossil fuel–derived energy and releasing carbon emissions at environmentally detrimental levels (Stead *et al.*, 2020).

Other technological interventions such as renewable energies, electric vehicles, and the transition to a circular economy are beset with similar compromises. It could also be argued that the latter promotes a utopian, monolithic vision for the future—one which responds to the problem of unsustainability from a privileged Global North vantage. Outside this lens, alternative forms of a circular economy are, to a degree, already flourishing. Born from necessity but built on resilience, in some Global South communities, product repair practices help older iterations of devices to continue to remain culturally, economically, and environmentally valuable. So would the Global North do better to follow the lead of Global South repair communities when seeking to transform its unsustainable material cultures? Should new technologies continue to be designed and implemented to remedy the environmental problems caused by earlier technologies? Might alternate forms of action, or even inaction, be more beneficial or worse for the environment and society?

Designing sustainable futures with and for wider sets of stakeholders has been key to our recent research. The Repair Shop 2049 (2023) project has been investigating the limitations of EU/UK Right-to-Repair policy, which currently does not sanction the repair and reuse of Internet of Things device hardware and software. Collaborating with our partner, The Making Rooms, Blackburn's digital manufacturing hub, we have brought together a variety of stakeholders including citizen groups, local government, and industry to start to understand whether design methods can help improve access to better repair knowledge, skills, and tools; increase smart device repairability; and develop more equitable technology infrastructures across local communities. For our Edge Computing projects, we have designed interactive games to highlight to stakeholders that there is a collective need to reduce our data-driven carbon emissions—just like there is to use less plastic and choose more environmentally friendly forms of travel. And to show that this decision-making often comes with uncomfortable trade-offs, our Edge game players must negotiate between improving their data sustainability while potentially forfeiting some of their data cybersecurity (Stead *et al.*, 2022).

Crucially, our projects directly engage with citizens and communities to begin to allow them to have their say in how the design of new devices, practices, and policies might positively and/or negatively affect the future of the planet—a planet whose fate is not yet set. For while it is imperative that we be extremely vigilant going forward, the future, like the past, will no doubt present a complex mix of opportunities and challenges for Earth and its humanity to flourish sustainably. "Change is not merely necessary to life, it *is* life" (Toffler, 1970, p. 342). By the same token, designing for sustainability will likely always be both a utopian and dystopian project.

Reference list

Escobar, A. (2018) *Designs for the pluriverse: radical interdependence, autonomy, and the making of worlds*. Durham: Duke University Press.

Morton, T. (2013) *Hyperobjects: philosophy and ecology after the end of the world*. Minneapolis: University of Minnesota Press.

Rittel, H.W.J. and Webber, M.M. (1973) 'Dilemmas in a general theory of planning', *Policy Sciences*, 4(155), pp. 155–169.

Stead, M. and Coulton, P. (2022) 'A more-than-human right-to-repair', *Proceedings of DRS2022 Bilbao: design research society conference 2022*, 29, Spain, 25 June 22. https://doi.org/10.21606/drs.2022.718

Stead, M. *et al.* (2020) 'Edge of tomorrow: designing sustainable edge computing', *Proceedings of the design research society conference 2020*. Situations edn, vol. 1, pp. 88–110. [293]. https://doi.org/10.21606/drs.2020.293

Stead, M. *et al.* (2022) 'More-than-human-data interaction: bridging novel design research approaches to materialise and foreground data sustainability', *Proceedings of the 25th international academic Mindtrek conference (Academic Mindtrek 2022)*. ACM, pp. 62–74. https://doi.org/10.1145/3569219.3569344

Stead, M. *et al.* (2023) 'The repair shop 2049: co-designing sustainable and equitable transitions for smart device repair with and for local communities', *Proceedings of the 5th product lifetimes and the environment conference*. PLATE 2023. Espoo, Finland. May–June. Available at: https://eprints.lancs.ac.uk/id/eprint/193011/1/405_The_Repair_Shop_2049_PLATE_Proceedings_2023_.pdf

Toffler, A. (1970) *Future shock*. New York: Random House.

Afterword

To flourish or not to flourish by design

Rachel Cooper

What can design do to help the planet and its inhabitants to flourish? Or are we on an inevitable continuum toward what Sudjic suggests is us 'being cooked and drowned'? Indeed, is there a collective role for design and how can we use it? What follows reflects my reading of the provocation chapters and the action we need to take.

Recognise design passion and diverse philosophies

This volume presents essays by people with extensive knowledge and experience of design and design research alongside early-career researchers, just beginning their careers with passion and curiosity. Hence, the perspectives covered are both broad and deep. Do age and experience engender pessimism and critique, and does youth spawn optimism and hope? Not necessarily, although I would say there is evidence of both here. These are all individual provocations and therefore come from an individual's experience and value system. Working in the field of design, especially as an academic, it is often more than a job; it is a vocation about which everyone involved is passionate. As a vocation, design research also offers a sense of purpose and meaning, and most of us know intuitively that we "experience the deepest satisfaction when we engage in meaningful activities and we feel fully alive, when we passionately purse a worthy life goal" (Wong, 2015). This passion and sense of purpose for design is what we have in common. However, what we decide is meaningful in design varies, just as does what we determine flourishing to mean.

As a general rule, those people who work in the field of design are optimists. Valentine, for instance, asserts that design is imbued with unconditional love. Paul Rodgers, while discussing design and flourishing, suggests that perhaps to design is to flourish. Indeed, there is a general belief that design is good and can do good, and Deyan Sudjic says there is a touching conviction that design can do good. Both Sudjic and Bruce Brown remind us that in the 1960s, Papanek illustrated the harm that design can do, and, according to Sudjic, design practice struggles between the philosophies of William Morris and Raymond Loewy—from being socially responsible to industry driven. And Brown refers to Herbert Simon seeking in 1969 to establish a new science of design that would shift its

DOI: 10.4324/9781003399568-37

focus from business and commerce to society and welfare. Today, design operates in multiple domains with multiple perspectives.

Stop defining design

In every situation in which design and design researchers come together, there is a general desire to specify what design is and what design does. This is often because we struggle to communicate the value of design and design research, to move it from a black box of magic tricks and creativity to a valued activity that can address global problems. Do we need a definition of medicine to understand the value of medical research? We just see its impact. Perhaps, then, we should focus on the outcomes and impact of design research as evidence of its value.

While Sudjic suggests design is a way of looking at the world from multiple perspectives, Davis emphasises how design must make a difference and focus on action, and Naidoo asserts that design without action is only a daydream. Buchanan suggests that design itself can flourish with a more expansive and plural concept of agency.

There is also a further area of contention, the difference between design (verb, noun) and design research (verb, noun). Sudjic criticises design research for being distant from design, and Brown warns us not to confuse advocacy with research. For the purpose of this essay, it is best to consider design and design research together, as both often take on activities related to each other; they are diverse and, as Ehrenfeld suggests, existential in nature.

What is important is that we define by doing.

Embrace multiple agency and specific contributions

Brown reminds us of Simon's (1996) influential phrase "everyone designs who devises courses of action aimed at changing existing situations into preferred ones", and this has become something of a mantra for contemporary designers. Brown also asserts that design is seemingly boundaryless.

Indeed, I like to use the quote by Norman Potter (2002) that "Every human being is a designer. Many also earn their living by design". We do have professional trained designers and design researchers who have specific skills and capabilities that help them to make sense of the world and create the world through their imagination and their hands. However, the reason we often refer to the phrase 'everyone designs' is that whoever makes decisions about the material (and now digital) world could be considered as designing that world.

Over the course of the past 40 years or more, with the rise of user-centred design and the importance of the customer, everyone has been brought more formally into design. This is illustrated by the emergence of co-design, participatory, and collaborative design that proliferate in many sectors and, as Perez states, returns power to people. Thus, engaging communities, groups, and the public in using design can, as Mullagh writes, contribute to public imagination and, furthermore, collective ownership of the outcome, in line with Siodmok's shared imaginaries. Christou advocates using design research to foster cross-relational efforts . . . increasing literacy, and expanding community ties and infrastructures.

At the same time, the recognition that collaboration across disciplines, professions, and sectors means that *inter-, cross-, and multidisciplinary* practices have been asserted. Jenny Sabin illustrates the value of and the need for interdisciplinary research to solve problems, bringing together science and design. Mullagh illustrates how to create public value by developing skills of public servants and embedding design in their everyday practice.

There are circumstances, however, in which such approaches draw criticism; for instance, the hype around design thinking leads Davis to suggest it is technocratic and meaningless. If we are not careful, the same will be said of co-design, interdisciplinary, collaborative, etc.

Therefore, whatever context we are situated in, it is important to clarify roles and contributions; as Buchanan suggests, we must understand "who gets to design, who gets changed by design, or who is doing and who is being done to".

Those in the profession may be agents of change (Brewster), and there may also be a specific design attitude as a mindset (Amatullo). We assert that design excels at bringing ontologies together (Ellsworth-Krebs); and some suggest we see design as a collaborative practice (Perez); and that design and design research can participate in nurturing, as change agents, and in knowledge transfer (Tsekleves). Whatever the case, global challenges mean a team-based approach—with qualitative and quantitative data—for design to be effective, that data must be thick (Mortati).

The answer for a flourishing world is that design research and action must be context specific.

Situate design beyond now and the human

Siodmok reminds us of the fourth industrial revolution and the need to rethink the common good. Sabin is optimistic about materials research, nano technologies, powered by AI, and new transdisciplinary research. Lee sees an opportunity for design as a means of problem framing, comprehending context, and how to work with AI for future generations. And KP Lee offers an insight into new organisational and business clusters . . . small, disruptive constellations with design enabling fluidity in the technological landscape. Yet Jacobs, looking at the use of memes in the transmission of knowledge in a digital world, suggests we need to be cognisant of the dangers and that we cannot flourish if we can't understand each other. Stead further reminds us of possible technological utopia or dystopia . . . and calls on design to look at technological solutions and to investigate alternative forms of action.

So we need to take a critical look at our horizons and our focus. Dunn gives us an example when he says, "Living in cities removes us from the rest of the world", and you could say we focus on the technical more than the human or the planet. Therefore, we need to design more-than-human urban places. Siodmok asks whether we have reached the limits of the modernist design paradigm, especially the notions of human-centred design. With the increasing interest in more-than-human–centred design, in centreless constellations and speculative ontologies (Pilling and Coulton, 2022), we are designing beyond the human focus. As Griffiths says, the Anthropocene warrants exploratory thinking, hearing nonhuman voices . . . imagining alternative futures, and possibly focussing on alternative perspectives like degrowth (Ellsworth-Krebs).

Question the purpose

However, as Sudjic suggests, "the more the world dematerialises the more we value physical qualities". But what do we value, and what gives meaning and purpose to our life and our work? If it is to have meaning and purpose, design agency must be linked to values and ethics. Surely, as Costa says, design research should be to help people flourish. It is important to link our purpose to our values, ethics, and principles.

Over 20 years ago, social responsibility became more prominent in design, even though, as Brown and Sudjic illustrate, social conscience has always been an aspect of debate for society in general and therefore in the profession. Rogers offers the notion of social responsibility as a new way of repurposing design to open new possibilities and thus the development of a caring theory of design. Cruickshank calls for design research to engage with social issues but criticises superficial collaboration, reminding design researchers of their ethical responsibilities. Indeed, Tsekleves tells us a story about a research intervention leaving without any thought for the people and place after the value had been extracted for the design research, thus leaving a negative impression and impact of design research. Valentine argues that in relation to societal challenges, design must be fully present, understanding what 'better' is in a specific context and how to embed value.

Yet Davis more specifically sees the benefit of design (arts and culture) and its relationship to public health, while Naidoo believes people are more likely to trust culture than politics. Thus, design can empower, as Dunn says, but we must do so with greater sensitivity. We must also consider the purpose and impact of how we do design research in relation to societal-readiness levels (Siodmok).

Forget manifestos, mantras, and slogans

The world of design and design research is littered with simplistic quotations, slogans, and manifestos (Brown). For instance, the design manifesto, Brighton 05–06–07, was created in 2008 by 12 scholars including Bruce Brown and Victor Margolin and published in *Design Issues* (Brighton 05-06-07, 2008). But what happened to it? While many design researchers hang on to revered academic statements, especially when they validate all our thinking such as design being "perhaps the most critical of all intentional activities that govern human life" (Ehrenfeld, 2019) or, according to Buckley (2020), "Design cannot change anything before it changes itself".

All very laudable but equally challengeable. What we need to do is do it with measurable impact.

Flourish by breaking new ground?

Siodmok asks, Do we need a new roadmap? . . . How can design respond to technologies and offer purposeful innovation? Speed says design enables multiple stakeholders within an eco-system to find voice and agency . . . to look at 'Thingness', but new design does not differentiate between things.

A VUCA world (volatility, uncertainty, complexity, and ambiguity) has been mentioned twice in this book, by Amatullo and Davis. It is a shorthand for multiple and complex concerns for planet and place. Van der Wacht calls for solidarity among designers. But as we have illustrated, we are not one force. Individually and collectively, we must find meaning and purpose; we must decide whether "we give a shit" (van der Wacht) and whether design does indeed care.

There are alternative perspectives, for instance, Siodmok cites RISE (responsive, inclusive, systemic, effective); Galabo suggests a challenge to capitalism through design, offering new commons ownership and new political belief systems. As Cruickshank states, exploring the radical can give design meaning and purpose. Naidoo states that to be a designer "is to be an optimist, dreamer, thinker, researcher, instigator, provocateur, demonstrator, visualiser, storyteller, educator, changemaker, activist, reformer and humanitarian".

Whatever a designer is, we are all humans, and surely, we want to flourish on a flourishing planet. Now, we must extract our values from that goal. Don't stay the same; challenge, question, provoke, do good . . . push the boundaries of knowledge for yourself, your community, and the rest of the world.

As Santamaria says, "a seed grows best in broken soil". Go and break some soil.

Reference list

Brighton 05–06–07 (2008) *Design Issues*, 24(1), pp. 91–93. https://doi.org/10.1162/desi.2008.24.1.91

Buckley, C. (2020) 'Made in patriarchy II: researching (or re-searching) women and design', *Design Issues*, 36(1), pp. 19–29.

Ehrenfeld, J. (2019) 'Flourishing: designing a brave new world', *She Ji: The Journal of Design, Economics, and Innovation*, 5(2), pp. 105–116.

Pilling, M. and Coulton, P. (2022) 'Shifting perspectives: a speculative ontographic approach', *Proceedings of Cumulus Detroit 2022: design for adaptation*.

Potter, N. (2002) *What is a designer: things, places, messages*. London: Hyphen Press.

Simon, H.A. (1996) *The sciences of the artificial*. 3rd edn. Cambridge, MA: MIT Press, p. 53.

Wong, T.P. (2015) 'Meaning therapy: assessments and interventions', *Existential Analysis*, 26(1), pp. 154–167.

Index

Note: Page numbers in *italics* indicate a figure and page numbers in **bold** indicate a table on the corresponding page.

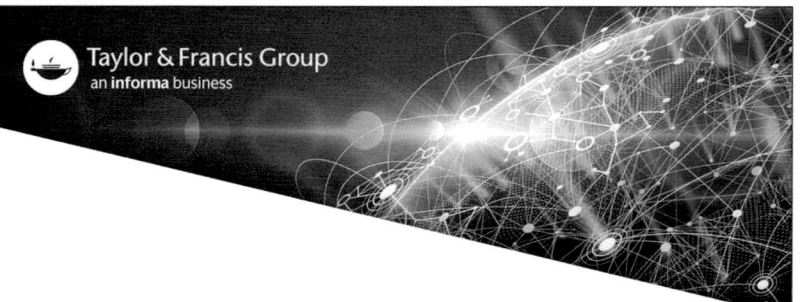